## "I NEED YOU TO CUT THE HANDS OFF!"

After we dragged the body from the pickup and laid it on the ground, we put lighter fluid all over it and lit it on fire. Thirty minutes later, the fire had barely burned through the clothes.

"I need you to cut the hands off," Will said.

"But—"

"Go and get the saw and cut them off."

So I took the hacksaw and began to cut. I had to hold each hand down as I worked. I was surprised there was no blood. I guess it was because we drained it out of the body the day before.

At first, Will just stood there watching and staring.

Then he said, "You're sick," and laughed.

# WAGES
# OF SIN

## *Suzy Spencer*

## PINNACLE BOOKS
## Kensington Publishing Corp.

http://www.pinnaclebooks.com

Some names have been changed to protect the privacy of individuals connected to this story.

PINNACLE BOOKS are published by

Kensington Publishing Corp.
850 Third Avenue
New York, NY 10022

Pinnacle and the P logo Reg. U.S. Pat. & TM Off.

First Printing: November, 2000
10 9 8 7 6 5 4 3

Printed in the United States of America

*In memory of*
*Ben Masselink*
*teacher, friend, mentor, hero*

# Prologue

Even in the dead of winter, when the tree limbs were bare, the wind around Lake Travis rustled. On Wednesday, January 11, 1995, its rustling coaxed handsome Chuck Register and his three-year-old son to Pace Bend Park, a rambling public facility along the long shores of Lake Travis and forty-five minutes from Austin, Texas.

Pace Bend, once known as Paleface Park, juxtaposed dirt trails with paved roads and cozy coves with wide open picnic areas. Register, a young corrections officer with the Travis County Sheriffs Office (TSCO), guided his white van from Pace Bend's blacktopped roads to its dirt paths.

He and his son had hopes for a good night of playing and camping. Register knew the area. He'd camped there on numerous occasions with his wife.

But Paleface Park had a dark past. In the 1980s, the Banditos, a Texas version of the Hell's Angels, partied on its shores. Dead bodies were discovered there about once a month. With an increase in the park's entry fee, the Banditos and dead bodies disappeared, and the darkside faded.

Register turned his vehicle toward Kate's Cove, a smooth palm of tan ground that allowed the water to slip between its fingers. He eased between draping mesquite trees, maneuvered past concrete picnic tables, and wound along the curving lakefront. The sun began a slow dip toward the water.

As he drove closer to concrete picnic table number 117, he

squinted into the oncoming dusk. A mannequin appeared to be lying in the fire ring closest to the table. The fire ring was a simple metal circle and grill on the ground used for barbecuing hamburgers and hot dogs. Register parked his van about ten feet from the ring and got out. "Stay in the van," he told his son.

Register walked until he stood two feet from two shoeless and sockless feet and stared at white, bare, dark-haired legs. He moved his gaze upward. He saw fragments of burned maroon briefs that just covered the pelvis. Register didn't want to believe that this inanimate thing was a human being.

He moved his focus toward the head, but there appeared to be no head. Not even a skull. The area where a head should have been was burned black. Register stared at the arms. One was limestone-white. The other was charcoal-black. Both arms were handless, as if the hands had been screwed off like those on a plaster window-display model. Then he noticed the skin around the wrists was jagged, and the left arm stretched upward, as if begging for help. It *was* very human. Chuck Register turned to go get help.

# One

The wind chimed and its music was sweet as it swept over the ears of Travis County park ranger Michael Brewster. Brewster stood silently at the front gate of Pace Bend and gazed at its cedar and oak trees. He loved his park. It was a place that protected and nurtured him.

On Wednesday, January 11, 1995, his park had been good to him. It had allowed Brewster to relax for nine and a half hours, as he'd sold only twenty park-entry permits. Only one other person, a maintenance man, had worked in the park that day. It couldn't get much deader than that.

With just thirty minutes to go before time to close the park for the night, Brewster decided to take a patrol through Pace Bend. Slowly he drove, his eyes and soul relishing the quiet of the slipping sun.

Five minutes later, lights flashed on his windshield from a white van trying to signal him. Pulling into a cove, Brewster climbed out of his truck to walk over to where Chuck Register was stepping out of his van. His three-year-old son remained in the passenger seat. At six feet two inches, Register towered over the shorter but equally handsome, dark-haired, young park ranger. "I've seen something that I think is a dead body," whispered Register.

*Here we go,* thought Brewster, *he's going to take me to another dead deer.* In his mind, Brewster rolled his eyes. The rangers constantly got those kinds of reports—dead body, pile of bones. It always turned out the same—pile of deer bones.

"I don't really know if it's a man or mannequin."

Brewster listened closer. That didn't sound like a deer being described. Still, he wasn't worried. Someone had probably just dumped something.

"There was hair on the legs."

Brewster stared Register in the eyes. "Tell me how to get there."

Register's directions were too vague for the ranger to follow. "I need you to lead me to the site," he said.

"I don't wanna go back." Register looked at his son in the van.

"It's starting to get dark," said Brewster. "If you don't lead me to the scene, then it probably won't be found before sunset." Pace Bend stretched across 1,500 acres of rugged hill country. "And we'll all be wondering if there's a dead body in the park."

Register got back into his van and led Brewster toward Kate's Cove. As Brewster drove alone in his vehicle, he mulled over Register's words—hair on the legs. *It might really be a dead body.* He picked up his radio and tried to contact his supervisor, Kurt Nielsen. But park after nearby park that he radioed didn't answer. It was, after all, closing time in the dead of winter. And it was past time for Nielsen to be off duty.

Brewster finally reached a familiar voice at Hippie Hollow, a local nude beach. "Please page park zero-three-one," he said, consciously calm, not wanting to arouse reaction from civilians who scanned the airwaves for entertainment. "Please page my supervisor, Kurt Nielsen. We have a law enforcement incident." He wanted to say "emergency," but he wasn't about to—not with civilians listening.

"I'm being escorted to the scene, and I really need to talk to Nielsen in five minutes. Send him whatever page you can, right now. Whatever's quickest. We have a law enforcement incident."

His repetition of "law enforcement incident" grabbed the

attention of park supervisors in Austin, who were listening to the broadcast as it bounced more than thirty miles, from tower to tower, over limestone hills, between scrub oaks and cedar trees, on channel six.

The county's top supervisor jumped on the radio. "Is there anything I can do for you?"

Before Brewster could answer, Nielsen called, "What's up?"

"Park zero-three-one, go to one," replied Brewster, telling Nielsen to go to channel one, which afforded them more privacy as it wasn't bounced throughout the county. "I'm following a guy who says he's seen a dead body. We're driving down the entrance to Kate's and Johnson's coves right now. It may be a false alarm. I'll let you know in two or three minutes. Just monitor your radio."

Nielsen called the Travis County Sheriffs Office.

It was about 5:50 P.M., still light, and easy to see. Brewster studied the terrain as he drove. He didn't spot anything until he was thirty to forty yards from the cove. Then he saw only a large object that looked like a trash bag lying in a fire ring. It certainly didn't strike him as a body.

He pulled up on a dirt road. As he made his final approach to the campsite, he spotted a left arm sticking up high in the air, with no hand. *Oh, this isn't a body. It probably is a mannequin.* It looked so unlike a human. Then he almost laughed to himself. *At least it's not a dead deer.*

Brewster pulled to within ten to fifteen feet of the fire ring. Legs protruded from the ring, lifelike and muscular. Inside the ring, resting on a large, flat rock, was the torso, which lay on its back. Brewster stared at the legs again. Something struck a nerve in him.

He parked. He started to get out of his vehicle. He'd parked too close, if this was a body. Still, he wasn't one hundred percent sure it was a body. The upper torso looked plastic.

He got out and walked to the body's left side and stood one foot away. He bent down. The head and neck were incinerated to ashes. There was nothing recognizable from the shoulders up. But in the ash, he did see small, concave, ash-colored debris. Skull fragments, he supposed.

He looked at the chest. The skin didn't look human. He stared at the wrist and looked for signs of blood. There was none.

He looked at the legs, slightly bent and leaning toward the setting sun. The left leg was bruised, and the left foot was bruised and swollen, freshly bruised.

He saw pubic hair peeking out from the burned-into-tatters underwear. *This is human. This is real. Oh, no, I've just walked into a crime scene. It's up to me not to disturb anything,* he thought.

Brewster planted his feet firmly and noticed exactly where he stood. He stood for only twenty seconds and took one more good look at the body to make sure it had been human. *Memorize where you walked,* he told himself.

He turned around and walked back to his vehicle, making sure he took the same path to his truck as he had to the body.


Register had already turned around his van, as if ready to leave. He walked over to Brewster. "What do you think?"

Brewster radioed Nielsen. "We need law enforcement." He faced Register. "We need you to hang around and talk to law enforcement."

"No, I really need to be going," Register said as his three-year-old son bawled. "He's very upset."

"We need you to stay."

"I want to leave." Register glanced toward his van, almost as if he were at a funeral home.

"But you found the body. They'll want to talk to you."

"I'll be staying inside the park. You can find me," he insisted. "I'll be at Mudd Cove."

Brewster listened to the cries of Register's son. He thought about how the ashes looked cold. The killer was obviously gone. Mudd Cove was just five minutes away. "You've got to at least give me your driver's license," he answered. "I've got to at least be able to identify you."

"Will you walk over to my van to write down the information?" Register said. "Talk to me within earshot of my son and talk to me about it just being a mannequin."

They did, and Register's three-year-old son wailed, "But I saw the legs. But I saw the hair on his legs!"

"Oh, no," said Brewster, his stomach squeezing tight with anxiety for the child. "They do this a lot. Don't worry about it. It just looks real."

Moments later, Travis County Sheriffs officer Chuck Register was gone, and Brewster was left writing down the van's license plate number as the witness drove away.

He turned up his radio. TCSO was en route. EMS was en route. His job, now, he knew, was to protect the crime scene, despite the urge to play detective.

He forced himself to stand only at his vehicle door. *Where are the hands?* Staying put, he scanned the campground for hands. He saw, maybe, some litter. *Gee, I'm handling this well,* he thought. *I've got my emotions under control. I'm gonna act professionally.*

Brewster reminded himself again to simply protect the crime scene. He stared over at the body.


After five long minutes of Brewster's staring at the mutilated body, Kurt Nielsen pulled up and parked next to him. "Mutilated" wasn't a fact Brewster had relayed.

Nielsen got out of his car to look. Shaken, he said, "This is bad." From the left, he walked up to the body. "We need to back up our vehicles to the road."

They moved their vehicles thirty feet away, canceled Pedernales EMS, the closest volunteer unit, and STARflight. Rescue AID 16 from nearby Highways 620 and 71 was still on its way without lights and sirens.

"Why don't we replace AID sixteen with the medical examiner?" Brewster suggested.

Dispatch insisted that EMS make the pronouncement.

At 6:05 P.M., in downtown Austin, Travis County Sheriffs sergeant Timothy Gage directed Detectives Manuel Mancias Jr. and Mark Sawa to respond to Pace Bend Park. Sawa left first, to service his vehicle; Mancias drove toward the park.

Despite the cancel call, Pedernales was still on its way to Pace Bend. When Brewster looked up to see the Pedernales EMS truck driving down the dirt road, he realized they'd forgotten to block off the entrance to the cove. "Kurt," he called.

Nielsen flagged down the EMS team thirty yards from the scene. Shortly after, Brewster handed Nielsen Chuck Register's driver's license and license plate numbers. He drove Nielsen's vehicle to his post at the park gate so that he could escort the sheriffs deputies to the crime scene. It was about 6:10 P.M., just forty minutes since he had decided to take a relaxing patrol through his park.

In the solitude, Michael Brewster wondered, *What's the world coming to?*

At 6:15 P.M., the first official Travis County Sheriffs deputy arrived at Pace Bend. Park Ranger Kurt Nielsen immediately turned the scene over to Officer Don Rios. Rios, who took his own quick look at the deceased, noticed that the genital area had been burned.

Five minutes later, Austin EMS unit AID 16 arrived. They, too, observed the scene, then contacted Brackenridge Hospital. At 6:30 P.M., the mutilated-and-burned white-male homicide victim was pronounced dead.

Mancias believed he was headed to a routine homicide. As he drove, the investigator was told, "The hands of the deceased were removed." He knew then this case would be different.

At 6:55 P.M., Brewster greeted Mancias at the park gate and

recounted how he'd learned of the body. Like Ranger Nielsen before him, Mancias suddenly had "this is bad" painted on his face.

Sergeant Gage arrived, and the park ranger led the two officers 3.4 miles into the park, wound them between trees and campsites, then stopped near the Lake Travis shore and picnic table 117.

Gage was a tattooed Marlboro Light smoker who only recently had begun working the Criminal Investigation Division (CID) and now was the unit's supervisor. Mancias was a handsome, physically fit, immaculately groomed detective with starched shirts and tight jeans who loved golf and referred to cigarettes as cancer sticks.

Gage and Mancias got out of their vehicles and took a quick look at the victim. It was even more gruesome than they'd imagined, as though the killer had purposely put his victim on display.

"Ritualistic," was whispered. "Who would do such a thing?" was said out loud. "Why would they cut someone's hands off?"

But the detectives knew why the hands were missing—the perpetrator had done it to hide the victim's identity.

"What kind of person can sit there and cut off somebody's hands?"

They began making field notes while waiting for the crime lab technicians. They noted the position of the body and how far it rested from the lapping water's edge. They wondered if they had multiple victims. The word "ritualistic" came up again.

Mancias shook his head. In truth, at this point, they just didn't know what they had. *How could anyone have done such a thing?* It was a thought that would not leave their minds.

Within an hour and a half, all necessary personnel were on the scene and the investigation began. Yellow crime tape was up. Sawa was on the scene, as was the county sheriff and captain. Gage had designated Mancias as the lead detective.

Mancias asked Sawa to track down Chuck Register. Sawa

and Nielsen left together to find him, stopping first at Nielsen's house to pick up the park ranger's children. He didn't want them home alone, in the park. Pace Bend just had something different in the air that January night. And it wasn't something anyone liked.

Crime Lab Technician Tracy Hill lit the area with a generator-powered spotlight. She and Gage searched the area in a clockwise direction. They placed black plates painted with white numerals around tire tracks, plastic bags, and footprints.

She photographed the scene with both a still camera and video camera. As she moved her lens around the fire ring, picnic tables, and trees, the night was pitch-dark and deathly silent. A flashlight rudely pointed out the evidence and her body cast a haunting shadow on the corpse.

Nielsen left his children with Brewster. Register still had his frightened child with him.

The officers listened carefully as Register quietly spoke. "I saw what I thought was hair on the legs, toenails on the feet, and underwear." He talked about the missing hands, the missing head, the charred black body with the pale white legs. "No," he said, "I didn't touch anything." Neither, he said, did Ranger Brewster.

Mancias approached the dead body. He studied its burned maroon briefs and noticed a burned T-shirt with the word "cowboy" printed across the front. There were other letters, but they were burned away.

A four-to-six-inch piece of blackened firewood rested like a necklace in the neck or chin area—or what should have been the neck and chin area. Like the face and skull, both were missing.

The burned right arm bent inward at the elbow toward the body. Underneath that arm, another piece of burned firewood rested against the right rib area.

Mancias glanced to the side of the fire ring. A piece of unburned firewood, still in its plastic store-wrapping, lay just four feet away.

The left upraised arm, which seemed to call for help, propped itself against the metal ring of the firepit. Mancias stared harder at that left arm. There were serrated cuts on its exposed bone; ligature marks appeared around the wrist area. The lack of blood indicated that the mutilation had probably occurred after the young man was dead.

The detective's gaze traveled back to the stomach, which was scorched, possibly from the burning shirt, and discolored, definitely by the flames.

He again studied the underwear. Around the left genital area and right hip, the briefs were partially burned into tatters. Around the left hip, they were burned to nonexistence.

But not a hair on the legs was burned. There was a one-inch bruise on the right leg. There appeared to be transferred blood on the left leg, but no burns. The bare feet were clean—even the soles were spotless. The toenails were perfectly clipped.

Mancias stared at the buttocks, which rested on the large flat rock. The rock elevated the hips three or four inches above the torso, almost like the body had tried to lift itself above the fire and away from the flames. The burn marks streaked from the torso to the pelvis.

Mancias stood and looked around the body. There was string near the right leg. Dribbles of bright blue plastic, almost like Mardi Gras beads, lay on the rock beneath the body and in the dirt beneath the left leg.

Gage discovered a white comforter and a black, blue, and gray sleeping bag in a fifty-five-gallon trash barrel close to another picnic table, a trash barrel next to an oak tree and sixty feet from the body. Blood soaked both the comforter and sleeping bag. The amount of blood stunned Gage.

The comforter, sleeping bag, and trash barrel were bagged for evidence by Hill.

The media were about to swarm like fire ants in heat, and Park Ranger Michael Brewster was ordered to protect the entrance to the cove from the press, while still watching Nielsen's children.

He loaded the kids into Nielsen's vehicle, drove to the entrance of Kate's and Johnson's coves, and blocked the entrance with the vehicle. One moment he fielded excited questions from the kids. The next moment he fielded excited questions from the media. To all, he tried to give vague answers. The kids were less persistent than the media.

"Look, sometimes you see a sight like that and you just need someone to talk to," said reporter after reporter. "If you want to get it off your chest, I promise, we'll keep the cameras off and I won't be taking notes. You'll have someone to talk to."

Brewster declined.

The sounds of night filled the winter air—raccoons roaming, owls calling, the occasional collision of tires spinning in hard dirt. Medical Examiner Investigator Bob Davis stared at the body. He spotted what appeared to be a hacksaw blade under the right armpit. The blade was burned but still intact. He left it beneath the armpit to be bagged with the body.

Davis rolled the mutilated corpse over on its side. What looked to be two large charcoal briquettes, or cow dung that'd cooked in the sun too long, lay beneath it. "They look like they're the hands," said Davis. "Dr. Bayardo will have to confirm that." Dr. Bayardo was the Travis County chief medical examiner.

Eventually Davis removed the body. Since it was so late in

the night, the detectives decided to secure the crime scene and return the following morning. A cover was placed over the fire ring to protect it from scavenging animals and the wind.

Park Ranger Daniel Chapman, an off-duty supervisor, spent the night at the crime scene. He was assigned to protect it from any campers.

Contrary to his statement to Michael Brewster, that he could be found at Mudd Cove, Chuck Register and his three-year-old son had already left the park.

As Mancias drove out of the quiet park, he noticed that the temperature on that January night was a balmy 70 degrees. The sky was partly cloudy to cloudy.

He stopped at the closest Circle K convenience store. "Has anyone bought any firewood from here lately?"

The cashier said no and glanced at the firewood propped outside the store, against the windows. The firewood was wrapped in plastic just like the single piece that lay four feet from the dead body. "But someone could have stolen some."

# Two

Thursday morning, January 12, 1995, Park Ranger Michael Brewster awoke to the sound of wisecracking disc jockeys laughing and joking on the radio about some people who had found a dead, mutilated body on a picnic table.

*Boy, what are the odds,* thought Brewster. *I found a mutilated body, not on a picnic table, but on the ground.* A couple of groggy minutes passed before it dawned on Brewster that the deejays were talking about the body he had found. It was going to be a strange day.

At 7:30 A.M., Detective Mancias, his partner Mark Sawa, Sergeant Gage, and Crime Lab Technician Tracy Hill were already back at Pace Bend staring at the fire ring in the gray light of the morning. Hill photographed the area again and made plaster casts of the tire tracks she'd photographed the night before.

Detective Jim Davenport, a trained arson investigator, arrived and looked through the firepit. He took a few samples, then Mancias, Sawa, and Hill began to sift through the ash. Using a screen, they filtered out bone fragment after bone fragment.

With an eye out for vultures, Hill left to take aerial photographs of Pace Bend. The helicopter made low repeated passes over the park. Texas Ranger "Rocky" Wardlow peered out of the chopper's windows and watched for more bodies. The word "ritualistic" still hadn't left the investigators' minds.


Just after lunchtime, Hill, Mancias, Davenport, and Dr. Roberto Bayardo gathered at the county morgue. A nearly nude, severed, blackened corpse lay on the table before them, its belly protruding as if it had just eaten too much, too fast.

Dr. Bayardo noticed a portion of charred brain. The neck was almost completely missing. A portion of the throat kept the skull attached to the thorax.

The numerous scorch marks indicated that a powerful, fast-burning accelerant, possibly charcoal lighter, had been placed on the victim's shoulders, back, and head and had been allowed to soak into the T-shirt.

Davenport believed that the burned logs he had seen at the park must have been soaked in accelerant and placed in the head and chin areas and the armpits. There were deep burn and char patterns on both sides of the body between the waistline and armpits, as if the flames had burned up and outward.

The maroon underwear the body wore had a white waistband with a label that read "HANES M (32-34)." The underwear was cut away and the corpse's pubic hair was singed.

Dr. Bayardo showed Mancias two X rays, one of the victim's hands, the other of the victim's chest and head. Dr. Bayardo had pulled out of a paper bag what appeared to be two hands. The left hand was better preserved than the right, which consisted of only two metacarpal bones.

Davenport noted that the hands, too, had been soaked in accelerant. They looked like barbecued pig's knuckles.

The detectives and coroner saw that the left hand perfectly matched the amputated forearm. There was an extra saw cut, as if someone had started to saw in one spot and then changed his mind and moved to another spot.

On the chest and head X ray, there were six small white dots.

The white dots were bird shot from a shotgun. A BB pellet located in the head area was removed and collected.

The victim was murdered by shotgun blast to the forehead, perhaps just to the right of the forehead, Bayardo determined.

The body measured sixty-eight inches tall, 160 pounds. Its age was less than twenty-six years and closer to early twenties. "The color of the head hair on the deceased was possibly brown, based on the color of the hair on the body's legs," he said.

Dr. Bayardo studied the victim's legs. There appeared to be eight abrasions on the knee. The abrasions were actually burn marks. The second toe on the right foot was longer than the big toe.

He cut open the body from the neck to the pubis. An undigested French fry was found in the stomach. No smoke was found in the lungs. More than likely, the victim was dead before he was burned.

The lungs were partially shrunken and coagulated from the heat of the fire. The myocardium of the heart was also partially coagulated, as was the esophagus, also from the heat of the fire.

Death, said Dr. Bayardo, probably happened the night before. Rigor mortis was slight. There was, perhaps, a couple of days of facial hair growth.

Dr. Bayardo moved back to the face and examined the jaw and teeth. One molar had been removed from the right lower jaw. There was a filling in the same area. All of the wisdom teeth were missing. "The upper lateral teeth were crowded," he added.

He noted a bit of white plastic substance on the upper lip. It measured three by one inches. Tracy Hill collected that substance for analysis. She also collected the hacksaw blade. She did not collect the French fry.

Hill left for the crime lab. Mancias went back to the office to meet with Detective Sawa. They had to sort through the missing persons reports, which were filing in after the media and disc jockeys had blared the story throughout several counties.

Sheriff Terry Keel had been quoted in the morning's *Austin American-Statesman* newspaper as saying the murder was "a typical gangland-style slaying" and that the victim had been placed in a manner designed to attract attention.


Friday, January 13, Mancias and Sawa spent the morning again tracking down missing persons leads. While Mancias returned to Pace Bend that afternoon, Sawa continued going through missing person after missing person report.

One person was too tall. One had motorcycle gang tattoos decorating his body. Another had a scar. Sawa's victim had clean, smooth skin marred only by fire. One was too dark. Another was in Florida. Another was in Malaysia. Sawa eliminated them all as possible murder victims.

Sawa received a call from Tracy Hill and joined her at the crime lab. Inside the bloodstained sleeping bag that had been found near the body, Hill had discovered "Hatton 9153" written on the care-and-use tag.

The handwriting looked frighteningly familiar to Sawa. It resembled that of a TCSO employee who had once worked the same patrol shift as Sawa, whose handwritten reports Sawa had often seen. It resembled the handwriting of Deputy Bill Hatton. Hatton now worked at the Del Valle county jail, just as Pace Bend camper Chuck Register did.

Sergeant Gage was called. It was 2:30 P.M., only three hours shy of the corpse's being unidentified for two days.


A veteran, Gage knew that military personnel often wrote their last name and the last four digits of their Social Security number in their belongings. Gage checked personnel records. Officer Hatton's Social Security number did not end with 9153.

The detectives were still at a dead end.

* * *

At four o'clock, Mancias and Sawa met at the coroner's office with John C. Schilthuis, DDS. The plan was for Dr. Schilthuis to X-ray the dead man's teeth to help, perhaps, in identification. In order to get a better view, Schilthuis wanted to do the X rays at his office. Plans were made for the doctor to do the X rays the following morning.

Sawa took the teeth into custody.


At 10:10 P.M., Mancias received a call at home from a TCSO watch commander.

The commander stated that he had gotten a call from Corporal Holly Frischkorn of the Round Rock Police Department. Round Rock was a thriving suburb north of Austin and home of Dell Computers. Frischkorn, said the commander, wanted to talk to Mancias about her missing nephew. Her nephew, she'd said, matched the description of the body.

Mancias phoned Frischkorn, who was at Dell Computers working an extra security job.

"I've been contacted by my nephew's supervisor at work," Frischkorn said into her cellular phone. "He's worried about my nephew Michael, who hasn't shown up for work since Wednesday, the eleventh." Her voice was cigarette deep. "When he heard the description of the body on the news, he got worried. That's when I called TCSO, who called you."

"What's your nephew's name?" said Mancias.

"Christopher Michael Hatton. I'm Bill Hatton's ex-wife. Bill and I adopted Michael several years ago."

"What does your nephew look like?"

"He's five feet, six inches tall, one hundred sixty pounds, clean-cut, dark hair, dark eyes."

"Has he been in the military?"

"The Navy."

"Do you know his Social Security number?"

"No, but his supervisor's standing right here." She looked over at Gary Thompson. "He might know."

Thompson got on the line. He didn't know Hatton's Social Security number, but he would go to his office and get it. "Chris checked out of work at nine-thirty on Sunday night," he said.

Hatton was known to his family as Michael. Everyone else called him Chris.

Thompson explained that Chris worked for Capitol Beverage, a supplier of Coors beer. "He was supposed to return to work on Wednesday but didn't. That's not like him. And that's why I'm worried something's wrong."

Frischkorn got back on the line.

"Do you know where your nephew lives?" asked Mancias.

"I only know that he lives in Austin in an apartment near Rundberg on North Lamar. All I have at home is his pager number and phone number. I've never been to his apartment." She could not, would not believe that her nephew was the body at Pace Bend Park. "Would you check his apartment and see if Michael is there?"

Gary Thompson said he would track down her nephew's address for Mancias.

"Does he own a vehicle?" said Mancias.

"I know he was trying to buy a truck. But he usually just rides his bike."

"Do you know if he's ever had any dental work, and if so, do you know his dentist's name?"

"He's seen a Dr. Jansa in Round Rock. I'll try to locate his address and phone number for you."

"I'll have to wake up my sergeant," said Mancias.

The officers hung up. Frischkorn called her dispatcher, Jim Fletcher, who was also her boyfriend and a friend of her nephew's. She asked Fletcher to phone Jansa and get her nephew's dental records.

Mancias paged Gage.

\* \* \*

It seemed that every time Tim Gage took his wife out to dinner he got a call-out. At 10:24 P.M., on Friday, January 13, it was no different. When he received the page from Mancias, Gage sat with his wife in the Bakehouse, a south Austin restaurant, on the opposite side of town from Round Rock.

Mancias arrived at TCSO headquarters before Gage and went to work alone. His partner, Mark Sawa, couldn't be reached.

Mancias ran a driver's license check on Christopher Michael Hatton: The address showed a North Lamar apartment, just as Frischkorn had suggested; an April 11, 1972, date of birth, making Hatton twenty-two years old; a height and weight of five nine and 165 pounds, just one inch and five pounds different from what the coroner had suggested; and dark hair, just as the coroner had said.

Gage arrived and began to cross-reference the address from Hatton's driving record. Learning the name and phone number of the residing apartment complex, he dialed the number. He reached an answering service. After identifying himself, Gage gave the operator his name and number, and the operator relayed the information to the apartment manager.

Minutes later, a sleepy Dawn Trevino called. It was eleven at night and the answering service had awakened her.

"Does a Chris Hatton live there?" asked Gage, explaining that he was investigating a possible murder.

Trevino gave the apartment number.

"Have you seen him lately?"

"Not since he paid his rent around January fifth. He has a roommate, but I haven't seen him in some time, either."

"Can you meet me at the apartment? In about an hour? We have some concerns and might need to access it."

"I'll do whatever you need me to do." She'd heard him say it was a matter of life and death.

They hung up. But a nervous Trevino pressed the reset button on her phone and dialed out again. She called a friend on the Austin police force and asked him to meet her at the apartment complex. She didn't want to go to the Aubry Hills Apartments at midnight by herself, especially since she didn't know if the caller truly was who he said he was—a homicide detective.

While Gage talked to Trevino, Gary Thompson phoned Mancias. He had Chris Hatton's Social Security number. The last four digits matched what was printed on the sleeping bag.

Round Rock Police Department dispatcher Jim Fletcher phoned Holly Frischkorn.

"Dr. Jansa's in Colorado, but his wife's going to the office and pulling the charts."

The information was relayed to Mancias, who then contacted the dentist's wife. Deborah Jansa and Mancias agreed to meet at her Round Rock home to get the charts.

The investigation had become an unstoppable, rolling boulder.

# Three

At 11:42 P.M., Friday, January 13, 1995, Mancias and Gage left TCSO headquarters. At midnight they obtained the dental records from Deborah Jansa and drove to the Aubry Hills Apartments.

The Aubry Hills was a gated complex with a swimming pool and tennis courts, large trees that smothered the noise of traffic speeding down multilane Lamar Boulevard, beat-up cars, crooked and bent mini-blinds, and razor wire atop one electric fence. Dawn Trevino anxiously waited alone in her office.

After identifying themselves, Mancias and Gage talked with Trevino for fifteen minutes.

"I spoke to Chris quite a bit during the week," she said. Trevino was petite with long, dark hair. "He was upset. His roommate had left—"

"When?"

"In late December, and Chris was concerned about being able to pay the rent. We talked about possibly transferring him to a smaller apartment or possibly adding a new roommate. He said he'd let me know. Later he said he'd possibly found a new roommate and would probably be staying in his apartment. Later he said the new roommate hadn't worked out."

"Who's his roommate?"

She showed Mancias and Gage rental applications filled out by Hatton and a William Busenburg.

"Do you have any idea who the new roommate was that he was referring to?" said Gage.

"No idea. Chris was evasive about that."

"Do you know why Busenburg moved out? Did they have a fight or disagreement?"

"I don't know," she said. "But they were two very different personalities. Chris was easygoing and easy to get along with. He was real quiet. Will was demanding and wanted everything done immediately."

"What do you mean by that?"

"If there was something wrong in the apartment, it was usually Will who came to complain and then he wanted it repaired quickly. And he said it in a demanding way. He just generally had a poor attitude. But with Chris, if there was a problem, he wouldn't ask. He was very timid about it."

She offered the officers copies of the rental application.

As Mancias and Gage studied them, Gage noticed that two vehicles were noted on the application, a 1994 Dodge Dakota and a 1994 Chevy Cheyenne. "Do you know which vehicle belonged to which tenant?"

Trevino didn't know. "Chris almost always rode his bicycle."

Busenburg had written on the rental application that his previous employer had been the U.S. Army, where he had been a medical specialist, and his current employer was Intermedics Ortho, where he manufactured artificial implants.

Hatton's previous employer was listed as the U.S. Navy, where his job had been BM—Special Warfare. His current job was entered as merchandiser for Capitol Beverage.

Mancias called the Austin Police Department and requested uniformed backup.

At 12:25 A.M., Saturday, January 14, 1995, TCSO, APD, and Trevino approached Hatton's second-floor apartment. It was toward the rear of the complex, next to an alley and a wooden fence without razor wire or electricity.

Gage knocked on the door. "Sheriffs department!"

There was no response.

Gage unlocked the door and opened it. "Sheriffs department!" He shouted it several times into the dark apartment.

Dawn Trevino waited a safe distance away. All of the officers entered the apartment, illuminating the room with their flashlights.

A single folding chair, a mess of items stacked against the wall, a can of Ajax cleaner, an opened box of Hefty Steel Sak, a *Playboy* magazine (the girls of the SEC issue), another adult magazine, and a plastic container for a tarp were all that filled an otherwise empty living room. *Disarray,* thought Gage.

A small divider wall or counter separated the living room and kitchen. On that wall was a note scribbled on an envelope: "Chris, I bought you a burrito and came by until Steph gets off from work, I'll be back around two or so to say hi, Will." And there was a later notation about eating the burrito.

There was also a pager, a guitar in a trash bag leaning against the wall, and plates on the floor.

In the kitchen sat an unopened box of tall kitchen trash bags and an open can of paint. In the dining area there were some cowboy hatboxes and cowboy boots on the floor and a dartboard on the wall.

The officers moved down the hallway. Gage entered a small bedroom on the left. He steadied his flashlight beam on a bed frame turned on its side. On the headboard were skull fragments with hair attached.

Mancias walked into the master bedroom. His light flashed across an almost empty room—no bed, but a computer desk, a pair of underwear, and a few boxes. He opened the closet. No one and nothing was there.

He met Gage in the small bedroom. Mancias noticed that there was no mattress or box spring. A large portion of three walls and the ceiling appeared to have been recently painted with a white-toned paint a few shades different from the old.

Gage pointed his flashlight onto a large stain that looked

like blood. It was on the carpet next to a wall. Someone, it appeared, had tried to clean up the blood. A small bone fragment rested near the stain and headboard. Another bone fragment lay near the door.

The window was open. The blinds were drawn. There were a chest of drawers, a nightstand, and a brown folding chair.

The officers checked the closet. They checked the bathrooms.

They had the murder scene.

"Ms. Trevino," the detectives called. "Would you come here?"

Trevino climbed the stairs to the apartment and entered the small bedroom on the left.

"Would you verify that this is not the condition the unit was in when they moved in?"

She did.

"Is it normally kept in such disarray?"

"I don't think so." She said the maintenance man would know better than she would. "He may have been in the apartment since I was. And he may know which vehicle belongs to Chris."

"Would you call the maintenance man and have him respond to our location?"

Trevino said she would. Everyone exited the apartment, and the detectives closed the door, securing it with yellow crime tape. Sergeant Gage requested a crime lab technician.

At one in the morning, Technicians Tracy Hill and Dolly Day were paged.

While waiting for Hill and Day, Gage and Mancias began questioning the neighboring tenants. Allen Cooper, who lived in the apartment that shared a common wall with the murder site, hadn't heard a thing. Most neighbors hadn't.

But tenant Aaron Green had heard "two pops" late one night, one night during the middle of the week.

"Could you be more specific about the time of day?" said Gage.

Green couldn't. "The sound of gunfire isn't uncommon around here, so I didn't give it much thought," he replied. "But I was asleep when I heard it."

Another neighbor, Mario Ybarra, told Mancias that Wednesday morning, around midnight or one o'clock, he had been awakened by something that sounded like a gunshot, one gunshot. Ybarra had waited. He'd listened. He hadn't heard anything else, so he'd gone back to sleep.

Maintenance man Rex Dorsett arrived. He couldn't tell Sergeant Gage which vehicle belonged to Hatton, but he could tell him that neither truck was currently parked in the lot.

Around 2 A.M., Gage requested the blood splatter knowledge of Detective Tommy Wooley.

Fifteen minutes later, Hill and Day arrived, armed with still and video cameras. They entered the apartment with Mancias, Gage, and maintenance man Dorsett. He verified the apartment was not usually in this state of disarray and left.

The detectives showed Hill and Day what needed to be photographed. As Hill photographed the living room, Mancias watched from outside. He noticed a waist-high blood smear on the front door frame and pointed it out to Gage and Hill.

Hill finished photographing the living room, so Mancias reentered it to take a better look. A TV and VCR sat on a stand against the living room wall. Nearby lay a stack of magazines with *Soldier of Fortune* on top.

Hill photographed the kitchen, the countertops, the stove, the floor, the overflowing trash cans. The countertops were a mess—a Halloween decoration sat on one, a Dr Pepper three-liter bottle sat on another. Christmas cards hung along one of the dividing walls/counter.

Mancias walked to the rear of the apartment. He stared at the huge bloodstain on the aquamarine-colored carpet of the smaller bedroom. The red blood on aquamarine carpet mixed to a near black in the stain's most soaked center. On its outer edges, the blood looked more like a large, spilled can of Hawaiian Punch.

Mancias stared at the walls and the fast, sloppy, unfinished paint job. It was obvious that blood would be splashed between the two white paints—one flat, one semigloss—like spaghetti sauce between two slices of bread.

Mancias focused his attention on the headboard, which was turned on its side but still attached to the bed frame, then on the closet door. A paper nametag with Chris Hatton written in bold black ink was stuck to the door frame.

Detective Tommy Wooley arrived and looked at the blood-splattered bedroom while Hill photographed the dining area, the items on the dining room floor, and a closet in the dining area.

She began to move to the bedrooms when she overheard Mancias and Wooley talking. "Do you think we should get a search warrant?" said Wooley. They decided they should. Hill ceased photographing the apartment.

Wooley and Mancias left for downtown Austin and TCSO headquarters to prepare an affidavit.

At 5:08 A.M., on Saturday, January 14, 1995, municipal judge David Spencer signed the search warrant for the apartment on North Lamar Boulevard in Austin, Texas. Two minutes later, Wooley let Gage know they had the warrant.

At 5:15 A.M., Hill and Day returned to the crime lab to mix up a batch of Luminol, the chemical that makes blood glow in the dark.

At 5:25 A.M., Mancias and Wooley arrived back at Aubry Hills, and Wooley began his close inspection of the apartment. In the master bedroom, he noticed that the boxes on the floor were empty gun boxes, one for a Winchester 1300 Defender 12-gauge shotgun, the other for a Savage .243-caliber rifle.

In the small bedroom, he noted cans of white spray paint sitting on a dresser. There was a large white fingerprint on the bed frame, another white fingerprint on a brown folding chair splattered with white paint. There were no blood splatters that could help the investigation.

The piece of skull on the headboard, however, told him that the murder victim had been lying in bed when he was blasted in the head by a shotgun, exploding his head.

Wooley left Aubry Hills to run checks on Chris Hatton and his roommate, Will Busenburg.

Hill and Day arrived back on the scene around 6 A.M. They completed photographing the apartment and began collecting evidence: a blue Lysol lid, a newspaper with a shoe impression on it, a VHS tape with "Chris 244-9739" on it, and two maroon T-shirts inside a Randalls grocery store bag, all from the living room.

From the dividing wall/counter separating the living room from the kitchen, they collected, among other things, the hand-written note to Chris from Will and the pager. The pager had five calls on it: 10:07 P.M., 1:23 P.M., 10:01 A.M., 5:21 P.M., and 11:15 A.M. Two of the pages were from the same phone number.

Time was ticking away. Daylight was approaching. The Luminol tests had to be done while it was still dark. Evidence collection was put on hold so that the Luminol tests could begin.

At 6:15 A.M., Hill sprayed the master bathroom with Luminol; then she turned out the lights. The showerhead glowed. The tile walls were illuminated. Foot marks on the wall shone. The dirty bottom of the bathtub glowed with blue light—the Luminol blue light of blood. The drain glowed. Gage saw the swirling path a gush of blood had taken as it washed into the drain.

Photographs were made of the Luminol blood glow.

Hill continued spraying. The outside of the tub glowed with large, running blood drips. The bathroom floor glowed in swirling mop marks, as if the blood had been scrubbed from the floor.

The vividness of the bloody cleanup stunned Sergeant Gage. The Luminol shine, he thought, told the story. The lack of shine also told the story. When Hill sprayed the hallway, there was no blood glow. Gage knew that the body had been dragged on a comforter or sleeping bag from the bedroom to the bathroom. Either had obviously caught the blood. Both had been found at Pace Bend Park.

Finally Hill sprayed the bedroom with Luminol. The walls and ceiling flashed like lightning. It was the quick glow of the blood beneath the fresh paint. Gage had never seen anything like it. Flashing blood. The sheer amount of splatter.

Hill sprayed again. The blood flashed again, streaking like electricity burning the sky, burning Gage's memory.

He thought about the living room and the dining room, the packed boxes, the stacked dishes on the floor. *The killer was packing up the apartment to move.* His mind went back to the bedroom; the blood must have dripped like a waterfall. *He spent a lot of time with all that wet blood, scrubbing, painting. He returned more than once.* Gage shook his head and walked out the door for a cigarette. He knew the killer would be back. The job wasn't finished.

Mancias and Hill returned to the bloody bedroom. He helped her cut out a piece of blood-coated carpet. The bottom of the carpet was saturated with blood, too. Between the carpet and baseboard, they found four lead pellets, shotgun shell BBs. Hill collected them.

Gage came back in and searched the wall. He noticed what appeared to be painted-over BB holes. It looked as though more shotgun pellets were embedded there.

Mancias aimed his knife at the drywall. He bore out a triangular-shaped piece and handed it to Hill for collection.

He then left for TCSO headquarters—he had a meeting. Gage's thick Texas accent was becoming thicker with exhaustion. Friday had turned into a long beginning of a Saturday.

From the dining room floor, Hill collected a hatchet and knife in a leather case. In the dining room closet, she and Day found and tagged a white-colored U.S. Navy cap with "Hatton 9153" written on it, just like the sleeping bag recovered days before; a red cassette-tape holder, also with "Hatton 9153" written on it; a Winchester model 1300 box; and one small blue dot—like those found near the fire ring at Pace Bend Park.

From the kitchen, rubber gloves with blood on them, trash cans, a Coke bottle, a cleaning rag, and an Oshman's Sporting Goods receipt were collected. The Oshman's receipt was for a shotgun. There were also letters to Will Busenburg from an attorney representing Oshman's demanding payment for the gun.

Hill collected a sales ticket for a $19.99 skull mask; stained paper towels; a flashlight; Coke cans; and a butter knife with paint on it. The knife lay in the sink.

She and Day tagged a three-quarters empty can of glossy white Rustoleum paint, a steel wool pad, the three-liter Dr Pepper bottle that had a white paint fingerprint on it, an Ivory soap bottle, a container of Copenhagen tobacco, a roll of duct tape, and an empty vacuum cleaner bag.

A honing stone with honing oil for sharpening a knife was also tagged.

In one bathroom, they collected a rug with stains, a small burgundy towel, and a cigarette butt from a trash can. She took two swabs for blood from the sink.

From the master bedroom, she and Day photographed and tagged the shotgun boxes and a green table box containing photographs. Also in that room was a plastic Halloween sickle, like the one carried by the Grim Reaper.

In the master bath, Hill and Day photographed and collected a blue-striped shower curtain and swabbed for blood on the side, back, bottom, and caulking of the tub.

Then they moved into the murder scene bedroom. They took close-up photographs of the blood, which dripped from the headboard. They photographed and collected the paint-covered folding chair. From a nightstand, they took a can of Lysol, a can of Woolite upholstery cleaner, and a bottle of All detergent.

From the drawer of the nightstand, they tagged a green address book, one empty 12-gauge shotgun shell, and an insurance packet containing a doctor's receipt. Also in that nightstand was a military photograph. Paperback books, including a book of poetry, were scattered throughout. A poster was on the bedroom door. There was a plastic milk carton full of change.

Near the nightstand stood a white bucket filled with milky-looking water, a red scrub brush, a red-handled paintbrush, and a blue-handled paintbrush. They collected it all.

They bagged bone fragments from the headboard and the floor, Krylon paint from the dresser, men's black Hanes underwear from the dresser drawer, and two Round Rock High School annuals on the floor near the dresser. Photographs of Hatton and Busenburg were in the annuals.

They took the headboard with blood on it and a portion of the brown metal bed rail. Gage broke them down to be removed.

A red Hoover vacuum cleaner sat in the closet. Still plugged into an outlet just outside the closet, it was stuffed beneath a high school letterman's jacket and crammed next to a fishing pole. Hill disconnected the vacuum's hose and found it to be filled with bone fragments and dried blood. She could see how the blood had dripped through the connections.

Hill then collected a piece of paper marked with a bloody shoe print.

Throughout the two-bedroom, two-bath apartment, she found twelve latent fingerprints on everything from the can of Krylon paint to the can of Copenhagen tobacco.


Sergeant Gage made sure that a surveillance team was requested. He wanted someone there to catch the killer when he returned.

At 7 A.M., Deputy Richard Hale was called. When he arrived on the scene, Hale told Gage, "I'll need backup for the surveillance."

About the same time, Detective Wooley returned with a date of birth, "10-22-72," for William Michael Busenburg. Busenburg became an official suspect.

The officers loaded up the crime lab van, and Hill and Day returned to the TCSO crime lab. Gage pulled down the yellow crime scene tape and purposely dropped it just to the left of the front door. He, Hale, and Wooley left to try to search out fingerprints for Will Busenburg and to access a call roster to find someone to work backup for Hale.

They didn't find fingerprints, but they did find an address for Busenburg. It matched that of the murder site. They also found a vehicle registration for a 1994 Chevrolet pickup truck, Texas license plate number KW3-883, in his name.


Detectives Manny Mancias and Mark Sawa walked into the office of Dr. John Schilthuis, DDS. It was about 9:45 A.M., Saturday, January 14, 1995.

Dr. Schilthuis looked at the X rays he'd made of the murder victim and those the detectives had brought from Dr. Robert Jansa. In Schilthuis's opinion, the X rays matched. But the detectives needed more confirmation. They took the X rays and teeth from Dr. Schilthuis and drove to the county morgue.

They handed the X rays to Dr. Roberto Bayardo. It was then official. The burned, handless, near-headless murder victim was Christopher Michael Hatton.

# Four

On April 11, 1972, Christopher Michael Hatton was born in Dadeville, Alabama, a town of fewer than 3,000 residents living in the lush foothills of the Appalachian Mountains and swimming in the clear waters of Lake Martin. It was a community where crosses were burned in yards and white police officers refused to ride with black police officers.

The baby's mother, Rhonda Hatton, was a pretty, dark-haired, thin, young woman from a large family of Native American descent, most of whom grew up to own their own successful construction companies. Christopher Michael looked just like his mother, and he grew up to hate that. He was short, handsome, dark-featured, and had thick dark hair with a widow's peak. He was, in all eyes, a beautiful child.

In his eyes, he felt his mother didn't want to touch him; she didn't even want to bathe her baby. She rarely hugged him, or told him she loved him. He believed his mother had only had children to suit his father.

His father, who was named Michael Hatton, was a tall, handsome man from a military family—the son of a sergeant major and a mother who had been a World War II POW in Poland. That background provided Christopher Michael's father with impeccable manners and a strong work ethic.

Together, he and Rhonda—who had dated Michael's brother Bill in high school—had Christopher Michael, and several years later, another son, Brian. Michael Hatton took his children to church, taught his sons to open doors for ladies, to respect their elders, to say "yes, sir" and "no, ma'am."

Still, Christopher Michael could speak disrespectfully of other races. He used the "n-word," and, as he got older, he often made negative comments about his mother. But the young boy felt he had his just reasons, and they had nothing to do with race. Rhonda Hatton had a reputation for picking on her eldest son and spoiling her youngest.

In the fall of 1986, Michael Hatton—who worked two jobs, held the family together, clothed them, fed them, and got the boys up for school—fell ill with a fever. As his temperature hit 105 degrees, he entered the hospital. Concerned Hatton family members flew to Alabama to be with him.

On the third day of the fever, Michael Hatton began hallucinating. When he became violent in the hospital hallway, the police were called. They struck him while subduing him, some of the blows hitting Michael Hatton in the head. That night, his fever broke. The following day, he was taken for X rays, and later the same day, died.

No one ever clearly determined the cause of death—fever, hospital staff negligence, or police brutality. But Michael Hatton was dead.

With her husband's death, Rhonda Hatton had two young sons, the boys' Social Security income, and, according to her son and other family members, a severe case of alcoholism.

Soon thereafter, Round Rock, Texas, police officer Holly Frischkorn married Travis County, Texas, deputy sheriff William Hatton. It was her second marriage, his third, and it got off to a rough start. The Bill that Holly married was not the Bill she had dated. A man who kept his emotions bottled, he changed the day his brother, Michael, died.

From Texas, the Hattons repeatedly called Child Protective Services in Alabama about Christopher Michael and Brian. Repeatedly a CPS worker drove out to Rhonda Hatton's home and sat down with the mother and boys. She questioned them about the allegations of abuse. They denied them all. With their mother sitting beside them, the boys couldn't tell the truth.

Within a year or two of his father's death, Christopher Michael, who went by "Mike" and "Michael," dropped out of school. He spent his days hanging out in the woods of Alabama. He spent his nights stealing stop signs and construction signs, then decorated his bedroom with them. It was easy for Mike to do this; his mother often went a week without seeing him.

When Rhonda Hatton finally walked into her eldest son's bedroom and saw his collection of traffic signs, she called the cops. The police showed up on her doorstep, took the signs from Mike, and laughed off his case. They knew too well his home situation.

Mike soon grew strong enough to fight back against his mother, so she sent him to live with his uncle Bill and aunt Holly in Texas.

Bill and Holly became Mike's legal guardians so that they could enroll him in Round Rock High School. His return to school was a stipulation of his move. Mike wanted simply to get his GED.

"It's school or nothing," Holly had said.

Holly was charmed by Mike. The 1988 day that she and Bill drove Mike home from Austin's Robert Mueller Airport, she picked up the young teen's luggage to carry it into the house. Mike ran to the front door, swung it open, and ran back to grab the luggage from Holly.

"Aunt Holly, you'll never have to carry anything again. You don't have to worry about anything anymore. I'm here." And he smiled.

Holly thought the polite, handsome boy was a godsend. She was a tall, kindhearted woman with a good smile, who had always wanted kids and couldn't have any.

* * *

Round Rock was a bit different from rural Alabama. It was in the process of forsaking its own rural, farming past to become a high-tech, booming suburb full of solid-income, churchgoing Republicans who flocked to the community from states north and west.

Its community leaders took pride in their urban sprawl and chain restaurants that popped up faster than weeds in the nearby sorghum fields. Its parents believed in protecting their children by banning books in the schools and preaching against abortion. They expected their children to grow into God-fearing, college-educated successes who married the opposite sex and produced athletic babies.

At Round Rock High, Mike Hatton decided to leave his Alabama past behind by changing his name to Chris. But he couldn't change his sweet, soft Alabama accent that Texans had a hard time understanding. And he couldn't bring himself to tell his family that at school he was called Chris. To Holly, Bill, and Brian, he was still Mike, the Mike who wore only Levi's 501 button-fly jeans.

"Michael, you're going to have to get away from those Alabama things. There's no sheep around here for you to sneak up on in those button-up jeans," Holly teased.

"Oh, Aunt Holly." He began to blush. "I can't believe you said that."

"Well, what the hell do you not want a zipper for?" she laughed.

His blush flamed beet red. He was very teasible, and Holly liked to tease the boy she now loved like her own.

"You need to call your mom. It's her birthday," said Holly.

He only phoned Alabama without prodding when he called to check on his little brother, Brian.


Hatton was quiet, shy, and kept his worries and thoughts to himself. Because of that, he didn't have a lot of friends and spent much of his time with family. Often he rode patrol with

Holly in her squad car. Often he ran two to six miles a day, sometimes with his uncle Bill. Mike was a sprinter on the track team.

But he wasn't comfortable at school. He was older than most of his classmates, due to his lost time as a dropout. He struggled with his studies, particularly math and English. He wasn't good at getting his homework done. He was a slow reader, although he loved to read James Bond-like books and stories about mercenaries and military missions. Following in the family tradition of military service, he joined the Junior ROTC.

In June 1991, Mike Hatton was scheduled to go on a ROTC trip to California. But he was running late, which wasn't uncommon. Often he slept through four and five alarms and fell asleep in the shower. This time, though, there had been a mix-up in communication as to who was supposed to drive him to the bus, Holly or Bill.

Mike frantically called Holly, who drove him in her squad car, police sirens blaring. Mike acted like he shrugged it off as no big deal. But to the ROTC students at Round Rock High, it *was* a big deal.

"Oh, my God, what's happened?" said fifteen-year-old sophomore Lisa Pace, staring wide-eyed at the flashing blue lights. "The bus is going to be detained by the cops. We're never going to get to Disneyland. We're never going to get to California," she panicked to her girlfriend.

Then she saw nineteen-year-old senior Mike Hatton step out of the police car. With his thick dark hair and ROTC body, he was teen idol gorgeous. And he *had* thought about doing some modeling.

"Who is that guy? He is so cute," said Lisa, panting like a groupie.

"You don't know who that is?" said her friend Debbie. *"That's* Chris Hatton."

Round Rock High was so large that first-period ROTC members didn't know third-period ROTC members. But Debbie knew all the cute boys.

"Oh, he's really cute," moaned Lisa.

Lisa Pace was a tall, dark-haired, voluptuous flirt, and at that very moment, she set her sights on Chris Hatton. Despite a little schoolgirl voice, Lisa Pace could be domineering.

Hatton stepped onto the bus.

"Oh, special you. You got a police escort," the students ribbed. "Yeah, we were holding the bus just for you, Mr. Important."

By the time the bus rolled back into Texas one week later, Chris Hatton and Lisa Pace sat side by side, holding hands, as they slept on each other's shoulders. When they stepped off the bus, Lisa made sure she had his phone number.

Hatton later asked her if she could get her friend Katy to go out with his best friend, Glenn Conway. It would be a double date. The foursome went to SPSJT, a Round Rock live country-music bar. Hatton nervously looked around. Through the din of smoke, couples shuffled roper boots against a wooden floor, their arms wrapped around waists and necks. Chris looked away. He was a rotten dancer.

Lisa grabbed him and dragged him onto the floor. She was a great dancer. He looked at his feet and he tried to shuffle in rhythm. He just couldn't do it. They wouldn't go where he wanted.

Where he wanted was to go to the movies. Hatton loved action-packed, thriller-killer, blow-'em-up movies. From that night on, he and Lisa spent most of their dates at the movies, alone.


In September 1991, just months after Chris and Lisa started dating, Lisa's father was diagnosed with cancer. Chris held Lisa in his arms as she cried. "I know you're having a hard time," he whispered. "This is a thing, you know—people die. And you have to get through. My dad died, and I got through it. Everything will be okay."

She continued to weep and hold onto him. "You don't have

to talk," he comforted. "You don't have to say anything. I'm here. And I'll be here for you. Just think about all the good times."

Lisa walked into her backyard, looked for a perfect rose, found it, clipped it, and took it to school for Chris, for no reason at all.

"This is so pretty." He nearly wept. "Nobody's ever given me flowers. Nobody's ever given me a rose or anything."

For her first birthday with him, October 10, 1991, Hatton gave Lisa a pair of opal earrings, a Garfield bookmark, and a carefully picked card telling her how special she was and how important she was to him. They constantly traded love notes between classes.

The following month, Lisa gave Chris her body, something she'd wanted to do for months. She believed she was his first because he wouldn't answer her questions as they drove through the Texas nights, cruising the country roads, listening to country music.

"Have you ever had sex in a car?" she asked, giggling.

"Yes."

"In a boat?"

"I don't know," he said, frustrated, embarrassed. "Stop asking me all these questions."

She believed she was his first because on their first two dates, he'd been all over her. "Slow down. Calm down," she'd told him. After that, Lisa had always had to make the first move.

That fall, Chris Hatton walked into a recruiter's office and signed up to join the Navy. *Awesome,* he thought. He dreamed of being a Navy SEAL.

Glenn Conway thought it was awesome, too. They planned on reporting together right after graduation.

"Excuse me?" said Lisa Pace. "We didn't discuss this, and we're supposed to be together?"

"What?" said his aunt Holly. She didn't want him that far away from her. It seemed like she'd just gotten him. She tried to talk him out of it.

But the female pleas fell on deaf male ears. *Navy SEAL.* The thought made Chris Hatton break into a smile that charmed. And no female could resist his smile.


"Every time my mother writes or calls, and that's not even once a month, all she does is say, 'I don't know how I'm gonna pay my bills. I've been working two, three jobs. I'm sick. I need somebody to help me. I can't do it on my own.' "

Chris's dark hair draped toward his dark eyes. He took a swig of Dr Pepper, then reached for Lisa's hand.

"All my mother wants is someone to help her. The only reason she wants Brian there is for the Social Security. The only reason Uncle Bill wants Brian is for the Social Security."

"I'm tired," said Lisa. "My mom came in again last night and woke me up, crazy, yelling, acting stupid. What's the worst thing your mom's ever done?"

Chris furrowed his brow and looked away. "One time, my mom tried to stab me. Another time, she tried to shoot me. Another time, she tried to run over me. You know," he said, looking back at Lisa, "I love your mother to death, but when she's drinking, I can't stand her. It's my mom all over again."

He shook his head. To Chris Hatton, alcohol meant abuse. Holly and Chris had had talk after talk about such things when his uncle Bill was away at National Guard school. He sat there in silence, but his aunt Holly's words were loud in his memory: "You have a history of alcoholism in the family. Keep in mind that it is hereditary. You have a tendency to become an alcoholic. Be careful."

Lisa Pace had been smoking weed socially since she was twelve years old. To her, it was no big deal—one joint shared among five friends resulting in two puffs each.

"What drugs have you done?" Hatton asked her. He turned to spit a long, golden drip of tobacco juice into his Dr Pepper can. He dipped Copenhagen tobacco morning, noon, and night, even while in school.

At school, rather than put a pinch in his lip, he tucked it in the chubby part of his cheek so that his teachers couldn't spot it, and he swallowed the juice.

He spat again. "How'd they affect you? Where were you when you were doing them?"

Lisa looked at her beautiful beau. To her, he seemed to love to hear her wild drug stories. *He's not known for his particularly exciting life,* thought Lisa, *but he seems to like to live vicariously through others.* So, she told him.

Two weeks before Valentine's Day, 1992, Chris wrote Lisa two Valentine's love poems and a letter. Letters, he said, were the best way for him to express himself.

He professed that he'd never loved anyone before, that the eight months they'd been together were the best time of his life, and that Lisa had brought more happiness into his life than he'd ever expected.

"I know that we've both had our problems in the past with life," he wrote, "but it looks to me like we've overcome them. Remember last night when you asked me to make a list of things that really bother [me about you]?

"Well, there isn't really much that bothers me except when you talk about drugs and people that you still know that use them. What I'm trying to say is that drugs scare me. And before I moved here, I lost two good friends to drugs."

As their relationship grew more and more serious, time and again, Chris Hatton begged Lisa Pace to get away from her drug-using friends and never do drugs again.

Lisa felt that that demand then extended to wanting her to sit by the phone, waiting for Chris to call. Not doing drugs—Lisa could handle. Sitting at home waiting—she couldn't go for that. But she loved Chris.

He added: "As of today I will no longer promise to quit dipping. I will quit dipping, but not for me but for you." He also promised to be more sensitive to the things he said that Lisa disliked.

"One other thing which has bothered me is that when I leave for the Navy, I worry that you'll find someone else while I'm gone because of our age difference and you're still in school and I want you to know that I'll be there for you when I'm gone."

He signed it, "I love you, Lisa, with all my heart, the good and the bad."

The phone rang in the Hatton house. It was Brian calling from Alabama.

"She put a loaded gun to my head last night," he told his Texas relatives. He looked around to see if his mother was coming. If she knew he was on the phone, he said, she listened on the extension. He told them that Rhonda Hatton had flipped a couple of vehicles, including a brand-new Corvette, with him in them.

Holly and Bill called Child Protective Services in Alabama.

"There's nothing we can do because there's no physical evidence," said the caseworker. "It's just your word against hers."

Chris sat down with Lisa. "I don't like Brian being so far away from me. I want him to move to Texas."

Brian's school called next.

"Brian came to school with a stab wound in his leg and came to school crying," said his school counselor. "His mother was home all weekend, and she stabbed him in the leg with a screwdriver."

In Dadeville, everyone knew everyone's business, and the

school counselors knew the Hatton boys' lives. They helped the Texas Hattons take Rhonda Hatton to court and get custody of Brian.

With the boys together, Chris and Brian finally felt free to talk about the many times their mother, who was fascinated by guns, had placed a gun to their heads.

As much as Aunt Holly tried to protect the boys, she couldn't. Holly, who'd served years in the military herself, felt that Bill treated the boys like buck privates. To her, it was abusive.

To Lisa Pace, it came across as jealousy—Chris and Lisa were having fun; Bill and Holly weren't; so no one's going to be happy.

Lisa and Chris made plans. Bill gave Chris a list of chores to do: clean the house, wash the car, mow the lawn. Bill Hatton lived in a black or white, right or wrong world. There were no grays, absolutely no mitigating circumstances. If the lawn wasn't mowed the way Bill wanted it, Chris had to mow it again.

Chris constantly was late for dates. He constantly didn't have money for dates. His excuses seemed bizarre—Bill's constant petty chores and remown lawns—that Lisa thought he was using his uncle to get out of doing things with her.

But Chris found a way. "Uncle Bill, I'm going running," he'd say as he jogged out the door, then he'd sprint two blocks. Waiting at the corner was either Glenn Conway or Lisa Pace. Chris would jump in the vehicle and they were gone—to a movie, McDonald's, or Old Settler's Park to sit and talk by the water.

Lisa was charmed by the movie idol–gorgeous young man in ball caps and cowboy hats, who could tease her and trick her into believing most any story that he told with his handsome poker face. In fact, Chris Hatton almost always spoke with a straight face. After tricking Lisa, he'd break into laughter. He loved playing mind games.

On April 2, 1992, at 10:02 P.M., just days away from his twentieth birthday, Chris Hatton sat in his bedroom writing Lisa Pace one more love letter. "I really don't understand my uncle and his way of thinking. I think most of all he wants me out of his house. And I can't blame him much because most people my age are out earning a living."

Chris Hatton may have always smiled, but inside, his sorrow was strong. "I can't wait until I get out on my own this summer so I can finally be a free man." He forced his pen forward and wrote of how his grades were a struggle, how he didn't want to lose his goal of graduating.

"Most of all I don't want to lose you, trying to reach that goal. You're very special to me and you've made a big difference in my life. And I want you to be a part of it forever. I hope you'll stick by me until I get out of school and long after. But for now, until I graduate, it's going to be hard to spend time together. And I want you to know that it's not that you're boring or anything like that. I have to play by my uncle's rules until school's out and then I'm on my own. And then it's to hell with him."

Chris Hatton pledged to see Lisa Pace that night, even if he had to sneak out.

# Five

In the spring of 1992, twenty-year-old Chris Hatton finally graduated high school. That summer, just before he left for the Navy, he phoned Lisa Pace. "Can you come over right now? Can you come get me? Can I stay there?"

"Sure, but let me ask my mom." Ten minutes later, Pace, in her mother's truck, pulled up in front of the Hatton house.

"We have to hurry before my uncle gets home because I don't want to look at him, I don't want to talk to him, I don't want to hear any shit. I just want to get my stuff and get the hell out of here."

He smashed pillows, then crammed them under his covers, making it look like he was in bed. He grabbed his clothes, still on the hangers, threw them in a blanket, grabbed the blanket full of clothes, and threw it all in the back of the truck.

Lisa Pace noticed one item on top of Chris's dresser, which he also took with him. It was the rose from her backyard that she'd given him almost a year earlier.

Aunt Holly couldn't really blame her nephew for his exit. In her eyes, it was as though Bill didn't even think the boys had a right to a life of their own.

As proof, Christopher Michael Hatton had developed ulcers

while living with his uncle Bill. When he left Bill's home, his ulcers left, too.

That fall, Holly also left. Brian was now alone with Bill.


Just home from work at Long John Silver's, Pace walked into her bedroom. At her feet were Chris Hatton's freshly packed bags.

"I can't trust you," he said, his dark eyes hard. "I was going through your things, and I found this bag of weed." It was about a quarter bag of marijuana. "And I found these pipes." He shoved the pipes into her face.

"Well, they're not mine," said Lisa. "I'm just keeping them for a friend of mine because his mom always snoops through his things."

"You're lying. You always lie to me."

"I'm not lying. For real, it's not mine."

"I want you to get rid of it. I want you to flush it down the toilet."

They argued until Pace stamped into the bathroom, opened the bag of marijuana, watched it fill the toilet bowl, flushed the toilet, and threw the pipes into the trash.

Hatton stomped out the door and didn't return until late that night.

"Where've you been?" she questioned, now the angry one.

"Out."

"You smell like smoke. Have you been at a bar?"

"No."

Hatton eventually admitted that he'd been riding patrol with a Round Rock police officer. That ticked Lisa Pace off. Sometimes she got sick of him desperately looking for excitement.

There was that Navy SEAL dream of his; when in reality, the job he had applied for in the Navy involved a lot of mundane painting of the ship. She climbed into bed and went to sleep. So did Hatton. He slept till almost noon.

Hazel Franzetti, Lisa's mother, couldn't stand the way Chris

Hatton slept all day and slept through everything, including roaring vacuum cleaners.

On July 20, 1992, Chris Hatton left for the Navy. That fall, he graduated from Navy boot camp in San Diego. Lisa Pace went to watch him graduate, and he gave her a sapphire-and-diamond ring for her birthday.

Several days later, he sent her flowers and a card, also for her birthday. By then, he was writing to her almost every day.

On October 3, 1992, at 9:40 P.M., on board ship, Hatton wrote Lisa: "I'm getting really good at this type of work. . . . If I could only manage money, too, I'd be the perfect housewife." He added, "There's only seventeen more days, and I'll get to see you."

From the time he hit ship, Chris Hatton hated the Navy and hated the ship—it was cold, it was dark, the food was horrible, he constantly had bronchitis due to the mold and stale air in the sleeping quarters. He hated the hours—painting all day, on watch all night, with only three hours of sleep. He could no longer watch TV all night and sleep all day. It was a far cry from swimming and fighting as a Navy SEAL.

On October 6, 1992, he wrote that he believed he and Lisa were truly meant for one another, that he wanted her to go to college, for him to get a "good-paying civilian job," and then he "would ask for your hand, actually all of you, in marriage."

On October 20, Chris Hatton flew to Texas on a two-week leave.

"My pass is for only three days," he told his family so that he could spend all of his time with Lisa. "I lied to them so I wouldn't hurt their feelings," he told Lisa. She noticed that Chris Hatton often lied in the name of not hurting feelings.

But the day before Halloween, he and Lisa drove to the small town of Copperas Cove to visit his grandparents. He wore jeans and a T-shirt, but Lisa thought it'd be cute if he showed up at the Hattons' door in his sailor suit, as if he were trick-or-treating.

So while Pace drove her 1980 Ford Pinto, Hatton changed into his Navy uniform. When he rang the doorbell, his grandmother looked at him as if to say, "Who's this?"

Then Chris smiled. There was no mistaking that gorgeous grin. His grandmother broke into her own huge smile. "Come in, come in."

Sounding almost like a bird, she ordered, "Eat, eat, eat. You need to eat. You're too skinny." The woman who was tiny herself hovered over her grandson's plate. "You're not getting enough food."

They didn't serve his favorites in the Navy—homemade fried chicken and Nutter Butter cookies.

The following morning, his grandmother, with loving, arthritic hands, cooked Chris and Lisa bacon, eggs, and biscuits. Chris and his grandfather left the room to let the women clean the kitchen. It was as though Chris expected to be waited on hand and foot, as if his grandfather thought a woman's place was in the kitchen, which was tremendously different from when Chris and Lisa were together. Whoever cooked, the other was expected to clean.

On November 13, 1992, Hatton wrote Pace and told her he'd been Christmas shopping and had found a sapphire-and-diamond necklace that matched her sapphire-and-diamond ring, but with "bigger stones." He underlined many times "bigger stones."

"Would this be nice for you?" he said. "Or would you like a ruby or just a diamond ring—like an engagement ring?"

Lisa jumped with excitement as she read. They'd talked for months about getting married, how they wanted to have three kids, all boys. "Their" song was the country-western tune "Two of a Kind, Working on a Full House."

"I promise, two years, and I'll be back in Texas with you. We can get our own apartment, you can go on to college, and I'll have a job to support us. And we can take it from there. How does that sound? I love you. And I just wanted to ask if we could get married this summer, or would you rather wait for me to get out of the Navy shithole. I can wait if you can. And if you can't, then I'll marry you tomorrow because you're wonderful, beautiful, special, one-of-a-kind, and I want to always be your man. . . ."

Lisa's father died on November 22, 1992. Three weeks later, she flew to California to see Chris Hatton. He had only one day off, which worried him. It was okay with Lisa—at least they'd get to see each other in the evening.

Pace stayed at the Navy lodge. They spent every lunch together in their room's kitchenette, eating sandwiches and junk food from the commissary. At night they each ate a pint of Ben & Jerry's ice cream, watched movies, sat and talked and laughed.

Two days before Christmas, Chris walked into their room. Clothes, suitcases, and junk lay on one double bed. The other double bed, they slept in. Lisa jumped up and greeted Chris. "I want my Christmas present now. I don't wanna wait till Christmas. And I want to give you your present right now."

After a bit of flirtatious bickering, they sat in bed, clothed, and Chris handed her a long, skinny box.

She gasped with excitement to him. To herself, she thought, *This is not a ring . . . unless he put it in a different box.*

Inside the box was a gold watch with two rubies and four diamonds on the dial. "Oh, this is so pretty!" She put on the watch and sat back.

"Okay, now let me give you your present." In her mind, she said, *Okay, I know I'm getting another present, but I don't want to ask him.* "Here's your present," she said, smiling.

He opened a box and found a $1,000 gold ring with three

channel set diamonds in it. "Wow, this is really nice," said Chris. It could be worn as a simple ring or as a wedding ring. He reached over and hugged her and kissed her. But the ring was a bit big on his finger.

"You'll have to have it sized," said Lisa.

"Okay, I have one more present."

"Oh, you do?" laughed Lisa, attempting to feign surprise.

"Well, only if you're really good," said Chris.

"Okay," she said, kissing him.

He handed her another box, this one much smaller.

Lisa opened it. "Oh, it's so pretty." It was a diamond engagement ring. "Will you put it on me?"

Chris slipped the ring on her left hand and whispered, "Lisa, will you marry me?"

"Of course I'll marry you!"


The following October, around Lisa's birthday, she boarded another jet bound for San Diego. In the romantic California evening, Chris handed her a gift-wrapped package. Inside was peach-colored lingerie from Victoria's Secret. She'd told him she'd wanted diamond earrings. She slipped on the lingerie.

"Uh," breathed Lisa. "This color. I don't think it really goes with my skin."

"Here's the receipt," he said, handing it to her. "You can take it back."

She dug deeper into the lingerie box and found another box. Inside was a pair of diamond earrings, a third of a karat each. Lisa Pace thanked Chris Hatton with sex.

Afterward, at dinner, Lisa reluctantly looked at her lover. "Uh, Chris." For once, her words leaked slowly from her mouth. "I went to this party at this guy's house. I drank too much. I spent the night, in his bed. But that was it, just slept there."

"Who?" said Chris. "Who was it?"

"I don't want to tell you his name or anything because that's irrelevant. We kissed." They kissed, hot, hungry, heavy-breathing kisses. "And it happened more than once. But I haven't seen him in, like, three weeks."

"I don't believe you." Hurt splashed across Chris's dark brown eyes. "You wouldn't be telling me this if you'd just kissed him."

"He had a king-size bed, and I slept on one side, and he slept on the other. Nothing happened. I promise."

"Well, how do you know if you were drunk?" Chris retorted.

"I wasn't out-of-my-mind drunk. I'd just had too much to drive. And I know that I didn't have sex with this person, and that's what you're implying. I think I'd know if I had sex with somebody or not."

"Okay." What else was there for him to say? He remembered all those times back in Round Rock when Lisa had flirted with him and everybody else in the room, all at the same time. He knew the way she touched him when they talked. He had seen the way she touched everyone when she talked. It intimidated him. And it scared him. Women just weren't trustworthy.

"Well, I'm sorry," Lisa replied to his silence.

"That really hurts."

"Well . . . I felt really bad about it, so I thought I had to tell you. And now I told you, and I probably shouldn't have told you. Whatever." But her carefree, disgusted "whatever" belied the fact that Lisa felt like dirt for her indiscretion. She truly loved Chris Hatton.

Hatton had truly trusted Lisa Pace. Suddenly that trust was forever tainted.


Not long after Lisa Pace left San Diego, Chris Hatton got caught for driving his Chevy S-10 truck on post without insurance. "Do not drive this vehicle until you get insurance for it," the MPs told him. Hatton didn't get the insurance.

He was promoted to E-4 Seaman and went out with his Navy buddies to celebrate. Sometime between two-thirty and three o'clock in the November morning, the celebration turned dark. Chris Hatton got stopped for drunk driving. He was written up for DUI, no insurance, and speeding. He was sent to jail.

His truck was towed, and when he got out of jail, he couldn't locate it. Nor could he locate his buddies. He didn't have any money to get back to the ship, and when he finally made it back, he was in big trouble.

Hatton was given extra duty, lost his promotion, and lost his Christmas leave. He was confined to the ship, allowed to work or eat, then go back to his bunk. If he went to the head, a guard accompanied him.

*I can't stand it, I can't stand it, I can't stand it,* went through Lisa Pace's brain. Those were the words Chris Hatton had spoken so many times when her mother had come home drunk. Now he'd gotten a DUI. And lost his Christmas leave.

Chris Hatton couldn't stand it, either. He put on his black Skivvies and a wet suit, tucked his cash and plane ticket into a plastic Baggie, crammed the Baggie between his body and the wet suit, slipped over the ship's side, shimmied down the anchor, swam five hundred yards to the pier, climbed up the pier to hail a cab, and raced for the airport. He walked through airport security with nothing but a wet suit and a wad of dollars.

On December 17, 1993, Chris Hatton had gone AWOL to Texas.

"What are you doing here?" said Lisa, surprised.

"I needed to see you."

"You're gonna get in really big trouble."

"I'm already in really big trouble. So what?"

She looked into his handsome face. She reached over to touch him. "You better go back. I love you to death, and I want you to stay. But you'd be much better off if you'd just hurry up and go back."

Pace felt Hatton knew something he wasn't telling her. In Texas he had worn Justin roper cowboy boots and Levi's jeans, listened to country-western and the mellower music of the 1960s and 1970s. With his move to San Diego, he was listening to Jimi Hendrix, the acid rock of the 1960s and 1970s. He began wearing sandals, shorts, a bit of a Ralph Lauren look. He even learned to dance by going to hip-hop clubs.

Chris Hatton returned to the ship on January 3, 1994, and was placed on restricted status pending "an administrative separation." Bill Hatton wrote Chris's commander regarding his "adopted son."

On January 11, 1994, the commander replied, ". . . as a result of [Chris Hatton's] multiple violations, apparent attitude of indifference, and lack of remorse, I have lost confidence in his trustworthiness and believe he lacks potential for future service." He said Chris would be discharged toward the end of January.

"I am truly sorry to inform you of this situation, but I believe your adopted son is getting exactly what he wants—an early separation because he simply wants to take the easy way out."

Seaman Recruit Christopher Michael Hatton was booted out of the Navy on February 11, 1994. Lisa Pace was about to graduate from high school. It was a huge defeat coupled with a huge victory.

Hatton moved back in with Pace and her mother, Hazel Franzetti. He was unemployed and drove Hazel nuts, as she came home for lunch only to find Hatton still in bed, snoozing. "This is not working," she told Lisa. "He needs to get out. He's a man. He needs to get a job." He'd been home for one week.

Lisa rustled Chris from his sleep. "Are you gonna have a paycheck soon?" she said in her little girl voice.


Chris Hatton stared at the envelope in his hands. The return address read U.S. Navy. Slowly he opened the package and pulled out a roll of microfiche—his discharge "papers." He and Lisa drove to the local library to read it. The papers pronounced "less than honorable discharge" for "misconduct—commission of serious military or civilian offense."

As he printed out a copy of the discharge, Hatton talked as

though being kicked out of the Navy was no big deal. Then he whited out the "less than" and "misconduct . . ." and altered his discharge papers to read that he had been honorably discharged. He photocopied the altered papers and placed them with his job applications.


Chris Hatton got a job with Royal Vans of Texas, a company that customized vans and was within walking distance of the Pace home. Sometimes Chris walked the half mile to work, sometimes Lisa dropped him off. On February 21, 1994, he bought a $270 bike to ride to work.

He and Lisa began to pay her mother rent. They helped buy the groceries and did chores around the house.

A box arrived addressed to Chris Hatton from the U.S. Navy. Lisa opened the box and unpacked the possessions he'd left behind after his discharge. She sorted through letters from herself, from Holly, from Brian, and letters with an Oregon postmark. Lisa slipped out one of the letters and read.

"Thanks for the flowers," a girl had written, "you're so sweet, hope to see you soon."

Lisa grabbed the phone and punched out the girl's number. "Did you have sex with Chris Hatton?"

"No," she replied. "We just kissed."

Lisa's memory raced as she tried to calm down. *Back in October, he totally blew up at me,* she recalled. She heard her apartment door open and looked up from the phone to see Chris walking through the door. She confronted him.

"No," he protested. "Lis, I was in Portland, and it was adopt-a-sailor day. I spent the day with her entire family, not just her."

*How much deeper is this going to get?* thought Lisa.

Nothing seemed to be working out. Hatton hated his job with Royal Vans, just as he had hated the Navy. He hated the sweaty, hard work in a facility without air-conditioning. He hated the glue on his hands, the glue on his pants. He hated the fact that he was on his knees for so long every day that they became scrubbed raw and then callused.

The young lovers wanted privacy, while Lisa's mother appeared to want someone to watch TV with her. Hatton went to Aunt Holly for help. She found her nephew and Lisa an apartment in her own complex, with Bill living nearby.

Chris and Lisa needed to furnish their new place, so they bought a couch and bedding from Montgomery Wards. Half of the cost was put on Chris's credit card. Half of it, Lisa paid for with cash.

They put $2,500 down on a 1994 Dodge Dakota Sport truck. The dealership told them that it would be easier to get their credit application approved if they were Mr. and Mrs. Hatton. Chris seemed apprehensive. Away from the sales staff, Lisa told him, "This is your decision."

They put Mr. and Mrs. on the title.

At Wal-Mart they bought a TV and VCR. At Levitz they purchased more furniture, all from the discounted section in the back of the store. Again they paid half with Lisa's cash, half on Chris's credit card.

By April 8, 1994, Hatton's credit cards were carrying $2,500, and Pace's savings were wiped out.

Lisa started shopping for a wedding dress.


In May 1994, Lisa Pace graduated from Round Rock High School. Less than two weeks later, she left town for four months of Texas Army National Guard training at Fort Sam Houston in San Antonio. She asked Hatton to drive her the two hours down I-35 to San Antonio. He said he couldn't.

Hatton had switched jobs and was working for Capitol Beverage, where he was paid $1,400 a month. He didn't want to blow the job, he said. With their own place and with Holly and Bill no longer living together, he wanted custody of his brother, Brian.

* * *

Hatton was drinking a lot and regularly, unknown to anyone in his family. Out of the Navy and back in Texas, with his honky-tonking friends, he became known for his affinity for Coors Light.

Hatton also became resentful. He resented that his Navy career was over because he'd gone AWOL over Lisa, while Lisa's National Guard career was going great guns.

His future, at least in terms of career and money-making potential, seemed bleak. In the past, he'd talked about becoming an architect—he did love to draw. But he believed he wasn't good at school and studying; he believed he wasn't university material. He'd rather order a pizza and watch a movie. And maybe have a beer.

In the summer of 1994, Chris Hatton began spending more and more time with Glenn Conway and his family. He grew close to Glenn's sister, Cathy, and especially close to Glenn's mother, June, who became a second mom to him.

Chris and Lisa began arguing regularly.

"Lisa, you need to pick up these shoes. You can't leave things all around the house. You've got to pick up these clothes."

"Whatever," she'd reply.

Like his uncle, Chris wanted a clean house. Saturday afternoon was dedicated to cleaning house. Saturday morning was dedicated to sleep, after staying up all night watching TV.

"I'm tired of everybody telling me what to do and running my life. Bill and Holly. The Navy. And now you. I'm not going to let you tell me what to do and control my life," he'd complain.

From Fort Sam, Lisa Pace direct-deposited her National Guard paychecks and sent Chris money orders or wired him cash when he was broke. "What are you doing that you need so much money all the time? I don't understand," she said to him.

He began lying to her. He even lied to her about who drank the last Dr Pepper or whether he'd been to Hardee's, even though she stared at the Hardee's cup. It drove Lisa crazy.

"If it's affecting us financially and we're not going to be able to pay the rent, of course I'm going to tell you you can't buy those jeans and you can't buy a two-hundred-dollar cowboy hat," she said.

"You think you're so smart."

"Well, I am so smart. So what's your point?"

"You can't just boss people around all the time."

"Well . . . why not? Sometimes people don't know what they want, so you have to tell them. Or, you have to help them decide what they want."

Chris Hatton gained weight. His color was bad. Whenever Lisa Pace touched her fingers to his hair, it fell out like so much burned brown straw.

She phoned their apartment time and again from Fort Sam only to get a busy signal or the answering machine. She left message after message. Her calls went unreturned.

Pace phoned one of their neighbors and asked him to call Hatton while she listened on three-way calling. When Hatton heard their friend's voice on the answering machine, Hatton picked up the phone.

"Yeah, I'm just watching TV and drinking a beer," he said.

They hung up. Pace immediately phoned back. This time Hatton answered. "I just walked in," he lied to her.

In July, Lisa Pace found a Yellow Rose stripper-bar T-shirt in Hatton's drawer. "What's this?" she asked.

"Oh, nothing. A guy at work gave that to me. He stocks the Rose."

She only partially believed him.

On July 19, 1994, Chris Hatton walked into Kay Jewelers and purchased $413.91 worth of jewelry, including a ruby pendant. He paid $90 via check; the balance he financed.

Labor Day weekend, a bus was scheduled to go from Fort Sam to Laredo, and the price was dirt cheap—$5. Lisa Pace wanted to take it. Chris Hatton didn't want her to go.

"Whatever. Fine. Okay." Her one-word sentences were like one-word period punctuations. "I'll just come home, then."

Days later, Pace received a card from Hatton that he'd made on a computer at H-E-B grocery store. The card was postmarked August 24, 1994. On the outside of the card was a big heart, with Lisa's initials in the middle, and the words "I love you, Lisa. I really do." It was signed with several more "I love you"s.

When Lisa called home that week, some days Chris's telephone worked; some days, it didn't.

Just before Labor Day weekend, Chris Hatton sat with Lisa Pace, Glenn Conway, and some friends in a neighboring apartment drinking beer and watching a movie. Lisa wanted to go home, but Chris wanted to watch the movie. She left. After the movie ended, Chris stayed and horsed around with the guys. Lisa phoned wanting to know when he was coming home.

"I'll be there in a minute," he said. But he wasn't. She called time and time again, and finally Hatton put her on speakerphone. "I'll be home when I'll be home," said Hatton, with his buddies laughing in the background.

Pace didn't like that.

According to Glenn Conway, Lisa Pace stomped over to the apartment, threw open the door, and walked in—without knocking—strode over to Hatton, and in front of everyone, slapped him hard across the face. "Get your ass home."

Right then and there, Hatton decided he was going to do everything he could to make Pace's life hell.

On August 31, 1994, he drove to Kay Jewelers and returned all of the jewelry he'd purchased the previous month.

# Six

Over Labor Day weekend, Lisa Pace and a male National Guard buddy drove up to the apartment she shared with Chris Hatton.

Pace glanced at the door and her stomach sank. Her glance froze into a frightened linger. A page of newspaper was closed in the door. *Why would newspaper be on the floor?* They didn't even take the newspaper.

She waved good-bye to her friend and rushed up to the apartment. *Something's not right.* She swung open the door to find the living room completely empty. The cherry wood dining table was gone. The sofa. The cocktail tables. Everything.

There was a note: "I packed for you. You're welcome. I'm leaving and no one knows of this. I let the truck get repoed, and I'm getting something for myself." Myself was underlined many times. "Have a nice life. Bye."

She walked into the bedroom. Chris's clothes were gone; hers were on the bed. Her bedroom suite from her mother's home was left. The housewares, which came from Pace's deceased father's home, were packed in boxes on the floor. The phone was disconnected.

She raced out of the apartment, rounded the fence that separated apartment buildings, and beat on the door of Glenn Conway, who lived within walking distance.

Glenn opened the door.

Lisa's face, scarlet with hysterical tears, greeted him.

"What's the matter?"

"Where is Chris?"

"I don't know. Maybe he's at work. What's the matter?"

Lisa was full of fear and anxiety. She thought Chris might be in Glenn's apartment. She looked around, hoping he was there. She tried to spot some of his clothes, Coors beer caps, anything.

"Lis, I don't know where he's at."

"You're lying. I know you know where he's at. You're his best friend. Goddamn it, don't lie to me!" She wept hard, heavy tears as her thoughts swirled at tornado speed.

"Lisa, please calm down."

She pushed him. "I don't wanna calm down. I wanna know where Chris is."

Conway grabbed Pace by the shoulders. "Calm . . . down. You need to calm down. I don't know where Chris is." His words were slow. "I don't know."

Pace ran to her mother's house, fear and adrenaline pushing her heart and legs so well that she was barely winded when she completed the four-mile run.

She wept to her mother, "He's gone. He left, and he took everything."

"What the fuck—that asshole," replied her mother.

Lisa's words were unintelligible as they were sandwiched between hysterical tears.

"Calm down," said her mother.

"I need to get my stuff out of there right away." She worried that Hatton might return to the apartment that night and take the rest of her things. *I hate him. I love him. I want to beat him up. I want to hug and kiss him.* There were too many emotions. Lisa Pace took a deep breath as a wagon train of family members in pickup trucks drove to the apartment.

She just wanted to be alone as they unloaded her possessions back at her mother's house. But she paged the love of her life twenty times.

In between pages, she noticed her ATM card was missing.

Lisa Pace thought back. The last time she remembered seeing it, the card had been lying on the counter in their apartment, and Chris Hatton knew her PIN number. She phoned her bank.

"Great," Lisa muttered as she heard her account balance. It was 10¢. Just the day before, she'd been paid. Chris Hatton had taken her money, too.

Finally Hatton answered her repetitive pages.

"What d'ya need?" he griped.

"What do I need?" said Pace. "I need you. I need to know where you are. I need to know if you're okay. I need to know what the hell's going on? That's what I need."

"Well, I left you a note," he said. "I left. I moved."

She begged and pleaded with him.

"I just need some time on my own," he responded.

"You have a place to stay?"

He told her the furniture was in a friend's garage.

She told him that he didn't have to tell her where he was living, what was going on, or give her his phone number, but he did need to return her pages.

"Okay."

Lisa Pace went back to her regimented life at Fort Sam Houston in San Antonio, with a pledge to Chris Hatton that she wouldn't try to call him, write him, see him, or contact him in any shape, form, or manner until she was graduated from National Guard school in one month.

Chris Hatton went to Levitz Furniture and purchased one more piece of furniture, one he picked out on his own. He went to the liquor store and bought Hot Damn cinnamon schnapps, Jim Beam, Everclear, Guinness, Keystone Light, and Coors Light.

Hatton, Glenn Conway, and Conway's girlfriend, Marlena Broyles, sat in Hatton's new Aubry Hills apartment and drank. The men chugged Jim Beam and Coca-Cola. Broyles drank beer. They peppered their livers with shots of cinnamon schnapps, followed by beer shooters.

An hour and a half and a fifth of liquor later, the three fell into Conway's pickup truck and wove their way down Interstate 35 to south Austin and the Dance Across Texas dance hall, a warehouse-size country-music bar with a flowing Texas flag painted across its wide side.

Hatton and Conway wobbled into the building, Broyles with them. The boys stopped and rocked on their rolling heels. "He's a Navy SEAL," said Hatton, pointing to Conway, as they made their way through the bouncers. "He's going through training right now. I'm in the military, too."

The bouncers motioned for the club manager. He walked out, then yelled over the music. Hatton and Conway tried to focus. They couldn't. He handed the boys a piece of paper. They bent down to write, but still they couldn't focus. They handed the paper to the bouncers, who slowly listened and slowly completed the job applications for Hatton and Conway. Right on the drunken spot, the manager wanted to hire Chris Hatton and Glenn Conway, the Navy SEALS, as bouncers.

Through their bleary eyes, Hatton, Conway, and Broyles saw maybe ten to fifteen people in Dance Across Texas, and one of them, a young lady, Chris Hatton thought was pretty. Since he was drunk, he was able to muster the courage to ask her to dance.

She accepted, but her sister jerked her away from Hatton. "You don't need to be talking to that kind of trash!"

Country music blared from every crevice in the bar. Hatton needed to sit down. He walked toward a table. The pretty girl followed and started chatting him up.

Again her sister yanked her by the arm, swirled her around and screamed, "You don't need to be talking to that white trash!"

With that, Marlena Broyles taunted, "You wanna come?" She was ready to fight. "Let's go!" She pointed to the exit.

The sisters mouthed off. Their guys joined in.

"Shut up!" Hatton yelled. "Y'all need to leave!"

They didn't.

Hatton grabbed an eight-foot-long folding table, chunked it across the room, and jumped toward the guys, the table bouncing to the rhythm of "Boot Scootin' Boogie."

Glenn Conway flew across another table, while Broyles dived for the girls. Chairs flew through the air. The three flew out the door, with the bouncers' help.

They ran for their truck, spotted the guys and gals who had gotten them kicked out of the club, jumped in Conway's vehicle, and chased the culprits around the parking lot. Hatton hung out the window and cussed and laughed the whole time.

Chris Hatton had finally begun the life he dreamed—where no one told him what to do.


When Lisa Pace's bank statement arrived the following month and detailed her ATM withdrawals for August, the month for which Chris Hatton still knew her PIN number, she discovered addresses she didn't recognize.

She tracked down the addresses. They matched those of Sugar's and the Yellow Rose, Austin's two most popular stripper bars. Time and again, Chris Hatton had told Lisa Pace that he hated topless dancers. "Fun to look at," he said, "not fun to take home."

On September 28, 1994, Lisa Pace graduated from National Guard school, her pledge to stay away from Chris Hatton was completed, and she phoned her ex-fiancé.

"It's been a month, so I thought I'd call and see where we're at and how things are going. Do you have a roommate, or do you live by yourself?" she asked.

"No, I have a roommate," Hatton answered.

"Is it anybody I know?"

"It's just this guy."

"Is it Glenn?"

Hatton never answered her.

Soon he knocked on her door. Ten minutes later, Chris Hatton and Lisa Pace were in her bedroom having sex.

Lisa's mom came home. "Open this door!" she screamed, pounding her fists on the bedroom door. "You son of a bitch, I hate you. I'm going to call the police! You did my daughter shitty, and I want you out."

Chris and Lisa escaped to Old Settler's Park, where they'd sat many times in high school and talked about how much they had loved each other.

"We can work on things," she said.

"I just need some space. I need some time."

"What about all of my stuff?"

"What about your stuff?"

They argued about money and possessions. He called her a "money-hungry bitch." She denied the accusation. Pace said, "You can just take me home. This conversation is not going anywhere."

Days later, Lisa Pace pulled on a short, tight dress, stockings, and high heels. She put up her hair, circled on the lipstick, and drove to the H-E-B grocery store. It was time for Chris Hatton to be there checking the beer shelves for Capitol Beverage. It wasn't the first time Pace had hit the H-E-B, hoping to run into Hatton.

She got a basket, stuck a couple of items in it, and strolled up the beer aisle. "Hey," she said casually, "how's it going?"

Chris Hatton's mouth almost hit the floor. "Wow, you look really great. You look awesome."

She damn well knew she looked great. She was 38-28-38 due to her National Guard training.

"Thanks, I just had a job interview this morning," she lied nonchalantly. "I'm on my way home. I just had to stop and get a couple of things." She waited to see what he would do.

He didn't do anything.

She wanted to touch, hug, and kiss him.

He acted as though he didn't want to talk to her.

Still, in Pace's mind, it had been a successful mission. She'd wanted to leave a hot, sexy imprint on his brain so that he wouldn't stop thinking about her for at least another week. She thought she had left that message.

Not many nights later, Lisa Pace again pulled into the H-E-B parking lot. This time she was with a male friend from Fort Sam, when she looked up and spotted her Dodge Dakota truck in the grocery store parking lot. "I bet Glenn's driving it," she railed and ran into the store, scouring the aisles for Glenn Conway.

"Where is Chris?" Lisa demanded when she located Conway.

"I don't know," he answered.

"If I had had the key to the truck, I would have taken it. Chris is lucky that he has both of the keys. Glenn, you tell him that I don't have a way to get around, and I don't have a way to look for a job."

The very next morning, Hatton phoned and asked Pace who her new boyfriend was. She denied having a new beau.

"Oh, yeah. Who's this blond guy with this teal truck?"

She told him it was a platonic friend from Fort Sam.

"You are such a slut. The whole time you were at Fort Sam, you were fucking around."

She hung up.

He phoned back and ripped her with more profane accusations.

The following week Chris Hatton picked up Lisa Pace in their Dodge Dakota truck, ready to turn it over to her.

"Are you sure," said Lisa, "that you want me to take you home?" Purposely she was trying to rile him. "I can just drop you off at the corner or at a bus stop or something. I don't have to know where you live."

He rolled his eyes at her.

They went to the Aubry Hills Apartments.

"Do you mind if I come up and see the apartment?" she said.

"I guess."

She walked up the stairs to the apartment and saw the couch, TV, VCR, lamps, and vacuum cleaner she and Chris had bought. *I paid for this stuff, too. And he's got this roommate, and they're enjoying* my *couch and* my *TV.* "Can I use your bathroom?"

He obliged, and she sifted through his things to see if there were any signs of a girlfriend. There weren't. But there were a few porn magazines.

"Interesting literature in there," she said, as she returned to the living room.

"You're a fucking snoop. You always have to look through everything."

She denied it. He denied that the magazines were his.

She didn't buy it. She remembered that a subscription renewal to *Penthouse* had arrived at their home after he was booted from the Navy. They continued to argue until their battling fell into silence, then into sex, as it almost always did.

Around 4:30 or 5 P.M., Pace crawled out of the bed to take a shower. She was in Hatton's bathroom for only five minutes when she came out and discovered that Chris had left, in the truck he was supposed to be turning over to her.

Without bothering to dress, Pace swiftly continued her investigation of the premises. She checked his nightstand—papers, books, magazines, watches. Hatton had always loved watches, to take broken ones and mix them with more broken ones to make them working ones.

She adjusted the towel on her head, the towel around her body, checked his closet, checked more drawers. By then, Pace was looking just for the sake of looking. She walked into the second bedroom, the master bedroom and bath. Again she found only men's items, a rifle on the bed, men's colognes in the bath. She picked up the colognes and read their labels.

She walked back out and found the telephone bill. It said Will Busenburg. Lisa Pace gasped. *He is living with Will Busenburg! Yuck. I hate that guy.* She remembered how in high school Will Busenburg had given her the creeps, how—in her opinion—he had never had anything nice to say, how he had asked Chris to skip school, how he had asked Chris to go to Hooters.

But she couldn't dwell on that. Minutes were ticking and she had to continue her search. Pace checked the refrigerator and looked in the cabinets to see what kind of food they had, if any. If one of them had a girlfriend, she believed, there would be more food in the house.

She opened the pantry doors. All the items in the pantry were from her pantry with Chris, with her handwritten labels in her handwriting. *He couldn't take everything in the house. He had to take everything in the pantry, too.* She wanted Chris back at the apartment, right then, so she could just leave.

Fifteen minutes after her investigation began, Chris Hatton returned. "I took some videos back to Blockbuster," he said. "Plus, I had to give you time to go snoop through everything, didn't I?"

She sighed, "Yeah."


The day before Lisa's birthday, she and Chris walked down his apartment steps, heading for their truck and dinner at the Olive Garden Italian restaurant, when they ran into Will Busenburg and Will's girlfriend.

"Hey, how are you?" said Busenburg graciously.

"Hi," said his girl, blond hair curling around her shoulders. "Nice to meet you."

She seemed pleasant enough. But Lisa Pace didn't really notice. She kept hearing Busenburg's words from high school. "We need to wipe out all the niggers," he had said. She just wanted to get out of there. She and Hatton exited quickly.

But not long thereafter, Lisa Pace was back over at the Aubry Hills Apartments seeing Chris. But Chris Hatton wasn't telling anyone he was seeing Lisa Pace, especially not Glenn Conway and his family.

He wrapped his arms tightly around her voluptuous body. "What do people act like when they're on acid?" he said. "What do people act like when they're on cocaine or speed?"

"People on speed get nervous, jittery. They talk a lot," she answered. "They move around a lot. Up and down a lot. Cleaning. Tidying things. Just nervous behavior. Or they look around, blink a lot."

"Oh," he said, "uh-huh," as if making a connection.

She turned around and looked him deep in his dark eyes. "Why do you want to know about these things?"

"Just curious."

"Why? Were you thinking about doing drugs?"

"No." He didn't hesitate. "I was just wondering. I think Will might be involved in some drugs. There's a lot of traffic in and out of the apartment, and I don't like it. I want him to move out. He's a slob. He doesn't clean up his share."

As Hatton walked Pace to her truck, Busenburg drove up, drinking Hot Damn cinnamon schnapps out of the bottle. Pace sniffed with disgust. Every time she saw Busenburg he was drinking.

"Hey, man," he cried, "you oughta have a shot of this."

"Nah, I don't want any," Chris said, looking at Lisa.

"This is really good."

Hatton looked again at Pace.

"I don't care if you drink," she said. "You can do whatever you want. I don't tell you what to do."

He took the bottle and swigged some down.

Busenburg offered Pace the bottle; then he realized he'd interrupted a conversation. "Oh, I'll see you later." He walked up the stairs but called back to Chris, "Are you coming?"

"I'll be there in a little bit."

It wasn't much later that Hatton once again asked Pace about cocaine.

"Why do you keep asking me about cocaine? Are you doing drugs?"

"No," he answered.

"People get hooked on it real easy, and it's not anything you want to have in your life."

They never talked about it again.


Around 10 A.M., on an October Saturday in 1994, Pace knocked on the door of Hatton's apartment. He had promised to make a small recall repair on their truck. No one answered the door. She leaned close to it. She heard voices and a TV inside. She knocked louder, and she knocked longer. She knocked for minutes. Still, no one answered. She was getting ticked.

Finally a bed-headed Hatton came to the door. "What!" he said.

"You said I could come over this morning," she griped loudly, "and you were going to do this. Now, what the hell? Nobody's answering the stupid door." She chewed him out long and vigorously.

He yelled back.

"Are you going to hit me or something!" she screamed. "You're right up in my face!"

He grabbed her shoulders and shook her against the iron railing. "I feel like throwing you down those stairs."

"Okay. Go ahead. Just go ahead, do it, Chris."

He pushed her toward the door. "You're not worth my time."

"Hey," a dark-haired girl called from the doorway, stove smoke billowing behind her. "Would you like some pancakes?"

"No. No," said Pace tersely. "We don't want any pancakes. Thank you."

The girl walked back inside.

"Who is *that?*" said Lisa.

"That's Will's girlfriend. You met her."

"That's the same girl?" She wore big, ugly, schoolboy glasses and her hair was dark rather than blond.

Lisa Pace said her last piece and left.

By the last week of October, Hatton and Pace were no longer speaking. Still, every time the phone rang, her stomach dropped as she hoped, just hoped, that it was Chris on the other end.

But Hatton wasn't there. He was over at the Conways, and the Conways liked that just fine. June Conway, Glenn's mother, was a heavyset country woman, with short hair and glasses, who was nice, open, talkative, and easygoing. She was just what Chris Hatton needed—she mothered him well.

Glenn's younger sister, Cathy, loved having Chris around, too. She almost melted when he smiled. At the Conways', Chris Hatton smiled a lot. He felt like family.

When Hatton said something there that seemed like baloney, June Conway looked deep into his brown eyes and said, "Aaaah, excuse me." It was much better than being bitched at by Lisa Pace or punished by Bill Hatton.

At the Conways', Hatton could wrestle on the furniture and only get a mild rebuff from June. Like Holly, June Conway loved to tease Chris about his shyness with the girls. By Halloween, shyness wasn't the worry.

Hatton looked into June's eyes, kind behind her glasses. "This girlfriend of Will's," he said, "I don't like her. And I don't trust her." Chris wasn't smiling. "One time she came on to me. I told her to back off and get out of the apartment, Will's not here. I don't want anything to do with her."

In November, Hatton and Pace spoke once or twice on the phone and once or twice at H-E-B. Hatton had survival on his mind, not Lisa. One night, while riding his bicycle home from Capitol Beverage, he was run off the road. After that, his boss, Gary Thompson, let Chris borrow a company truck to drive during his personal hours.

Thompson liked Hatton, and Hatton liked Thompson. He was a loving Christian man who listened patiently.

In December, Hatton phoned Pace to say Merry Christmas. She asked him about his Thanksgiving. He said he went to his grandparents; he drove a company truck to get there.

A few nights later, he was out drinking with Glenn Conway and Glenn's mother. June was driving when Chris demanded that she stop the truck. He jumped out, grabbed a huge Christmas wreath from a storefront, and handed the wreath to June. It was his gift to her.

June Conway got Chris Hatton a Christmas stocking to hang with the rest of the Conway family's.

Chris gave June and Holly each a red metal vase with a candle in the middle and fresh flowers around the candle. He tried to hide the flowers behind his back as he walked up to the Conways' front door. But Chris's big grin couldn't hide anything.

June set the flowers on her entertainment center and kept them there until they started dying. Then she moved them into the bedroom and placed them by the headboard of her bed.

Hatton talked to Glenn and June Conway more and more about his concerns about Will Busenburg. "Will drives to San Antonio or Houston, gets out of the car, goes to lunch, comes back to the car, drives home and makes one thousand or five hundred dollars. He brags about it all the time. It's easy money." He worried more that Busenburg was into dealing drugs.

Time and again, Chris Hatton told the Conways that he despised Will's girlfriend. The Conways tried to convince him to move in with them.

"Pack your stuff. We'll move you out tonight. Just get your stuff."

He laughed. "I'll be fine." Chris Hatton wasn't about to let Will Busenburg get him down.

Eventually Hatton paid Pace back $400 of the $2,500 he'd taken from her. Then his phone was disconnected.

But he could still smile. Chris, Glenn, Marnie, and June went out drinking at Dance Across Texas. They laughed, acted silly, and Hatton got up enough nerve to ask a girl to dance. Then Marnie got into a fight, and they had to leave, again.

"Damn," said Hatton, "and I just met this girl."

"I know," joked June, "and I just started dancing."

Two days later, he and Conway went out looking at used trucks for Hatton to buy. He phoned Lisa Pace one last time. It was January 5, and he called to tell her he was selling their furniture. He sold the couch for $20 to help pay the rent.

On January 6, he drove the Capitol Beverage truck up to Holly's. He brought her flowers. He and Jim Fletcher, Holly's fiancé, fried chicken tenders, one of Chris's favorite foods. He told Holly how lucky he was to work for Gary Thompson.

She walked Chris to the truck and gave him a huge hug good-bye.

Hatton bought a pickup truck. It was an ugly, dented, scratched-up, beat-up clunker of a brown 1979 Chevy, which his grandparents helped pay for.

He drove straight over to the Conways'. "How do you think I should fix it up?" he said, giddy. "You gonna help me?"

He drove over to his uncle's to show it off, then retreated to the Conways' for support. "Uncle Bill said, 'How can you afford this? Why did you ask your grandparents?' " Chris shook his head. "He was down on everything about it. When I asked him to come outside to look at it, he didn't want to."

Chris, Glenn, and Glenn's father started cleaning up the truck's engine and talked about how they could repaint the vehicle.

Hatton spent the night. With Busenburg as a roommate, Hatton had become a regular overnight guest at the Conways'. He spent the next few nights there, working on his truck each time until 1 A.M.

On Monday evening, January 9, 1995, Chris Hatton was again with the Conways. They shared dinner from McDonald's, and Chris shared his heart with June Conway. "Guys come over, they leave packages for Will, and Will leaves a brown paper bag for them," he said.

About 10 P.M., Glenn walked in. Exhausted, he went straight to bed.

June continued listening to Chris.

"Will brags all the time about making all this money."

June Conway grew more concerned and begged Chris to spend the night.

"I've gotta go to work in the morning and I don't have a uniform here."

"I'll get you up in time to go home and get cleaned up."

"No, I'll be all right. I'll go on home."

She begged him to move in with them. She wanted him away from Will Busenburg. "We'll move you out tonight."

Hatton just laughed and smiled. Besides, Will Busenburg was in the process of moving out his belongings.

"Move in here with us," said June, again. She just didn't trust that Busenburg, moving out or not, especially not if he was dealing drugs.

"I don't know," Hatton answered.

"Well, you need to at least go down to the manager's office, explain to them the situation, about Will moving out, and say you need to get the locks changed, that you want it done immediately."

But she knew the manager had recently installed a dead bolt and Hatton didn't think he needed anything else.

Around one in the morning, Chris Hatton got into his beat-up pickup truck and left the Conways' home. He never returned.

# Seven

On Saturday, January 14, 1995, Holly Frischkorn's doorbell rang. Tired, worried, she opened her apartment door to find Lieutenant Dan LeMay of the Round Rock Police Department. She knew this wasn't good. Holly lit a cigarette as her dogs ran anxiously around and between her long legs.

"They believe the body is Michael's," said LeMay. "You need to get dressed and come down to PD."

Frischkorn inhaled deeply as she sat down across from Detective Manuel Mancias. It was a typical nondescript law enforcement room—papers, clutter, cases. She didn't even notice.

Calmly she told him about Chris's background—that his family called him Mike; that Deputy Bill Hatton had legal custody of Mike and his brother, Brian; that despite her divorce from Bill Hatton, Holly was still close to Michael.

She spoke about Mike's relationship with Lisa Pace; that she didn't know Mike's roommate's name but she did know they weren't getting along; that Mike had complained about the roommate not paying his share of the bills and rent.

Holly wanted to light a cigarette. She talked about Glenn Conway being Mike's best friend, and that she last saw Mike on January 6.

"He told me he was going to purchase a pickup truck." She told Mancias that TCSO deputy John Phillips, who was a corrections officer at the Del Valle corrections facility, was also a high school friend of Mike's.

Then Corporal Holly Frischkorn lost her police composure. She began to cry. "Michael's roommate dated a topless dancer. He brought other dancers to the apartment on a regular basis. And Michael didn't like that."

She shook her head. "Michael didn't have an enemy in the world." Holly recalled the sweetness of her nephew, the way he'd carried the bags on his first day in her home: *"Aunt Holly, with me around, you're never gonna have to worry about anything again."* The words rang in her head. "His roommate could be involved in his murder."

"Why do you say that?"

"The ill feelings between them . . . that they weren't getting along."

Holly Frischkorn was told she could leave. She asked to see the body of her nephew.

The TCSO detectives didn't want her to view him. Chris Hatton's burned head looked more like that of a dead coyote's picked over by the buzzards. The Medical Examiner's Office refused her.

But Holly Frischkorn, the former military woman, was determined—she didn't believe anyone had the right to make the choice for her. She pressed on.

She was told that there wasn't a private room at the ME's office to view the body without other bodies around. *Don't you think that should be important enough to make a room for viewing by family members?* she thought.

Sergeant Gage called Bill Hatton and arranged to meet him at TCSO headquarters.

At 3:50 P.M., Saturday, January 14, 1995, Deputy Bill Hatton arrived at the downtown office to learn that his nephew had been brutally murdered, mutilated, and burned.

"Mike was a very quiet person," said Hatton. "I knew he

ad a roommate, but Mike never told me who he was." Hatton
ooked down at his large hands and told Detective Mancias that
is nephew's roommate dated a topless dancer, brought dancers
o the apartment, and Mike hadn't liked that.

Mancias listened carefully as if this were his first time hear-
ng this information. Confirmation was always good. Mancias
eaned back in his chair.

Stoically Hatton said that Mike's roommate had moved out
vithout paying his share of the rent or bills. "Mike recently
ought a truck," he noted. "I think it was a 1979 Chevrolet
nd was brown in color."

"When did you last see your nephew?"

"It was Tuesday."

That was January 10, the day before the body had been
ound.

"I received a call from him," Hatton continued. "He asked
ne to help him get his truck started. After I helped him get it
tarted, Mike left, and that was the last time I spoke to or saw
im." He sighed. It was the heavy sigh of a big man in loss.


At 4:35 P.M., Deputy Richard Hale sat in his unmarked ve-
icle watching the Aubry Hills Apartments. Backed into his
arking spot, he'd been sitting there for six long, boring hours,
taring at the steps that led up to Hatton's apartment.

Suddenly Hale shifted in his car seat to full alert. A black
ickup truck drove up and parked six or seven spaces from the
partment, despite closer parking being available. A white
nale, with a white female, got out of the truck and walked
oward the apartment of Chris Hatton.

Hale glanced at a driver's license photograph of Will Busen-
urg and reached for his radio. He called Deputy Bruce Harlan.
Harlan sat in his unmarked vehicle watching the back side of
he apartment.

"The suspect has arrived. Cover the south side of the apartment. When the location of the suspect is determined, we'l both take him into custody."

But Harlan didn't respond. Hale tried again. He needed t get out of his vehicle, fearing he was about to lose his suspect With one leg almost out the door, he tried Harlan one last time Harlan had been in the middle of changing his radio battery.

Hale, quietly and quickly, exited his car and walked close t the stairwell that led up to the apartment. His suspect unlocke the door and entered. Hale stayed downstairs. Harlan joined him "A white female and a white male have entered the apartment," Hale whispered to Harlan as they stood underneath the stairs.

Hale knew that the suspect would immediately know tha the police had been there—a search warrant lay in purposefu open view in the apartment, rubber gloves left by the crime la team were in the trash, a section of the carpet in the bloody bedroom was missing.

"I'll talk to Busenburg if you'll talk to the female," he con tinued whispering.

The deputies heard the apartment door open. Hale steppe out from beneath the stairs and watched the couple exit th murder site, then lock the door behind themselves. The suspect began walking down the steps. The woman, empty-handed passed Hale. Harlan stepped between her and Hale so that sh was separated from her companion.

Nonchalantly Hale pulled his badge out from beneath hi plainclothes shirt and drew his weapon, while keeping it tucke behind his back. Harlan pulled his weapon and held it close t his leg, its barrel pointed toward the ground. Hale stepped i front of the man.

"Travis County Sheriffs department," he called. "What i your name?"

"Will Busenburg."

"You're being placed under arrest for suspicion of murder Place your hands behind your back."

Busenburg did, and he was cuffed.

Hale secured his weapon. Harlan tucked his in his belt lin

behind his back. Then Hale read Busenburg his rights. "Do you understand your rights?"

"Yes. Murder?" Busenburg was emotionless. "What's going on?"

"I'll talk to you about it in a minute," Hale said.

"Murder?" the female companion chimed in. "What are you talking about? What murder? I don't know what you're talking about? I don't understand. Who's been murdered?"

Hale glanced up at the apartment. *Yeah,* he thought. The yellow crime scene tape pulled down by Sergeant Gage lay by the front door.

He patted down Busenburg. In the suspect's right front pants pocket was a small, folding knife. Hale walked the cuffed young man over to the unmarked vehicle and called Sergeant Gage.

# Eight

As gospel hymns played, the choir sang, and a crowd of churchgoers watched, ninth-grader William Michael Busenburg walked down the aisle of First Baptist Church Round Rock. He stopped in front of the pulpit, shook hands and prayed with a kind gentleman, and made a public profession of faith in Jesus Christ. He melted with relief. Will Busenburg had finally found a family that would love him kindly.

Since his first cry at 4:35 P.M. on October 22, 1973, in the Murphy Medical Center of Warsaw, Indiana, Will Busenburg had longed for sweet love. He had been the eight-pound, one-ounce new baby boy of Raymond Devon Busenburg and wife Frances Carol.

Warsaw was a small community just east of Fort Wayne and less than an hour's drive from South Bend, which supported itself through the manufacture of orthopedic implants.

Will had inched the population of the town closer to 8,000. He was the youngest of four children: Michelle, seven years older, Heather, five years older, and Adam, two years older.

Despite the fact that Will lapped at his mother's breast morning, noon, and night, he and Fran, a native Kentuckian who worked in the orthopedic industry, never quite connected.

But Will's father, whose own father had died when Ray was nine years old, felt close to his new son. He desperately wanted to share with Will the father-son activities that Ray had missed out on as a child.

At ten months, Will was walking. At fourteen months, he
was toilet-trained. His parents claimed he was ahead of sched-
ule on the development calendar.

By elementary school, the dark-haired child with hazel green
eyes was still looking like a boy of advanced achievement—
earning mostly A's and B's. But in the schoolyard, Will Busenburg got into fist-flying fights with other students. He wanted
to be a "man's man."

Will and his father hunted together. They shared sports together. In Ray's eyes, he and Will were closer than Ray was to
any of the other children.

But at age ten, Will Busenburg had developed a nervous
stomach. Both his mother and maternal grandfather had stomach ulcers. Will's mother often complained of stomach ulcers,
back pain, and difficulty sleeping. She was an attractive blonde
who could present herself as emotionally fragile.

In 1985 Will traveled to Arizona on a school trip. As he
swam with the other adolescents, water suddenly gurgled into
his lungs. The sky went black, and Will Busenburg fell unconscious. "I almost drowned," he claimed. "I was unconscious
for ten minutes."

His mother said she saw a change in her son after the near-
drowning—he became a loner. Will was busy constructing
emotional walls of protection from a large family with parents
who were beginning to have marital problems, but he couldn't
build them strong enough.

Heather slammed a fist into Will and, according to Will,
"beat the hell out" of him. His dad, he said, was on a coke
binge at the time and "had everyone stressed out."

Then, said Will, Heather got him into trouble with their father. "So after he was done with me," Will boasted, "I shot
her in the butt with my BB gun."

Sometimes Heather lived with the Busenburgs, and sometimes she didn't. When she did, Will told himself that they were
close.

In 1986, the year after Will's near-drowning, the Busenburgs moved to Texas without Heather, who stayed in Indiana with her maternal grandmother. Will's mother and other family members said Heather was the victim of much physical and emotional abuse by Ray.

According to Fran, Will, and Michelle, all the children—with the exception of Will—were physically abused by Ray Busenburg. According to them, Ray had broken Michelle's and Adam's noses and Heather's fingers, in addition to other unnamed abuses.

Will continued shoving his fists into other children. In one fight, jabbing a mean right, he injured his writing hand. He complained about that injury for years.

Not long after the move to Texas, Ray and Fran separated. Will's jaw began to pop when he opened his mouth wide. He got into more fights. In December 1988, the Busenburgs divorced.

Michelle, who had married years earlier, lived in Round Rock with her husband. Adam stayed with Fran in Austin, and Will stayed with his father in Round Rock.

Together, Will and Ray moved in with Ray's new love, a woman named Sylvia, fifteen years younger than Ray and the mother of two young children, who also lived with them.

Will Busenburg's grades began to slip. By ninth grade his Round Rock High School report card was mostly C's. That same year, he went out for smashmouth football and track. But the roar of the student body and the victory hugs, he didn't hear or receive. Busenburg dropped off the teams. His parents wouldn't drive him to practice, he said.

His frustration grew. His anger queased his stomach into relentlessly tight knots. Busenburg slammed his fists into more students—two fights within two weeks with the same boy. "Come to my office whenever you need to cool down," said Round Rock High School counselor Grace Finto. Busenburg did and Finto became his advocate. She knew his problems at home.

Busenburg walked down the aisle at church in hopes of find-

*Suzy Spencer*

ing a new family. He was desperate. In the eight months since his parents' divorce, Will Busenburg had packed his bags and moved back and forth between his parents' apartments, trying to get along with first one, and then the other, and back again.

At one point, he brought his possessions over to his sister Michelle's house. But that living situation also did not work out. Will packed up his T-shirts and jeans and returned to his mother's apartment.

He stayed only briefly, running away twice and disappearing for a month. When he resurfaced, he found himself knocking on his father's door, his stomach still queasing. According to family members, Will was still jealous of his father's new family—nine-year-old Sara and six-year-old Steven. Will ran away, twice more.

On his own, Will Busenburg found three families to take him in. Not one of the situations worked out. Church seemed like a good option to the teenager.


Will Busenburg announced to both his mother and father that he wanted to live at the Texas Baptist Children's Home (TBCH) in Round Rock, a loving Baptist community of Christian adults who were willing to help in a healthy way.

Busenburg had become religiously unhealthy and religiously rigid—furious at his parents for not living up to his Christian standards. He demonstrated that anger by staring long hours at the flashing light of the TV.

His father and stepmother complained that he wouldn't work or do household chores. Others griped that he was compulsive about cleanliness and table manners.

The Busenburgs argued that he had no motivation and was lazy. He did, though, attend church and its youth activities. "But he uses that time with the church and its youth ministers to create problems for us at home," they said. "These people have taken Will in, and not once have they spoken with us to confirm Will's stories."

He created a reputation for playing the role of evangelist at home, which only distanced him further.

On the Fourth of July, 1989, the day before Will Busenburg was to leave for church camp, he grabbed his stomach and pushed hard on his belly trying to ease the pain. He threw his head into the toilet and vomited.

The next day, Busenburg went to camp. As the other kids sang, laughed, and played, he moaned of stomach problems and complained about how much he didn't want to go back and live with his father.

His obvious physical and emotional pain touched the hearts of Ken and Rusty Long. The Longs, with three children ages nineteen, eighteen, and twelve, were a stable, respected family involved in the *Round Rock Leader* newspaper and First Baptist Church Round Rock. They agreed to take in Will and phoned the Texas Baptist Children's Home asking to be approved as foster parents.

On July 16, 1989, just before fifteen-year-old Will Busenburg was to enter the tenth grade, Raymond Busenburg signed a placement application for his son at the Texas Baptist Children's Home.

By then, Will no longer wanted to live at the Home. He was against placement, said the application, "because someone informed him that there would be strict rules to follow such as being in at a certain time." Busenburg had a girlfriend from his Round Rock Baptist church group.

His living situation with the Longs wasn't working out, either. Busenburg was constantly yearning for the reassurance of physical touch and taking the possessions of the Long children.

On July 27, 1989, eleven days after Ray Busenburg had signed the Children's Home application, it was marked received. It stated in part, "Will has no medical problems. He does very well in school life if he wants to. He's very well liked by other kids. Will's only problem, I feel, is that he wants to be the center of attention at all times. . . . No matter how hard we try to include him and make a place for him in *this* family, he won't give it a chance. Will is only happy when there is plenty of money and no rules to follow."

The application was filled out from the point of view of Raymond Busenburg, but the handwriting on the application did not match the signature of Ray Busenburg.

Under "Parent's Expectations of Placement," the application stated, "I would like for Will to work through his anger and disappointments. He doesn't want to accept the way things are. He is loved in both [of his parents'] homes but would rather have the attention of outsiders with whom he can manipulate with tales. I would hope that he can learn that things can be better for him. But only he can make that decision. He can't spend his life spreading tales and inventing problems."

The very last question on the application was, "What do you like about your child?" In handwriting that did match the signature of Ray Busenburg, there were the words "most everything."

On August 4, 1989, Ray and Sylvia Busenburg drove onto the 122-acre campus of the Texas Baptist Children's Home, located on the eastern edge of Round Rock at the corner of Highway 79 and Mays, just across the street from the local H-E-B grocery store.

They walked into the office of social worker Sharon Willis. It was a plain tan-colored but friendly room with photographs and Bible verses. Willis extended her arm to shake hands and smiled. The staffers of the Children's Home were always ready to smile.

Ray Busenburg grasped her hand. He was a large, muscular forty-two-year-old with hair pulled back in a long ponytail. He was eager to talk about his own childhood, the death of his father when he was nine, and complain about his son's mood swings.

That same day, Rusty Long drove Will to see Dr. Ben White, an Austin pediatrician.

Busenburg was rigid but pleasant when he walked in and sat down in front of the doctor. "The past few days," he said, "I've vomited bright-red blood, had diarrhea, and ran a lower than normal temperature."

Dr. White thought Will was on the precocious side.

"I know that my stomach pains are due to my problems with my father." But other than making sure that the physician knew his staunch views on religion and his parents, the teen tried hard not to reveal anything about himself.

Dr. White reached for his prescription pad. "I'm ordering X rays to rule out a peptic ulcer."

"I get headaches every afternoon," Busenburg said.

The doctor told Will to start wearing the eyeglasses the teenager already owned and suggested a visit with an ophthalmologist. He also recommended a visit to the dentist as Will hadn't had his teeth checked or cleaned in several years.

Then Dr. White sat down with Rusty Long. "Give him three teaspoons of Maalox after each meal and at bedtime. If, after a couple of months, the antacid isn't working, I'll prescribe Tagamet."

He looked Mrs. Long straight in her eyes and pointedly talked about the problem of Will's black-and-white attitude and told her that Will was anxious about being released from medical care.

An August 7, 1989, review of Will Busenburg's X rays revealed no ulcers, and the next day, social worker Sharon Willis met Will's mother, who was then going by her maiden name of Fran Wallen.

As they talked, Willis thought Wallen was worried about the situation with Will and angry at her ex-husband for not making a home for their youngest child. Like Ray Busenburg, Fran Wallen complained about Will's mood swings.

"I offered my home to Will," she said, shaking her head, "but he wouldn't attend school and he drove his brother Adam's

car. And Will didn't have a license and didn't have permission."
She looked down. "We can't get along, so we only see each
other once or twice a month for a couple of hours."

Willis later wrote, "Will's parents see him as not being able
to accept the realities of their broken home and imperfect life-
styles. They see him as placing too much emphasis on material
possessions. Both parents feel Will needs a stable placement,
since he is unable to live with either of them."

On August 10, 1989, Willis sat across from Will Busenburg.
As she tried to talk to him, he withdrew almost completely, in
both speech and body language, until he could assess the situation. *That seems to be his way of gaining some control,*
thought Willis.

Finally he said, "I want a family, and my own parents aren't
available to me. My dad's home is one of drinking and fighting."

New Christian Will Busenburg resented his father's involve-
ment with the new wife and her children. His own fistfights,
he explained, were an attempt to win his father's approval.

"My mother has her own life that doesn't include me. We
get on each other's nerves."

Sharon Willis wrote, "Will has very high expectations of
himself, his parents, and others. He has difficulty facing reality
and he tends to see things the way he wants them to be."

She also wrote, "He has little insight into the impact he has
on others and tends to have a magical view of things rather
than a realistic view."

Will Busenburg, at the referral of Sharon Willis, met on August 19, 1989, with J. D. Ezell, PhD, for a psychological evaluation. With achievement tests and Rorschach tests at his elbow,
Ezell wanted to know why Busenburg couldn't get along with
his parents or anyone else the teen tried to live with.

The boy appeared older than his years to the psychologist.

"I like doing things as long as I don't have to do them," said

Will. "I like always having a choice." He laughed nervously and compulsively. He seemed distracted. "I fear going to Hell. God's an angry, punitive God." He also appeared to be blocking certain thoughts from his mind. "I love guns, and I want to be a cop because of that."

Busenburg repeatedly told the psychologist, "I don't know myself. I'm trying to figure out who I am. I'm trying to form myself, to be what I am. I don't know who I am." Busenburg was only fifteen years old and asking the questions of a man in a midlife crisis.

He complained of having trouble falling asleep and of having trouble staying asleep, constantly waking in the early-morning hours. Again he talked about his stomach problems and said he had appetite disturbances. Busenburg had downplayed those pains to the doctor.

He was tense and anxious as he reached for a pencil to begin the achievement tests. He scored 109, average to bright average, on his IQ. Ezell thought Will was really smarter than that. He thought Will's anxiety over the tests had reduced the boy's scores.

Ezell wrote, "[Will] reveals that he has difficulty dealing with expectations, authority, and structure, and it appears that he is apt to rebel against performance expectations, confident in the knowledge that he has the ability to succeed if he applied himself, which is of course how he rationalizes his under-achievement."

Ezell's personality evaluation of Busenburg revealed no severe emotional disorders or serious personality disturbances. Busenburg seemed pretty much the typical teenager. However, he was "moralistic and disapproving of his parents' lifestyle, and his implicit devaluation of them mirrors his own feelings of being devalued and rejected by his parents."

Busenburg's attitude toward other parent-authority figures, Ezell thought, was currently ambivalent but could turn hostile. His religiosity, reported Ezell to Willis, conveyed both externalized anger or judgmentalism, and internalized, self-punitive anger, or excessive guilt complexes.

"It is doubtful that he can reconcile his newfound religious convictions with his basic feelings and attitudes, laden with so much hostility, and he is certainly in need of some sensitive and informed counseling to help him sort through these issues," said Ezell.


On September 7, 1989, as the summer days were beginning their melt into fall, Will Busenburg moved into the Texas Baptist Children's Home—a series of neat cottages and a simple limestone chapel.

He was assigned to caseworker Chuck Lentz and houseparents Terry and Kay Williams, the "pop" and "mom," as they were called, of cottage number 9. There was a piano, a living room that wasn't used much, a dining room with several dark-toned tables combined into one huge dining table, and chairs propped atop the tables. "Everyone eats together, just like a family," he was told.

Busenburg quietly looked at the simple ruffled curtains, the cheap but comfortable carpet that wouldn't show stains, and followed the aroma of baking into the large, spotless kitchen. There were two refrigerators that assured him that this wasn't a typical home. He walked on through the house, saw the laundry room with its row of washers and dryers. "Everyone has his assigned chores and is expected to do his own wash."

He set down his things in the homey bedroom he was to share with one other boy. There was a desk for each, drawers beneath the two beds, and small closets. Everyone would have to share the bathroom.

In the den, TV and Nintendo were ready. Most of the boys spent their time there laughing with each other, or in the kitchen. This could be a home. Busenburg appeared to make an easy entrance into his cottage of six boys.

That very night, he left his newfound family and went to a

play with his "thespian club." By the next day, he was asking when he could go to "his church."

Six days later, Kay Williams reported that it appeared there would be a lengthy adjustment period.

Seven days into the young man's stay at TBCH, Will Busenburg came home from school early due to a queasy stomach, dizziness, and a sore throat. He said he was nervous about his parents going off duty for a few days. The following day, he threw up four times at school, but stuck through the complete school hours.


When school had opened that late summer, Will Busenburg had enrolled in Junior ROTC and was on the ROTC drill team color guard. Through ROTC, he was making friends with Chris Hatton and Glenn Conway. He often told people that Chris was his best friend.

# Nine

The sun's rays were slipping into the sloping angles of autumn as the occasional cool front finally blew through Texas and lowered the temperature below 90 degrees.

On September 22, 1989, before Will Busenburg left the Children's Home to spend the weekend with his sister, Will and "mom" Kay Williams sat down to discuss his progress. Kay looked at his theater arts grades of 58, the low 60s, and 86.

"Why are you failing the class?" she asked.

"I have a memory problem," Busenburg answered. "I can't memorize vocabulary."

Williams looked at his Spanish grades and did a quick mental tally. *He has a 97 or 98 average, and Spanish is another class requiring memorization.* "If your memory is so bad, how do you explain this eighty-six?" She pointed to his one good theater arts grade.

"A girl sitting next to me gave me the answers," he replied. "I've gotta succeed at any cost."

"That's cheating," Kay answered. *Rather than a problem with memory, Will Busenburg has a problem with ethics.*

"It's not dishonest or cheating," he said. "It's only success or failure."

Kay Williams walked away to write in her daily report that Will seemed more interested in being treated as a special case than in striving for real accomplishment. To ensure that he was treated special, she believed Will attempted to manipulate oth-

ers and situations and made constant requests for outside in-
tervention—such as doctor's appointments and medicines for
his stomachaches, his headaches, his bad eyesight, which was
caused primarily by the fact that he refused to wear his eyeglasses.

The following Monday night, Round Rock schoolteachers
filed into the Children's Home gym for the Home's annual open
house. The residents, including Will, had asked their teachers
to the event by presenting them with a lollipop and a written
invitation.

Two of Busenburg's teachers showed up, ready to sip punch,
eat cookies, and tour Will's cottage, with Will leading the way.
He smiled and seemed to be adjusting better to cottage life.

One of Busenburg's teachers tugged on Kay Williams's elbow and motioned her over to the side. "I'm very disturbed
and concerned about Will," said the teacher. "Can you come
see me Thursday morning?"

Busenburg must have watched and overheard, because the
next morning, when he woke, he was depressed, and he show-
ered his depression on everyone. By the time school was out,
he was ticked off at Kay Williams—she wouldn't let him leave
the Children's Home campus like he wanted.

"You can't go off campus anytime you like," she explained.
"The rules that apply to the other children here, apply to you."

"I don't like being told what I can and can't do!" Busenburg
flared.

Twice that day she had to talk to him.

"My sight's not good and my glasses don't help much," he
griped. "And the school nurse told me I need a tetanus booster."
He turned away. "I don't feel anything anymore. I'm harder
than ever. What anybody does to me, I pay back double. I care
about those that care about me."

That night, he settled down, and was in relatively good spirits
the next morning. On Wednesday evening, he went to chapel
at the Children's Home rather than at First Baptist Church. He
walked in, sat down with the other kids and houseparents,

reached for a hymnal, and began to sing and pray as he stared at the stained-glass windows—the story of Jesus on the western windows, the stories of parentless children from the Old Testament on the eastern windows.

On Friday, September 29, 1989, Busenburg strolled into the Round Rock High School football stadium to watch his team, the Dragons, battle it out on the field. Fans screamed, bands blasted their fight songs, and cheerleaders tried to dance their sexiest.

After the game and the dance that followed, Terry Williams drove up to the school to see Busenburg walking toward him, his hands dramatically grasping his side.

"This black guy jumped me at the football game." Will breathed hard. "And I didn't do anything to cause it. It was totally unprovoked on my side. He kicked me in the ribs. And I bloodied his nose and laid him out."

Within fifteen minutes of returning to the cottage, Busenburg walked into the kitchen and moaned to Kay. "He kicked me in the ribs and hit me in the face between my left eye and ear."

Kay wiped her hands on a dish towel, reached over to the boy, put her hands on his face, and looked closely. She saw a tiny red mark between his eye and ear, but she wrote that up as just typical Busenburg exaggeration.

On Monday she watched Will scrubbing dishes spotless before putting them in the dishwasher. "You only have to rinse them off," she said.

He continued scrubbing madly. Again she told him to just rinse. Still, he scrubbed. Again she said rinse only.

Finally he raised his head. "I was obviously half asleep when you told me, out of it."

Later he asked Kay and Terry not to use big words around him. "I don't understand them," he said. He reeled off some words he didn't understand. They were very common words.

The following day, Busenburg asked Kay Williams to help

him with an English assignment that was late. "I need you to help me identify the parts of speech," he said. "I don't know any of them."

Kay looked at the paper. The boy didn't appear to know nouns and verbs. "How did you get to the tenth grade without learning some of these things?"

He smiled slightly. "I always went with the right girls. They would do my homework. And I copied from other people's tests." Then he talked again, on and on, about his memory problems.

Will Busenburg was supposed to catch an early school bus for a meeting of his thespian club, but he was late finishing one of his chores and missed the bus. Furious at himself, he clenched his teeth and stomped out the cottage back door.

That night Busenburg was still angry. "I need to go to school early tomorrow," he said. "I have to retake a test that I made about a thirty on."

When Kay Williams pointed out that his teacher was trying to work with Will and help him, Busenburg responded with derogatory remark after derogatory remark about teachers.

Kay Williams wrote in her cottage report: "Will has told me that he's been on his own since he was 12-years-old. At that time, he said his dad rented an apartment and Will cared for himself and lived there alone with his dad checking on him about once a month. Will says that's exactly why he doesn't like anybody telling him what to do."

A few days later, he was telling other boys in the cottage the same story, and he added that he had been dealing drugs.

*One thing is certain,* thought Williams, *Will has a lot of anger inside.*

His English teacher passed him with a 70.


On October 10, 1989, caseworker Chuck Lentz noted in his plan of service for Busenburg that neither Will nor Will's father was open to therapy. Lentz thought it was necessary to clarify

he father and son's relationship. He planned to work with the
een to eventually urge Will and his father into counseling.

On her cottage report the same day, Kay Williams wrote,
"Will has *very poor* eating habits." He ate only meat and po-
atoes, sometimes fruit cocktail, and lots of sugar. She often
aught him eating fistfuls of cookies, cake, or whatever sweets
e could find.

The following day, Williams sat down again with Busenburg
nd enumerated lie after lie he had been telling.

"I didn't remember things right," he said, and then snapped
is mouth shut, refusing to say another word, with a look on
is face that was harder than Texas marble.

The next morning, when he walked into the kitchen, he still
efused to speak to Williams. He refused to speak to her
hrough breakfast or as they cleared the table. If she asked him
a question, he muttered a quick reply.

Busenburg oozed negativity.

"I hate this place," he said. "I hate it. I hate it."

On October 24, 1989, two days after Will Busenburg's six-
eenth birthday, he turned to Terry Williams and asked, "What
vould it take to go live with my mother?"

"To begin with," Terry replied, "it would require her con-
acting Chuck Lentz and discussing the matter with him."

As central Texas waited for its first frost, the Texas Baptist
Children's Home waited to hear from Will's parents. And they
vaited.

In mid-November, Busenburg's caseworker, Chuck Lentz,
ent Fran Wallen a letter telling her he had tried to phone her
a couple of times at her office and that he "very much" would
ike to talk with her about Will.

"Will, from time to time, mentioned he might be able to
come live with you," wrote Lentz, and Lentz wanted to sit down
with Wallen and see what she saw as a plan for her son. Lentz
wanted to have that meeting just after Thanksgiving.

Busenburg spent that Thanksgiving with his sister
Michelle.

By December 1, 1989, Will Busenburg was doing better at
the Children's Home. He agreed to see a counselor. On a cottage deer hunt, he shot two does.

Days later, three hundred people packed the Children's Home
gym. Will stood anxiously in an elf costume and watched his
brother, sister, and brother-in-law take their seats in folding
chairs that crowded the floor. They were there for the Home's
annual Christmas program, and Will was to recite a few lines.

He stepped in front of the audience. He barely bobbled a
word. The crowd smiled. Terry and Kay Williams smiled. Will
Busenburg fumed. "I forgot my lines. And in front of my
brother-in-law who was there to see my major screwup."

"I thought you did a great job," Kay reassured.

Will stomped off.

He left the Home on December 15, 1989, to spend his Christmas holiday at Michelle's. Two weeks later, on New Year's Day
1990, he returned in a good mood, to the shock of almost everyone.

Around the first of the year, his girlfriend dumped him. He
even handled that well. Three weeks later, he was still in a good
mood and expressed a desire to have a meeting with his father.

The last day of January 1990, Ray Busenburg called to check
on Will. He seemed genuinely concerned about his son's well-
being. Will didn't become angry, as he usually did, when told
that his father had phoned.

The next day, February 1, 1990, Will Busenburg started work
at a local McDonald's. A few days later, he called his dad and
talked for a half hour. That weekend Will asked Terry Williams
if he could call his father and go out for dinner.

"That needs to be cleared with Chuck Lentz," said Williams.

When Williams and his wife left for the evening, Will Busenburg grabbed the phone and called his father, who drove over
to the cottage for a visit.

Busenburg went out to dinner with his father on February
9, 1990.

Kay Williams believed he was politically posturing himself

to live with anyone. "I want to be with a family," he told her. He saw his father as the most likely candidate.

Will Busenburg was caught weeks later taking the "gentle-men" sign off the men's room door in the gym. When con-fronted, he denied it, then said, "I took it as a joke." To his Christian houseparents, it wasn't funny.

By March, Will and Ray Busenburg were seriously discuss-ing the possibility of Will moving back in with Ray, his wife, and two children. The plan was for some time after the school year ended.

Terry Williams sat down with Will and discussed the impor-tance of emotional preparation for the move. He had the same conversation over the telephone with Ray.

Ray and Will agreed to start meeting jointly with a therapist. On March 8, 1990, Chuck Lentz prepared his six-month evaluation on Busenburg. He thought the young man was doing well. He planned to do another evaluation in another six months.

Terry Williams wrote on March 9, 1990, in his cottage re-port, "Will Busenburg is in a holding pattern waiting to go home with [his] dad. He has started putting as much distance as possible between himself and the cottage. I believe that real preparation needs to start towards Will's return to [his] dad's home."

On March 20, 1990, Busenburg came home from school early. "I need to go to a doctor," he said. "I got mad and hit a wall at school." It was his right hand, the hand that he had said had been hurting him for years. "I can't move my little finger and ring finger."

A week later, Will and Ray Busenburg came by the cottage to pick up Will's belongings.

That same spring of 1990, through First Baptist Church Round Rock, Will Busenburg met Emily Eaves. Emily was a smart, pretty, hardworking, down-to-earth young girl with a devoted family and a devoted life to Christ. She had shoulder-length brown hair, a slim, taut body from running cross-country and track, and seemed to be running her life on a smooth track.

Eaves and Busenburg started dating. Sometimes they double-dated with the shy, good-looking Chris Hatton. Like others, Emily believed Will and Chris were best friends.

Sometimes, but rarely, Busenburg talked about his father. "He's abusive and uses drugs," he said, without ever going into much detail. Emily, a ninth-grader seeing a tenth-grader, met Ray Busenburg only once. The rest of the family, Will never mentioned.

"I used to use drugs," he said. She looked at him in horror. "But that's all in the past," he reassured. Emily Eaves certainly never saw Will Busenburg use drugs. They spent their time at church events.

But Emily did hear Busenburg talk on occasion about his hatred for African Americans, and she heard him talk on occasion about killing someone. Emily Eaves didn't take that seriously. She just thought her boyfriend was venting his anger. He did that sometimes. Sometimes he lied, too, mostly about other girls.

On occasion he tried to control Emily, but she didn't think much of that, either. She thought that was just the way teenage boys and girls were. In her memory, she refused the attempts to be controlled by Will Busenburg.


In the hallways at Round Rock High, Lisa Pace watched Emily and Will. As Emily sat down in art class, Lisa asked, "Are y'all going to go out to the SP this weekend?" She meant SPSJT, the country-western club.

Lisa Pace didn't need Emily Eaves to answer her question. Pace often saw Busenburg at SP's, always alone, never dancing, and always with booze on his underage breath.

Lisa Pace thought more about the way Busenburg stood in the school hallways, and seemed to be lurking after Emily.

She'd heard him rave about the Ku Klux Klan: "The KKK rules; the KKK needs to run the government; we need to wipe out all the niggers." It turned her stomach. She thought he was rude and that Emily deserved better.

Chris Hatton and Glenn Conway didn't feel that Will Busenburg was so bad. They just felt that he was always trying to live his life to everyone else's expectations, trying to fit in with whatever crowd he was with.

When he was with Emily Eaves, Busenburg was all Jesus this and Jesus that, even wearing Jesus T-shirts to school. When he was with Hatton and Conway, Busenburg was one of the boys—or at least tried to be. He wasn't really the type they wanted to hang out with. He was a misfit, and he knew it.

"I've always been an outcast," he said often, frequently to sympathetic female ears. "I've never fit in. I've never had very many friends." It seemed almost like a pickup line with the girls. With the boys, they heard it, but that was about it. They heard lots of talk from Busenburg that they dismissed.

He talked like he wanted to go party with the boys. But when they grabbed some beer, drove around, partied, and tried to raise a little ruckus while listening to country music, Busenburg sat in one place and didn't join in the rowdiness.

When Hatton and Conway went camping at Lake Georgetown with the idea of hiking in five miles, raising their tents, and building their own campfires; of getting their water from a stream, purifying it themselves, eating what they could find in the wilds; of roughing it like Junior ROTC boys would do, Busenburg went along once or twice, but he didn't act like he enjoyed it.

To Hatton and Conway, Busenburg's idea of camping was to take an RV. Busenburg was right—he just didn't fit in. He talked gung ho military, but he didn't ever look like he was actually enjoying playing military.

Hatton and Conway pulled out their paintball rifles and fired at each other. Busenburg fired, too. The paintballs slammed their bodies with chest-pounding splats. Hatton and Conway laughed. Busenburg didn't. In fact, he wasn't very good at paintball, just like he wasn't very good at camping.

Still, Will Busenburg wore his battle dress uniform (BDU) to school at least three times a week. That was just one more sign to Hatton and Conway that Busenburg was weird. They glanced down the hall toward the ROTC room. There stood Busenburg in his BDUs with a khaki shirt, or in a T-shirt with the sleeves rolled up. He just didn't get what one had to do to fit in.

When Chris Hatton and Glenn Conway drove over to Busenburg's house, they were never invited in. Busenburg just ran into the house and ran back out.

It was so different from Conway's home where friends were always welcomed and laughter was always plentiful. It was a house where Busenburg would have wanted to stay.

In 1991, during Will Busenburg's junior year, he and Emily Eaves broke up. He wanted more physically, he told Hatton and Conway. He wanted more emotionally.

Like Lisa Pace, they also knew he was obsessed with Emily, calling her all the time, going wherever she went. The only time Emily got a break from Busenburg was when she was in class. But he didn't come across to anyone as a crazy, psycho lunatic. The relationship just wasn't going anywhere, and it ended.

A month later, Busenburg told Eaves he was moving to Montana. His sister Michelle had moved there. He said he was going to finish high school in Montana and then go on to college.

Busenburg should have graduated from high school in the late spring of 1992. He told people that he had graduated from Skyview High School in Billings, Montana, with a 2.8 GPA out of a possible 4.0.

Will Busenburg's birthday suddenly changed to October 22, 1972, rather than 1973. In April of 1991, while still seventeen years old and a year before he should have graduated from high school, Busenburg joined the Army National Guard.

A small announcement ran in the "Military Notes" section of the *Austin American-Statesman* on September 12, 1991. It said, "National Guard Pfc. William Michael Busenburg has completed basic training at Fort Dix, N.J. He is the son of Fran Wallen . . . Round Rock."

From July 21, 1992, to September 29, 1992, Private First Class Busenburg attended and completed the Medical Specialist Course at Fort Sam Houston, Texas, and earned a U.S. Army diploma of the Academy of Health Sciences. He told others that he had graduated with a 3.9 GPA out of a possible 4.0.

Reportedly, he stayed in the National Guard in Billings, Montana, until May 1994. His job was medical specialist, combat medic, and Hum-Vee ambulance driver. His knowledge of his job was considered "excellent" by his platoon sergeant Don Hammel. Hammel believed that Busenburg's ability to work with others and his reliability and dependability were both "very good."

Busenburg, thought Hammel, was a "self-starter who was always volunteering, he was very loyal, very smart, and an excellent person to work with."

During a portion of Busenburg's tenure in the National Guard, he was also working for his sister Michelle and her husband, Ron Burchette. Busenburg was a deliveryman for their Bighorn Orthopedics company in Whitehall, Montana. He worked for his sister and brother-in-law from January 1992 until May 1994 when he moved back to Austin, Texas.

Busenburg said he had been honorably discharged from the National Guard, and on his arrival back in Austin, he immediately went to work at Discount Cinema 8, a huge nondescript gray block of a building between Austin and Round Rock. He said he was an assistant manager with a starting salary of $4.25 an hour that rose to $5.50 before he left.

Busenburg's mother, Fran Wallen, suggested that he work for Intermedics Orthopedics, as she did. On July 24, 1994, he applied at Intermedics for a job as a polisher. He passed a drug test for Intermedics on August 9, 1994. On the consent form, he said he was currently taking Demerol.

Intermedics phoned Busenburg's platoon sergeant in Montana two days later for a recommendation. He was given a positive referral.

Intermedics also phoned Busenburg's sister. She, too, gave him a glowing review. Michelle said her brother delivered implants, laid out instruments, and did inventory at Bighorn. He was very familiar, she said, with implants and instruments. He worked well with others, he was very quiet, and he was always there. "He never had to be asked twice to do something." Will, she said, was very motivated and very loyal.

On August 15, 1994, Will Busenburg was hired as an $8.13-an-hour knee polisher at Intermedics Orthopedics.

In the late summer of 1994, Chris Hatton and Will Busenburg ran into each other. "I'm living with my mom," said Will. "And it's not working out. Y'all know anyone who needs a roommate? I'm looking."

So was Chris Hatton.

By Labor Day weekend, they were living at the Aubry Hills Apartments. A few days later, on September 13, 1994, Busenburg purchased a Winchester 12-gauge 1300 Defender shotgun from Oshman's Sporting Goods. With tax, the price came to $260.56. Busenburg wrote out a check.

# Ten

As TCSO officers Richard Hale and Bruce Harlan stood outside the Aubry Hills Apartments on that Saturday, January 14, 1995, with Will Busenburg in handcuffs, Busenburg's female companion continued to excitedly batter the cops with questions. "What murder? Who's been murdered?"

"Will you come with me to my vehicle?" Harlan said to her. "I need to secure it." He'd rushed from his vehicle to the apartment stairs so fast that he'd left his car door open. "I'll explain as much as I can, if you'll come with me," he said, wanting to calm her down.

They walked toward the back of the apartment and to his car. She got in the passenger seat; he got in the driver's seat. As he drove past the apartment's fence with the razor wire and circled the complex to go back and meet Hale, the woman identified herself as Stephanie Martin.

"You're not under arrest," said Harlan as he drove. "You're not charged with, or, as far as I know, even a suspect in any crime. But because of my limited knowledge of the case, before I talk to you, I want to make sure you understand your rights." At 4:40 P.M., Harlan Miranda-ized her, just to be on the safe side.

He pulled up close to Deputy Hale's vehicle and turned to face Martin. "What's your relationship to Busenburg?"

"We've been dating for about three months."

"Did you know his roommate, Chris Hatton?"

"Yeah. Uh, we didn't like each other."

"When was the last time you saw Hatton?"

"Uh, I haven't seen him in a couple of weeks. My boyfriend, Will, we've been dating for two or three months, and that's caused some problems between me and Chris. Like I said, we didn't like each other. Will's moving out of here and in with me. We just, uh, came to move some of his stuff."

"When's the last time you were here at Busenburg and Hatton's apartment?"

"Will and I came by Sunday or, um, Monday to pick up some of Will's things."

"Can you account for Busenburg's whereabouts over the last week?"

"We've been together pretty much the whole week," she said quickly.

At 5 P.M., Sergeant Tim Gage was informed that Deputy Richard Hale had in custody Will Busenburg and a female companion. Gage and Mancias left for the Aubry Hills Apartments.

Hale walked around Busenburg's truck and observed a paint pan and rollers in the bed, along with a piece of rope with dark-red stains on it. He turned to face Busenburg, who sat in the deputy's backseat. "Why'd you come to the apartment?"

"I moved out about two weeks ago, around the end of December, and moved in with my girlfriend." He nodded his head toward the outside of the vehicle to indicate his female companion. "I moved out because Chris, my roommate, wasn't keeping up his end of the apartment and owed me some money. I paid the deposit and the first and second months' rent, and Chris owed me the money."

"When'd y'all move in?"

"August or September. I met Stephanie"—again he nodded toward the outside of the vehicle and his female companion—"about three months ago and we're thinking about getting married. She works at the Yellow Rose. We came here to pick up some clothes."

Hale thought about how Busenburg and his companion

didn't have any clothes in their arms when they exited the apartment. "An investigator is responding to the scene, and you can speak with him. More than likely, your vehicle's going to be seized as evidence. Do you own any weapons or do you have any weapons in your vehicle?"

"There's a hunting rifle in the toolbox of my truck, and I own a Mossberg shotgun that's either at my mother's house or Stephanie's apartment."

"What do the keys on your key ring go to?"

Busenburg politely and methodically pointed out each key—the apartment door, Hatton's pickup truck (which he then described), a toolbox key, a key to Stephanie's apartment, a mailbox key, and a key to a safe that he said Chris had stolen from him.

When Gage and Mancias arrived at the north Austin complex around 5:30 P.M., Hale still had a handcuffed Will Busenburg in his car. Busenburg was clean-cut but with the beginnings of a new beard. They glanced over at Harlan's unmarked vehicle. In it was the white, female subject. She was pretty and petite with long, dark hair.

Hale and Harlan relayed the facts to Gage and Mancias: the couple's arriving and then departing moments later from the apartment; their saying they were there to get Busenburg's things, but leaving empty-handed; the couple saying they knew nothing about a murder; both subjects had been read their rights.

"The truck the two subjects drove up in," said Hale to Mancias, "it's parked just east of the front door of the apartment." He pointed to the black pickup.

Mancias walked over to the truck and stared at the paint residue on the paint pan and rollers, residue that matched the freshly painted spots in Chris Hatton's bedroom.

Harlan led Gage over to Busenburg's truck. Gage carefully circled the outside of the truck in search of blood. He didn't see any.

Mancias walked back over to the composed Will Busenburg.

"We're investigating the possibility of a homicide. We'd like you to come to the office with us."

"Okay," Busenburg replied without one iota of emotion.

Martin was told the same thing. She, too, agreed.

Mancias led Busenburg to the front seat of Mancias's vehicle. Gage led Martin to the backseat of Mancias's vehicle. "Stay here with the truck until further advised," said Gage to Harlan and Hale. Gage and Mancias left with Busenburg and Martin.


Holly Frischkorn and Bill Hatton walked into Bill's Round Rock apartment. Together, they wanted to tell Brian about Chris.

But Brian was at one of his friends, and he thought he was in really big trouble, since he wasn't allowed by Bill to go over to any friend's. When Holly and Bill told Brian that his big brother was dead Brian ran into his bedroom and screamed, "My father, not my brother!"


Sawa got on the phone and made arrangements to meet with a TCSO officer and Chris Hatton's friend John Phillips. When Sawa tried to phone Glenn Conway, June Conway answered.

"This is Detective Mark Sawa with the Travis County Sheriffs Office. Do you know Christopher Michael Hatton?"

"Yes," said June.

"I hate to tell you this, ma'am, but he was killed at Pace Bend Park."

June cried.

"Are you okay?"

She tried to mutter yes.

"I'm sorry that I have to give you this type of information, but I've got to talk to your son."

"He's at work," June answered.

"Can I call him at work?"

"No. No. You are not calling my son at work. This will

devastate him. I do not want him driving home by himself being upset. I will call him at work."

She told the detective that Chris had spent the night in their home on January 8 and 9 and that on January 11, she misspoke, he had been at their house until 1 A.M. talking with her.

She phoned Glenn's boss, who was June's brother, and relayed the information to her brother. "Do not tell Glenn Junior what happened," she ordered. "Just tell him I need him at home and that it's very important."

When Glenn was told to go home, he wouldn't go. "Not until you tell me what's the matter."

"It's something about Chris."

John Phillips's interview with the detective at TCSO was brief. Phillips didn't know anything. He hadn't seen Hatton in months.

Glenn Conway was different. The cops escorted Glenn, his girlfriend Marlena, and Glenn's cousin to the downtown headquarters. For safety, they led Glenn and his companions up the back stairs, then quickly separated him from Marlena and his cousin. They also escorted Glenn to the water fountain when he wanted a drink.

"Will often thought he was as good a friend with Chris and me as Chris and I were friends. But he wasn't. I didn't even particularly care for Will. He's self-centered and a habitual liar."

Conway told the detectives that Busenburg and Hatton hadn't been getting along, in part because of money, in part because of Will hanging out with strippers and dating a girl from the Yellow Rose. "It severely conflicted with Chris's lifestyle."

"Do you recall exactly what he was wearing when you last saw him?"

"A pair of blue jeans and a black T-shirt with a bronco rider on it that said 'My Heroes Have Always Been Cowboys.' " He and Chris had been wrestling in the yard and in the battle Chris had gotten his shirt dirty. Glenn had offered his buddy a T-shirt. That T-shirt was imprinted with the words "My Heroes Have Always Been Cowboys."

"I don't know if he took it or not," said Conway, "but I do know the shirt's not at the house."

Sawa remembered the fire ring at Pace Bend Park. On the remaining piece of burned T-shirt was the lone word "cowboy."

Detective Mancias walked in. He pulled his partner out of the office. "Will Busenburg and Stephanie Martin are in my office and Gage's office," he said quietly. "Both subjects were seen by Harlan and Hale going into Hatton's apartment. We need you to help with the interviews."

Sawa stepped back into this office. He looked at Conway and said, "They caught Will and Stephanie at the apartment cleaning up the murder scene."

One thought went through Glenn Conway's mind: *I want to see Will right now.*

While Sawa completed and closed his interview with Conway, Mancias took the handcuffs off Will Busenburg and began reading him his rights. It was 5:40 P.M., Saturday, January 14, 1995. After each sentence, Mancias stopped and asked Busenburg if he understood. Busenburg said he did.

"With this," Mancias ensured, "you are acknowledging that you have read and understood the warnings which I read to you."

Busenburg voluntarily signed the green card printed with the Miranda warning. It was 5:43 P.M. He then waived his right to an attorney and volunteered to answer any of Mancias's questions.

"Did you know Christopher Hatton?"

"We were roommates."

"Beginning when?"

"Since September of '94."

"When did you first meet?"

"Chris and me met in eighth or ninth grade when we were in ROTC together at Round Rock. After high school, I moved to Montana and was in the National Guard. Chris joined the Navy. After I was discharged because of my bad back, I moved back to Round Rock."

"When did you move back?"

"In May. That's when I decided to look Chris up. At the time, Chris was living with his girlfriend. A few months later, she joined the military, and Chris and me moved in together at Aubry Hills Apartments."

"Where did Chris work?"

"He was a driver for Coors."

"Where do you work?"

"Intermedics Orthopedics. I manufacture artificial knees. In the National Guard, I was a medic. That's the same as an EMT."

"Did you or Chris have any weapons in the apartment?"

"Chris owned a shotgun that he kept in his bedroom loaded with bird shot. I own a shotgun and a .243 rifle."

Lisa Pace's pager went off while she was at work. When she looked down and saw that the caller was her mother, Lisa reached for a phone.

"Lisa, I've got some pretty bad news, and I need you to come home."

"Yeah, Mom. Whatever. I'm at work. I don't have time to play these games." Lisa's family was notorious for making calls of fake emergencies or bad news to get out of work, only to go home to celebrate and party.

"No, really, Lisa, you need to come home."

"Mom, just tell me. What is the news? What is the big news, okay?" *Who's visiting? An aunt? One of my uncles probably just got out of jail,* she thought.

"Lisa, you need to come home."

Lisa Pace needed to make money. The last thing she wanted

was to go home and celebrate the arrival of a car thief. "Mom, *what?*"

"Lisa, it's Chris. He's been killed."

"Chris who?"

"Hatton!"

"What? What do you mean he's been killed? He's like run off the road . . . like drinking and driving . . . and killed himself, you know, like that type of he's been killed or what?"

"No, he was murdered."

"What? . . . What did you say?"

"He was murdered. I think you need to come home. Holly wants to talk to you."

Lisa started crying. She couldn't remember where she'd put her purse or where she'd laid her keys. She walked around in circles. She didn't know what to feel. But no longer would her stomach drop with hope every time the phone rang, hoping it would be Chris Hatton calling.


Gage sat down with Stephanie Martin. Her skin was pale; her eyes were determined. He again read her her rights.

"Do you understand your rights?"

She said she did.

"Do you read, speak, and understand the English language?"

Again she said she did.

"Will you sign this card then?" At 5:50 P.M., on Saturday, January 14, almost four days from the time the sheriffs department had been alerted to the corpse of Christopher Michael Hatton, Stephanie Lynn Martin waived her rights.

"You have been brought to this office in relation to a murder investigation," said Gage. "Can you tell me what you know about Christopher Hatton?"

"I know Chris as Will's roommate, and I, uh, lived with Will and Chris when I first met Will back in October."

"What were you and Will doing at the apartment today?"

"We went there to get some things that belonged to Will."

"What things?"

"Some clothes."

He remembered that the place had been almost empty of clothes, except in Chris's room. There had been only the one pair of underwear he'd spotted near the shotgun boxes in the master bedroom.

"Bathroom stuff. Mail," she said.

"Do you know where Will was this past week?"

"I was with him." She stopped, then changed direction. "He was with me, uh, for the past three weeks to a month." Then she changed again. "We were, uh, at Will's this past weekend, and Chris was there on Saturday."

"Can you tell me about Chris?"

"He used to go visit his uncle. He drank J.B. Scotch, whiskey, and beer. Chris owed Will some money and hadn't been paying his share of the bills. He had a reputation for being an asshole. He was constantly getting into fights at the Lumberyard and Dance Across Texas. He liked to hang out at those places," she volunteered. "I met Chris when Will brought him in to the Yellow Rose, where I work."

"What do you do there?"

"Dance."

Gage knew that meant topless.

"Chris, uh, used to come in there and watch me dance."

"Everything you're telling me, Stephanie, is contrary to what I've heard about Chris, and I feel like you're lying to me."

"If you're going to accuse me of something, I'm going to quit talking to you!"

"I'm not accusing you of anything but being less than truthful with me."

She shook her head. "I don't know what to say. I don't want to get Will in trouble."

"I just want to get any information that you can provide me about what might have happened." Gage leaned toward Martin. As he did, he noticed paint on one of her dark shoes. "Where'd the paint on your shoe come from?"

"It's not paint." Then she looked down at her shoe. "I, uh, don't know. If you're going to accuse me of something, I'm going to stop talking to you."

# Eleven

Detective Mark Sawa walked into the office, staring for the first time at Will Busenburg. Busenburg's brown hair was thick. His eyes were intense. His chin receded behind his stubble of new beard.

Mancias introduced Sawa to Busenburg. Sawa looked again at Busenburg, then glanced at the desk. Lying on top of the desk, he saw the signed green TCSO Miranda card—Busenburg had been informed of his rights. He and Mancias were already in the middle of the interview.

Busenburg politely turned to include Sawa in their conversation. "I was moving out of the apartment and in with my girlfriend, Stephanie Martin. By the end of December, I'd already moved ninety percent of my stuff, almost everything except for my computer desk."

"How'd you and your girlfriend meet?"

"I met her at the Yellow Rose, where she works as a dancer."

Sawa next went to Sergeant Gage's office.

Gage told him he'd also already started his interview with Stephanie Martin.

"Miss Martin, this is Detective Sawa."

Sawa sat down, listened, and watched. Martin was calm, very calm, and relatively relaxed. He asked her about her work hours, about Will's work hours, and then Sawa got up and went back to Mancias and Busenburg. This was tag-team interviewing.

* * *

Gage looked into Stephanie Martin's eyes. "Did you work any this past week?"

"No. Uh, I don't want to get Will in trouble." There was silence in the cluttered room. Stephanie finally spoke. "I can't remember if it was Tuesday or, um, Wednesday, but one of those days we moved a couch. Will's sick; he contracted a terminal disease in the Persian Gulf War. Because of that, I'm not sure which days he worked. He may have taken off a half day on Wednesday, uh, being sick, you know."

"Does Will have any guns?"

"Chris has a shotgun. I have, uh, a green shotgun, and that's the only gun I have. Will has lots of guns."

"What about Chris's truck?"

"He used to have a dark-blue Dodge Dakota truck, but his ex-girlfriend has it now."

"Do you know her name?"

"Uh, Michelle, I think. She lives in Round Rock."

"How did Chris get to work?"

"He walked or had people give him a ride."

Sergeant Tim Gage left the room to confer with Mancias.


"What were you and Stephanie doing at the apartment?" asked Mancias as Sawa listened.

"We were there to clean it up," said Busenburg, not hesitating a millisecond.

"Do you know anybody who'd want to hurt Chris? Do you know any enemies of his?"

Busenburg sat passively.

"Do you know anybody who would want to kill Chris?"

"Stephanie killed him."

Busenburg said it placidly. It had taken him all of a half hour to come up with that answer. Mancias tried not to show his shock.

"Stephanie killed him."

The detective had psyched himself up to be ready for the long haul. Now there was no more need to pick a story apart. He had to change tactics, and change tactics rapidly.

"She shot him after he tried to rape her."

Mancias walked out of the room. Gage needed to know this.


"She's real cold," said Gage. "She's not saying anything."

"He says she killed him," Mancias replied, and then walked back to his office.

Gage returned to Stephanie Martin. "Are you going to give me a truthful statement as to the events surrounding the death of Chris Hatton?"

She glared back at him and repeated for the last time, "If you're going to accuse me and Will of something, I'm gonna quit talking to you."

Gage acted as though he was going to walk out on her. Then he turned and casually said, "That's fine. We'll just use Will's statement."

Martin's eyes widened. "What'd he say?"

"Enough."

"I'll tell you," she cried. "I shot him."


Mancias and Sawa both stared at Busenburg. "You want to explain the events that occurred that led to the death of Chris?"

Busenburg was still composed. "About a week ago, I was missing a money order that was made out to GMAC for fifty-seven hundred dollars, and it was taken from a lockbox I had in my bedroom. I suspected Chris had taken the check.

"On Monday, January ninth, sometime after I got off from work, I went over to Chris's. Chris and me had a couple of drinks. We drank until eleven-thirty or twelve o'clock."

"What hours did you work that day?"

"I worked from two P.M. to eleven P.M."

"What happened then?"

"Then I went back to my girlfriend's apartment."

"Where's her apartment?"

"On Cameron Road."

"What's the address?"

"I don't know. But it's behind Pappadeaux's."

They knew Pappadeaux's. It was a seafood restaurant off of I-35 that was popular with locals and traveling businesspeople on an expense account. But it wasn't exactly a neighborhood considered to be high apartment living.

"When I got home, Steph wasn't there, and I wondered where she was. Then around two A.M.—"

"You're talking about Tuesday now?"

"Yeah. So, around two A.M., she came home. She was frantic, and she was crying. I asked her what was wrong, and she said she'd shot Chris because he'd tried to rape her. She said she'd gone there to try to get Chris to give her the money that he owed me. She said while she was there, Chris was drunk and tried to rape her."

With a stone face, he looked straight at Mancias and continued to speak in a calm voice.

"She said he tried to drag her into his bed, then she broke free, and grabbed Chris's twelve-gauge shotgun. She told me she pointed the shotgun at Chris and pulled the trigger."

The detectives thought about all the shotgun boxes that littered the bloody apartment, and in particular, the boxes in the bedroom empty except for a computer desk.

Tiny tears began to well in the eyes of Will Busenburg.

"I know that Chris kept the shotgun loaded and ready to shoot."

"How do you know he always kept his shotgun loaded?"

"I know from previous experience."

Their looks indicated he should continue.

"Stephanie said she just sat and stared at the body for a while and then drove back to our apartment. That's when she told me what she'd done. Then we both drove back over to

Chris's. It was only when I walked in that I realized how bad he was shot and that he was dead. His face was no longer there. From the nose up, his face was gone.

"When I stared at Chris, the wheels in my head started spinning. All I could think about was how I loved Stephanie, and I didn't want to lose her. That's all I knew. She's the only person who's ever loved me. So we decided to do something with the body." He sat erectly.

"What was Hatton wearing?"

"A dark-colored T-shirt and underwear. He was lying on a sheet and a sleeping bag. We wrapped him up in them and carried him into the bathroom that I used when I lived at the apartment. We put Chris's body in the bathtub so that the body would drain out all of the blood. Then, around four-thirty or five-thirty in the morning, we left and went back home."

"Still Tuesday morning?"

"Yeah, that was Tuesday morning, the tenth. I went to work that day. But I was sick all day. I got sick whenever I thought about Chris or Steph. After work I went to Stephanie's apartment, and I just sat and thought for about an hour.

"I'd had Stephanie go buy a tarp during the day. Then that night we went back to the apartment and wrapped Chris's body up in the sheet, sleeping bag, and tarp. We carried him out to his pickup truck. We put the body in the bed of the pickup, and we drove from the complex."

"Who was driving?"

"I was driving Chris's truck, and Stephanie was driving her cream-colored Nissan Stanza. I followed Stephanie as she drove for what seemed like three hours. We drove out to Paleface Park and a campsite. I'd never been there before. But Stephanie had. It was the only one that Steph could think of. When we got there, I helped Steph move Chris from the truck to a campground fireplace."

"How'd you start the fire?"

"We'd stopped at a Randalls and bought firewood and lighter fluid." Randalls was a grocery chain with a store in just about every Austin neighborhood. "Then after I helped move the body, I sat down on the bench for a while and then went to the rest room that's out there because I had diarrhea."

"What about the hands?"

"We'd brought a hacksaw that I had in a Sears tool chest. We were so afraid, even though we knew that there was nothing else we could do to stay together. We knew we had to hide Chris's identity so that Stephanie wouldn't go to jail. She took the hacksaw, and she sawed off Chris's hands. We then set the fire."

Mancias walked out of the room to go work on a search warrant for Martin's apartment and Busenburg's truck.

"What about the hands?"

"The hands were thrown in the fire, and the fire burned Chris's face. When I looked at Chris, it was like he wasn't real. We took the sleeping bag and sheet and put it in a trash can by the campsite. Then we left."

"What time was it?"

"We left the campsite about five or five-thirty on Wednesday morning."

"Where'd you go?"

Mancias came back in and listened quietly.

"We drove east on Highway 71 West." That was back toward Austin. "And I noticed that Steph was falling asleep behind the wheel, so we stopped at a gas station at Bee Caves Road and Highway 71 west. We left Chris's truck there and drove back to Stephanie's apartment together.

"I was sick all day, so I called in sick to work. The next day, we drove back out to the gas station to get the truck. But we found out the owner had had it towed to Bernie's Towing.

"On Thursday, January twelfth, we went back to Chris's to clean up the apartment. I brought a can of paint with me to paint the walls and the ceiling with the blood on them. We scrubbed the carpet with beer and Vanish. I drank Dr Pepper during the cleanup trying to make my stomach feel better. We painted the walls, and we wore surgical gloves during the cleanup."

"Where's Chris's truck and his shotgun now?"

"His truck's at Stephanie's apartment complex, and his shotgun is in her apartment."

"How'd the truck get there?"

"On Friday the thirteenth, I got Chris's military ID and went to Bernie's to get the truck out of impound. I paid eighty dollars to get it out. Then I drove the truck back to the apartment and sat around."

Mancias left again to work on the search warrants.

"We also went back to the apartment to check on the bloodstain."

"When was that?"

"Still Friday the thirteenth. We only stayed about five minutes. The bloodstain was just as bad as it ever was, so we decided to return on January fourteenth to finish the cleanup."

While Mancias waited on the warrants, he phoned Bernie's Wrecker Service. He was told that a 1979 Chevrolet pickup with the Texas license plate 531 IPN had been stored by their company and that it had been taken out of the yard by a Christopher Hatton at 4 P.M. on Friday, January 13.

Mancias went back to his office to listen to more of Busenburg's statement.

"When we got back on Saturday, we met the police. I feel bad now that I tried to get away with this. I wish Chris was here so I could say I'm sorry. I can't believe I thought everything would be all right and that Steph and me could live happily ever after."

Sawa volunteered to transcribe Busenburg's statement. He once again read Busenburg his rights. It was 8:30 P.M., almost three hours since Mancias had first read Busenburg his Miranda warning.

\* \* \*

About the same time, Gage said to Martin, "Do you want to give me a statement?"

"Yes," she answered. "Can I call my father?"

"You can do that later," said the detective.


Lisa Pace was on the phone to Holly, and Holly Frischkorn was crying. "They killed him."

"Who's they?" said Lisa.

"Will. Will and Stephanie."

"Who?" She knew Will, but Stephanie didn't ring a bell. But nothing much rang a bell.

Lisa cried and cried and went to sleep.


At 9:25 P.M., Busenburg signed his statement. Martin was still talking. Mancias and Sawa sat with Busenburg until the search warrants for Busenburg's truck and Martin's apartment were obtained. Busenburg repeatedly asked about Martin and repeatedly said how much he loved her and how he didn't want her to get in trouble.


"I was going to report this after I talked to an attorney," said Martin as she began her statement. "On Monday, January 9, 1995, at about two-thirty or three o'clock in the morning, I went to tell Chris that Will didn't have as much money as he used to and I told him that I wanted him to give back the money. I told him that Will was too nice to take back the money because he thought Chris needed it.

"Then he started saying that he deserved the money, Will had money, and he didn't know what it was like. Then he started saying that Will didn't deserve me. He was drunk and he started pushing me against the wall saying that I took Will away from him. He started throwing me, pulling my hair, and slapping me in the face." Martin nervously stroked her dark hair.

"He would hit me but mostly he hit himself and screamed about his problems. He said it was his girlfriend's fault that he got kicked out of the Navy and he hated women. I tried to run but he kept pushing me and then he picked me up and threw me on the bed. He said that was the last place his girlfriend had been. And he started screaming and slapping me.

"Then he put a blanket on me to keep me from screaming. I tried to kick him in the nuts but he was too good." She brushed her hands through her hair again. "I started to manipulate him, I don't know how, he was drunk, he was sloppy and stupid. I started caressing him and then I saw the shotgun. I put his hands down like I was going to kiss him. He grabbed me and called me a bitch. I thought he knew I was faking and he was going to kill me. I tried again to act like I was going to be with him. That's when I grabbed the shotgun and I cocked it and it didn't go off. So I cocked it again and it went off."

Martin stared at the wall and said she was cold; Gage gave her his coat.

"Then I puked and then I sat there in the corner for thirty minutes. I was in shock. I couldn't move. I called Will and told him what had happened. I was in shock when I called him.

"I thought about everything. I couldn't believe that nobody had busted through the door. I told him what happened, and he said to sit there and wait. He was concerned about me. The first thing he said was, was I hurt. Then he came over and he held me and he said I wasn't going to go to jail for something that his roommate did to me.

"We sat there for a long time. I was in shock." She still stared at the wall, only occasionally glancing at Gage for his reaction. "I couldn't move. I felt like I was in a dream state, just floating there. We waited for the people to come any minute, but nobody ever came. I told Will that I didn't want to go up there. He said we had to do it as quick as possible and that he would do it all. He didn't want me to go in shock or do something crazy. He didn't know what I would do.

"He went to Chris's room and was in there for what seemed

like thirty minutes. He told me that we had to drag the body
into the bathtub. I couldn't believe what we were doing. I kept
telling him we should call the cops. It kept flashing in my mind
that I was a dancer and people would not believe me. We
dragged the body on a blanket and then we threw it in the tub.
He did most of it. Will then threw something on the bed to
cover the blood. We left and went home where we sat on the
bed wondering what to do."

Martin paused for a moment to wipe away tears. "He was
scared for me and felt like it was his fault for what his roommate did. We stayed there in my apartment on Tuesday morning. Will went to work Tuesday afternoon and tried to do
everything normal. He was sick at work, so he left early. I
couldn't take it anymore. About eleven P.M., we went to the
apartment and I tried to make myself hate him. I didn't want
to go to jail. I'm stupid and naive." She looked directly into
Gage's eyes.

"Will and I put Chris's body in a tarp and then put him in
Chris's truck. He drove Chris's truck and I drove my car. We
stopped at Albertsons on one-eighty-three where we got firewood and lighter fluid. Will knew from the Army that we had
to burn the body to get rid of him. Will is strong because he
has been through a lot, and I knew that he knew the best thing
to do.

"We drove everywhere and went to different campsites and
finally found Paleface at about three A.M. Wednesday morning.
He rolled the body out of the pickup."

"How?" said Gage.

"I don't know how, I was still in shock. Otherwise, I would
never have put a body on a fire. Will started the fire and I
helped him. Chris's body wouldn't burn well, so we poured
more lighter fluid on it.

"Will said we needed to cut his hands off because they could
identify him by his hands. He didn't want me to go to jail. Will
was puking, so I cut Chris's hands off with a saw blade and
put them in the fire. Will cried," Martin wept to Sergeant Gage.

He couldn't believe his roommate would betray him. He was
sick and had pains in his stomach, so I knew I had to be strong
and I told him we should go.

"That's when I had to push the body more into the fire."
Martin's body shook with the memory. "I hated Chris for doing
this, and I started feeling very bitter. Will drove Chris's truck
to the Mobil station at Highway Seventy-one West and RR
six-twenty, where he parked it.

"We went to my apartment where we finally got two hours
of sleep. Will was sick and throwing up blood, so he couldn't
go to work. I started thinking that we had to fix up the apartment. On Wednesday night, around seven or eight P.M., we tried
to cover it up. I went to my mom's and we got paint." She
nervously stroked her hair again.

"There was blood on the carpet in the bedroom where I shot
him. I didn't realize what a shotgun would do. It was the only
thing I had to use. We tried to soak up the blood with beer in
the refrigerator and carpet cleaner. I've used the carbonation
in beer before to get up stains. We took the mattresses and put
them in Will's truck. I thought there was a dump in Round
Rock, but we threw them in a big trash can at some apartments
on Highway seventy-nine in Round Rock.

"Saturday, we came to get the rest of Will's stuff out. We
thought everything was all right. When we saw Chris's room,
we just thought the landlord had been in there." Martin looked
up at Gage. "I was going to report this after I'd talked with an
attorney."

At 11:12 P.M., Stephanie Martin read her statement, approved
it by initialing each page, and signed the statement.

Gage walked out the door to tell Mancias and Sawa that the
statement was completed. They were still waiting for search warrants, so Gage walked back into his office and pushed the phone
over to Stephanie Martin. "You can call your parents now."

# Twelve

When Stephanie Martin was in elementary school, the family cat, Kitty, disappeared. The Martin family sat devastated around the kitchen table, veils of gloom covering their faces. Kitty was renowned as the perfect pet.

"Shush." The family went silent. "I thought I heard Kitty."

They listened. They did hear him. The Martins flew to the door to greet Kitty with open arms.

Several months later, Sandra Martin, Stephanie's mother, was cleaning her daughter's room and putting away Stephanie's Bible when she noticed a note sticking out of the Bible. Sandra pulled out the note and read: "Dear God, please help Kitty come home." The note was in Stephanie's schoolgirl handwriting.

Sandra and Robert Martin had always wanted a girl. So when Stephanie Lynn Martin was born on June 17, 1972, in Lake Charles, Louisiana, her father smiled and said to his wife, "Can we stop now, dear?" They already had two boys—Cid, nine years older than Stephanie, and Jeff, who was one day shy of being one year older than his sister.

Stephanie had a head full of shining black hair—and was full of independence. She became her daddy's girl, with Robert Martin showing her off everywhere he went. She was easy to show off.

The Martins were having a party at their Lake Charles home, when Stephanie was three years old. Little Stephanie came barreling into the living room wearing nothing but her sandals. The guests looked up. The little girl jumped on her hobbyhorse and rode—bouncing on the toy with glee. The guests laughed, and the Martins photographed their daughter's naked ride.

She was a happy, giggling five-year-old when they moved to Mississippi that summer. Stephanie began taking dance lessons and didn't stop until her senior year, when the family moved from Oklahoma to Texas.

Stephanie spent most of her youth in Oklahoma. The family moved to Ponca City, Oklahoma, when she was in the second grade. Ponca City, which was named after the Ponca Indian tribe, was an oil company town just thirty miles south of the Oklahoma-Kansas border, a land where it was freezing cold in the winter and sizzling hot in the summer.

It was a fancy oil-company town with a company gym and indoor swimming pool, with well-educated white-collar workers toiling in research and development, computer support, and in the company's business office. There was a lake nearby for camping and waterskiing, which the Martins did regularly.

Stephanie Martin appeared to live the quintessential Norman Rockwell life. Every summer the family traveled together throughout the United States—camping in Montana, Wyoming, and Colorado. Every summer her mother took the kids to Midland, Texas, to see their grandparents. There the Martin children fed the chickens and gathered the eggs with their grandfather.

Stephanie Martin was especially kindhearted when it came to animals. She stood in her yard and stared down at a near-featherless, fragile baby bird, its fresh, cracked egg nearby. She looked up and spotted the nest from which the injured creature had fallen. Stephanie walked into her home, filled a shoe box with cotton, went back outside, and carefully placed the baby bird in the box. The bird didn't last more than a day, but Stephanie Martin wept the big tears of a little child when he died.

As she grew older, when folks commented on her looks, Stephanie often told her mother that she didn't like that, that she didn't know how to handle it. She also told her mother that she didn't want people to just think of her as pretty.

To Sandra Martin, Stephanie was more than pretty—she was sweet, loving, and tenderhearted. She was the type who always wanted to stop the car to give money to a panhandler.

"Oh, Stephanie, you can't believe all those people," her mother often said to her.

In Ponca City, Stephanie won the dance competitions she entered. In her mother's mind, Stephanie liked school, made good grades, liked to go to church, liked to sing in the church youth choir, and had plenty of friends. They were in church almost every Sunday morning and many Sunday nights.

In her father's eyes, Stephanie hated the church they attended. She thought the kids were snobs. She begged and pleaded to switch churches because all of her friends went to First Baptist Ponca City. Her father finally said she could attend First Baptist, while her parents stayed at the small church Stephanie abhorred.

At twelve years old, Stephanie Lynn Martin was baptized.


"Wanna play house?" said Stephanie to her sixth-grade friend.

The girl giggled yes.

Stephanie took her by the hand and led her into the bathroom, locking the door behind them. The girls then rubbed their bodies together, kissed, and touched each other.

In seventh grade, Stephanie attended Falls Creek summer church camp. Her best friend, who she'd met in seventh grade and who went to camp with her, was Roxy Ricks. Roxy was a tiny, lively, hyper young girl, whom the Martins didn't approve of. A girl who some might consider to be from the wrong side of the tracks and the wrong income bracket, the Martins thought she was simply too wild for their daughter.

Roxy was just a troubled orphan. Her father had been killed by the police. Her mother and baby sister had been killed in a car wreck. Roxy had been in the car with them. At five years old, she had been the lone survivor coping with the trauma of survivor's guilt.

Roxy had been physically injured in the wreck so severely that she was told she'd never walk again. With the help of her devout, churchgoing grandmother who reared her, Roxy went on to swim and dance. With Stephanie Martin, Roxy learned to laugh again.

The girls went inner-tubing—a ski boat pulling their tube so fast over the water that it skipped, bounced, and flipped over every rough ripple. They screamed, water spraying hard in their faces, as they clung to each other. The tube flipped, nearly throwing Stephanie into the lake. Roxy grabbed her and tugged her back onto the tube. It seemed like they were fighting for dear life—a team, them against the boat driver. They had to win. The boat turned, they flipped, and fell off together.

"Let's do it again!" they screamed into the air.

At school, Stephanie and Roxy were two popular kids. Their friends roamed the income brackets and the cliques from hoodlums to preps. They were renowned as "spazzes," two girls who ran around making stupid faces at each other and photographing those faces to determine who could make the silliest.

While Stephanie's parents didn't approve of Roxy, Roxy's grandmother didn't approve of Stephanie—Stephanie Martin was the ringleader of the girls' troublemaking escapades. She was the one who said, "Let's go vandalize this."

Stephanie and Roxy used thick red marking pens to write on the seventh-grade school hallways: the principal "is a bootyhead." They called their principal "Lester the Molester" because he made the girls bend over and grab their ankles before paddlings. In their minds, he took an awful long time staring at their bottoms before beginning the paddlings.

Roxy and Stephanie often got "swats," as well as detention. After the red marker incident, they were threatened with expulsion. Ordered to sit out of class and clean the wrestling room, they spent the time doing gymnastic flips across the room. Stephanie and Roxy never picked up a mop or a broom.

The church camp–going girls repeatedly got into trouble for typical, silly things like toilet-papering houses and talking too much. They got into trouble for sneaking out in the middle of the night to meet on their bicycles at the Dixie Dog drive-in restaurant to talk girl talk. Stephanie quietly crawled in and out of her basement window those nights.

"Stephanie," her father yelled, "you can't do that! You can't go out at one o'clock in the morning!"

"Oh, yes, I can!"

She and Roxy constantly wrote each other notes in their notebooks, drew silly cartoons, wrote about sex. Stephanie's mother found one such notebook. In Roxy's eyes, it increased Mrs. Martin's disapproval of Roxy. Mrs. Martin eventually forbade the girls to see each other. In Roxy's eyes, it was rather silly because she believed neither adolescent had any experience with sex.

In seventh grade, Stephanie arrived at school wearing a denim miniskirt. "Look," said a laughing and excited Stephanie to Roxy, "look at my underwear."

Roxy squinted her face at Stephanie like her friend was crazy.

"Just go down and look," begged Stephanie. "I have on these really funny underwear. Look, just go down and look." She kept laughing.

Roxy reluctantly looked. Her head popped up with eyes wide. "Stephanie, you don't have any underwear on."

"Oh," Stephanie exclaimed.


Robert Martin had never seen anything like it—the metamorphosis his daughter went through from sixth grade to seventh grade. Before, she'd been an easy child. After, she was a rebellious kid. Her exploits worried him. She had his attitude about having a good time.

Stephanie's grades dropped, and while they weren't bad, they included more B's than A's and a few C's. She and Roxy sneaked out and took joyrides on Stephanie's brother's scooter. They took dishwashing detergent and spread it over cars to ruin the paint. They opened other people's mail, then put it back in the mailbox. "Yeah, let's do it!" Stephanie always cried, with a giggle in her eyes.

They "lusted" over Rob Lowe and Billy Idol. At school Stephanie was voted "most likely to become a bus driver." She laughed. Roxy Ricks and Stephanie Martin laughed a lot with each other.

Stephanie had screaming, yelling, notoriously loud fights with her parents. Her father called them "violent arguments." Her mother, an unctuously pristine housekeeper, constantly rode Stephanie about her slovenly ways, the magazines and the clothes that were strewn across her bedroom floor.

She was like her father in that she was quick and hot tempered, a nail-biter.

Her father often stepped in during these fights, sometimes slapping his daughter in the face. Ten to fifteen times, he slapped her, according to Stephanie. "He didn't punch me, nor was it much physical pain," she wrote a decade later. "But it was rough, and it was wrong. He'd tell me he was sorry afterward, then after he got help with his temper and some medicine, he never did it again."

He pushed her and bellowed, "Get away! You've gotta stop!"

Stephanie never stopped. It was one of her character traits. She never seemed to understand why she couldn't do something that might endanger herself—like being a child strolling the streets in the depths of the nights.

It was frustrating. Robert Martin pushed and dragged his daughter into her bedroom. "Stay in here and settle down! This can't go any further! This is not working!"

Other times Martin physically picked up his daughter and

dragged and carried his screaming child out to their corner yard. There were no neighbors close enough to hear her tirade.

"When you can settle down and talk, we'll do it!" Martin yelled. Then he locked the door behind himself. It only made his daughter scream louder and longer.

Cid and Jeff heard it; they closed their doors and tuned out the battle. Indeed, Jeff often pointed the finger at Stephanie over a misdeed he had done.

That wasn't the end of it. In front of her best friend, Stephanie and Robert got into a fight over a radio. The next thing Roxy heard was the sound of breaking and Stephanie's screams. With a crazed look in his eyes, Mr. Martin was striking his daughter with the radio's electrical cord. *What do I do now?* thought Roxy. *Call the police or what?*

The Martins were devout Baptists, she knew. And it was hard for a child to hear the sermons of a loving Jesus while watching and feeling the repercussions of raging arguments by the very persons professing Jesus' forgiveness and grace. Roxy refused to go to church anymore. She felt that religion caused a lot of problems.

Robert Martin ripped Stephanie's rock 'n' roll posters off her walls. The church burned her albums.

The Martins briefly went to counseling for their loud, physical battles between parents and daughter. They met as a family. They met individually. They met maybe twice a month for about six months. Robert Martin didn't think it helped a bit.


Stephanie Martin wanted to do things with the older kids, but her parents didn't think she was ready, especially for the older boys who were attracted to their young daughter. By then, she and Roxy had outgrown their "spaz" stage. Thin, stylish Stephanie exuded such sexuality that Roxy's boyfriends took one look at Steph and wanted her instead. Robert Martin was nervous.

The Martins unloaded their pop-up camper at Beaver Lake

in Arkansas. It was their annual summer vacation, and Stephanie was a fifteen-year-old who loved to lie outdoors in the night and watch the constellations.

She also liked to watch her brother Jeff's best friend, Mike. Mike swung a ski rope high above his head like a lasso and tossed it into the water with a plop. He was a good-looking sixteen-year-old who constantly glanced and smiled at Stephanie.

As the sun set and the moon rose over the lake, Mike and Stephanie sneaked out of the pop-up and over to a picnic table to watch the stars. They kissed beneath the moon. They necked under the stars. They crawled to the ground with the lake water lapping nearby.

They pulled each other's clothes aside and placed their lips on each other's private parts. They also had intercourse. It was Stephanie Martin's first time.

The sex was pretty good, thought Stephanie, but it wasn't like she dreamed—like with a guy she loved. But that was one reason she went with Mike; it was easier with him because she didn't know him that well. Her boyfriend back in Ponca City knew her too well, so she feared what he might think.

Stephanie's mother found out about Mike. She exploded. Robert Martin led his daughter outside, sat with her on the swing, sipped a soda with her, and talked to her about boys and sex—about what boys really wanted.

Stephanie was allowed to only go on group outings to the movies, with parents doing the driving. Robert Martin talked to her more about boys and sex. Her sophomore year, she was allowed to date.

Roxy Ricks and her boyfriend drove over to the Martins' to pick her up. Stephanie wasn't ready, as usual. She still needed to iron her shirt. In bra and panties only, Stephanie Martin walked into the room holding her shirt in her hands, ready to iron it in front of Roxy and her boyfriend.

"Uh, Stephanie, that's kind of rude," said Roxy, who was

self-conscious and shy about her body, believing she was all
hips and no breasts.

Nothing deterred Stephanie. She was always confident and
comfortable showing off her body.


At sixteen years old, Stephanie Martin was pregnant.

Robert Martin sat down with his daughter. "Stephanie, how
could this have happened? Are you going to be able to keep
the baby? What's the boy going to do?" Robert Martin believed
he knew what the boy was going to do. "The boy's going to
do nothing but maybe send you fifty dollars."

Robert Martin thought the boy was nice, but he was young,
like Stephanie. Martin believed his sixteen-year-old daughter
had the maturity level of a twelve-year-old, and a twelve-year-
old wouldn't make a very responsible parent. Stephanie Martin
wanted an abortion.

He heard the words in his mind, *The parents inherit the sins
of the daughters. The parents have to either take their daughters to the hospital to have a baby or have an abortion.* It was
not a grand option. There was a part of Robert Martin that
wanted his daughter to have the child. *That way, she'll understand what's going on,* he thought.

Against their Christian beliefs, the Martins got their teenage
daughter an abortion. *I wouldn't do it again. Not ever. That was
a mistake for my daughter,* thought Robert Martin. *But she's
so young. It's a onetime boo-boo. She'll learn from it, and we'll
go on.* He just wanted his daughter to feel okay, and he just
wanted his wife and himself to feel okay. But they didn't.

It was also at that age, that Robert Martin had his proudest
moment from his daughter—she placed in the top five in a
statewide jazz dance contest. He smiled big that day. He knew
that if he and his daughter had been teenage boys together, they
would have been holy hell on wheels.

That same year, she smoked her first marijuana joint, and
dedicated herself to Jesus Christ. Stephanie Lynn Martin often

dreamed that she met God and He told her that she was to be a great leader. She also often dreamed that Satanists were trying to kill her. Stephanie Lynn Martin watched a lot of horror movies.

She felt she finally, fully understood that God had sent Jesus to save her from her sins and that she could have an intimate relationship with God.


Stephanie and Roxy were on the high school drill team. Just before drill team practice, the best friends sat eating in a Ponca City restaurant. The restaurant's outdoor umbrella, thought the teenage duo, was really cool.

"Yeah," breathed Stephanie with excitement, "let's take it."

"Okay," said Roxy.

"Go get your car, pull around, and open the hatch. I'll throw the umbrella in, and we'll leave."

So they did.

During drill team practice, a cop walked in and asked them to come with him. "Is that your umbrella?" he said, pointing to the rear hatch of Roxy's car.

"No, we stole it."

"You know, I could arrest you for grand larceny. Just give it back, and we'll mark it off."

Rarely, however, did Stephanie Martin get to dance with her drill team. Her grades were too poor.

One of the few times she did get to dance, Martin allegedly forgot to wear her briefs, which were supposed to be worn over her pantyhose. When the dancers lay on the floor with their pom-poms and did X's with their legs, teenage Stephanie Martin flashed an entire side of the pep rally. The boys went wild with their screams.

Roxy never dreamed, and certainly never believed, that perhaps Stephanie Martin knowingly "forgot" her briefs for the second time since seventh grade. Roxy just thought she and Stephanie were airheads. She thought Stephanie was gullible.

With high school, Roxy Ricks and Stephanie Martin began to establish different friends. Roxy began to tire of Stephanie's shenanigans, particularly that Stephanie was always late, as well as that they each had boyfriends. Stephanie dated a young man who was as daredevil as she was. The two constantly got into trouble. Ricks presumed it was for the thrill of getting away with it.

# Thirteen

Just before the start of Stephanie Martin's senior year in high school, she and her mother and father moved to Round Rock, Texas, the growing northern suburb of Austin. It was a huge change of pace.

Ponca City had one high school. Round Rock had three. In Ponca City, Mrs. Martin was a stay-at-home mom. In Round Rock, she went to work for the First Baptist Church of Round Rock as a secretary.

Brothers Cid and Jeff stayed behind in Oklahoma. Stephanie Martin's boyfriend was in Oklahoma. Roxy Ricks was in Oklahoma. The only one who wasn't there was Stephanie. She cried the entire first day of their drive toward Austin. That bothered her father—he'd never seen her do that.

Once they settled into an apartment, to wait for their house to be built, he let her phone Ponca City relatively often for ten-to fifteen-minute conversations. He even let her boyfriend come down for a visit.

Despite the fact that they had been going in different directions, even separate states, the move upset Roxy Ricks. No one knew her like Stephanie did. Stephanie understood her weirdness and stood up for her with the Martins.

Stephanie and Roxy planned visits. Stephanie's parents didn't approve when Roxy came to Austin. Unlike the boyfriend, Ricks absolutely was not welcome under the Martin roof. They set her suitcases on the front porch of their neat, upper-middle-class Round Rock home.

By then, Robert Martin had bought his daughter a car. Senior high students Stephanie Martin and Roxy Ricks drove into Austin, rented a Motel 6 room, and partied the weekend away on Austin's Sixth Street, a wild and loud few blocks of downtown, notorious for falling-down drunken college students doing Jell-O shots, dancing until the sweat forced the clothes from their bodies, and easily obtaining one-night stands.

*Oh, my god, what have I done?* thought Robert Martin as he heard about Sixth Street. *I've moved to the party capital of the world.*

Stephanie Martin scurried one block off Sixth Street and threw open the dark doors to Ohms. With its pulsing dance music, throbbing lights, and vampire-dressed teens, Ohms was Martin's favorite club.

Grinning and grinding to the music, she pumped her body out to the back patio, stared at the murals on the walls, and slipped herself a hit of Ecstasy. *Dancing on X,* she thought, *this is better than sex. Then again, sitting down and eating a whole cheesecake can be better than sex.* Martin laughed to herself and danced. She started doing X every other weekend for three or four months.

Martin and Ricks drove down the streets of the party district and passed a man leaning against a pay phone, wearing a trenchcoat, and looking and behaving, they thought, like a crackhead. Martin noticed the bum just as she wondered what time it was.

She jumped out of the car. "Hey, what time is it? Do you know what time it is?"

He grunted at her and slapped toward her, urging her away.

"No, what time is it? Do you know what time it is?"

"Go away," he drunkenly muttered.

"No, no, what time is it?"

He reached into his trenchcoat.

Ricks jumped out of the car, grabbed her friend, and pushed her to safety. "What are you doing!"

At eighteen, Martin dropped her first LSD. She went to class at Austin Community College during the week, and partied with dancing and drugs on the weekends. She danced until the sun rose and the club owners forced her out their doors.

As she had done with X, Martin dropped a bit of acid on her tongue every other weekend for several months. She simply slipped from one drug to the other, like a girl hooked on Oreos, then on moon pies, and back again.


Robert Martin wanted his daughter home at what he considered a decent hour. She wanted to drive fast and party with her friends, often getting speeding tickets, sometimes getting dents. Whenever she dented the car, she told her father immediately, never trying to hide the accident.

Her freshman year in college, Robert Martin gave his daughter an edict—"I think it's time for you to get an apartment." His was sick and tired of her refusal to come home at a reasonable hour. "That's got to stop."

With the edict, Stephanie phoned Roxy Ricks and asked her to move to Austin. It had been two years since the Martins had moved to Texas, and Ricks was sick of small-town Oklahoma. As she wanted to go to the University of Texas, she jumped at the chance to room with her best friend.

When Stephanie told her mother, Sandra Martin responded, "Oh, no. Not that Roxy."

Ricks immediately drove to Texas and moved in temporarily with another friend. She got a job hostessing at Bennigan's restaurant making $100 a week.

"How can I afford to get an apartment on this?" she asked.

Stephanie Martin had just quit her job as a nursing assistant at a home for the elderly, realizing that she didn't like working with old people despite dreaming of a career as a nurse. She looked at Ricks and her roommate, her hazel eyes twinkling.

"I know how we can make money." She paused and grinned for dramatic effect. "We can dance topless. We can strip for money."

"No way," cried Ricks. "I don't have any breasts. Come on."

Martin's smile danced. "Someone just told me what them bars are like." Her voice grew deep as she relayed the information to the girls. "It'd be fun. It'd be on the edge."

Roxy Ricks sighed. "Let's just go look and see what's out there."

They jumped in the car and soon careened into the parking lot of Sugar's, an upscale strip club. They walked in, their eyes having to adjust from the brightness of the summer sun to the darkness of the smoky room. Music blasted. Young, shapely girls moved slowly, their hands rubbing across their bodies, their knees grazing the men's thighs. They eased their fingers between their bodies and G-strings and slowly pulled the thin material, allowing the men a glimpse of intimacy.

Ricks blinked with embarrassment. She hadn't realized the girls wore only G-strings.

They were asked if they wanted to dance.

"Oh, no," said Roxy. "We're just thinking about it."

"But that looks so easy," said Martin. "They're not even dancing." She laughed. "They're just moving real slow, right."

The dancers' looks were so good, their bodies so hard, it intimidated Roxy.

They walked out of the bar and drove a few quick miles to the Yellow Rose, at that time, perhaps, Austin's second most popular strip club. While its clientele was a bit more blue-collar than Sugar's, it still had its fair share of U.S. representatives and senators and high-end attorneys on its customer list.

Martin's eyes grew bright as they stepped into the Rose's darkness. The stage at the Rose was bigger, much bigger than Sugar's. Martin loved that stage. Its atmosphere seemed slower, mellower, and there weren't as many girls dancing—less competition for the bucks and the men.

They walked out the door. Martin and her friends were comfortable at the Yellow Rose, with its white warehouse look on the outside, fancy cars parked in the front, pickup trucks parked in the back. That was the place for them.

They made a plan. They'd go home, they'd work and whip their bodies into shape for the next week, then they'd start taking their clothes off for money at the Yellow Rose. They'd work their way up to Sugar's. They'd strip for only a year.

And that's what they did, partly.


It was a slow day shift in 1991. Stephanie Martin and her friends stood in the Rose, adjusting their T-backs and slamming back a couple of Long Island iced teas. Waitresses, sedate in black pants or skirts, white tops and black bow ties, wove between girls naked except for their G-strings.

The veteran dancers looked relaxed, as if they were simply sitting at home naked on their beds manicuring their toes. As they danced in the men's laps, pushing their breasts and swirling their groins into the men's noses, the dancers continued to look as excited as if they were manicuring their toes.

They stared back over their shoulders to check out the women and men. They talked to each other. They reached for cigarettes.

Martin and Ricks reached for another iced tea. Ricks pulled out onto the stage, grabbed the pole, wrapped her legs around it, and swung her body to the music as sports and news flashed on every TV in the room.

It felt like power!

Martin blasted onto the stage, with Ricks cheering. She thrust and throbbed her body in a routine heavy on aerobics. Martin danced as though she'd been stripping for years.

When Martin climbed off the stage, her smile was huge.

No one in the club could believe this was the girls' first time. Martin walked over to a table, made eye contact with a customer, and sat down to talk to him.

The girls earned about $175 that day.

Soon they switched to the more lucrative and prestigious night shift. Around 10 P.M., the Rose transformed itself from a slew of unsmiling loners to a wailing crowd of free-spending, gangly university students and wealthy professionals.

The men were louder, faster, and wilder. The music was louder, faster, and wilder. But the job wasn't as easy as it looked. Stephanie Martin knew she had to learn how to hustle the men. She watched and she learned.

She walked up to a table. "Would you like some company?" The customer could barely hear over the deejay and music, but that didn't matter. Martin steadied her hazel eyes on him. She knew when it came to table dances, the eyes were the most important asset.

He gestured for her to sit. "Can I buy you a drink?"

Talk was the second most important asset.

Martin leaned close to listen. The body was merely the third asset. She smiled. "Would you like me to dance?"

He shook his head. She moved to the next table. She was learning, time was money. Conversation was money. The next man said yes to her offer to dance. She started earning $500 a night.

Martin got into the life of topless dancers, though not so much the drugs. She had Roxy to keep her away from that. They had watched too many dancers enter the bar depressed and crying, do a line of cocaine, and be ready to party.

But the rest of the stripper world, especially the money, Stephanie liked. "I'll pay you three hundred dollars if you'll go eat breakfast with me." Stephanie Martin went and ate breakfast. She also liked the men at the Rose. She thought they were young and good-looking.

"C'mon, c'mon, c'mon. Take me home with you," a patron said, as she danced, her thighs sliding up and down his.

"No," cried his buddies. "Don't take him home. He's getting married tomorrow."

"I know," said Martin, her hands slipping down his body. "I'm not going to." *God, he's good-looking.*

"C'mon, c'mon, c'mon," said her customer. "I'm not really in love with her. I'm just gettin' married because she's pregnant."

"That's even worse," laughed Martin. *But, God, is he ever attractive.* She left with him.


After a few months at the Rose, Stephanie Martin met a customer who was a bit older than she—Todd Brunner, a smart and successful mechanical engineer in the high-tech industry. They started dating, and Martin quickly got pregnant.

"I don't want a baby," she heard Brunner say. "Here's the money. You better go get an abortion."

Martin didn't know whether she wanted to have an abortion. It wouldn't be, after all, her first. She was nineteen years old, and she seemed to suffer morning sickness morning, noon, and night. She got an abortion, got depressed, and moved in with Brunner.

"Stephanie, think," Brunner constantly scolded her as she drove down the streets of Austin too fast, or as she did anything he thought was stupid. "Stephanie, think."

Martin started having migraine headaches. *I have nobody to support me emotionally,* she thought.

"I'm sorry," she heard Brunner say about his insensitivity regarding the abortion. She thought they'd eventually marry. She thought he was a "good, good boyfriend" who never got loud or violent with her, who complimented her on her grades and her workout regimen.

"I will not marry a woman who'll get fat, who'll be lazy, and who'll have a lot of kids," she heard Brunner repeatedly tell her.

"I want to go to church," she said. "I want to join Riverbend."

Riverbend, on Austin's expensive west side, was a church that many local fundamentalist Baptists considered sinfully liberal because its preacher didn't scream "sinner" each Sunday morning. "Sinner" is what Martin believed she'd heard her parents call her as a child. She *really* liked Riverbend.

"I don't want to go," argued Brunner. "They're all judgmental hypocrites."

"Why don't you give this church a chance?" said Martin. "It might be different."

"No, Stephanie. That's where you're so naive. You don't know people like I do."

Stephanie Martin felt that Brunner was always telling her she was dumb. She went to a psychiatrist and was put on antidepressants. Less and less, she wanted to have sex with Brunner. More and more, she thought of him as her best friend, as a father figure.

And with Todd Brunner in Martin's life, Martin didn't see Roxy Ricks as much—Martin didn't have time for friends when she had a lover.

Besides that, Ricks was sick and tired of always waiting on Martin. She'd been three hours late just to dress to go to Lake Travis and hang out in the sun. If she went to Lake Travis with Stephanie and Todd, Roxy spent her time listening to Brunner's foulmouthed berations at Martin.

"Goddamn it, you bitch! You stupid bitch!"

Roxy still loved Stephanie, but she was disappointed that her childhood friend dated stripper bar customers. That was a rule that one just didn't break.

Martin danced in the lap of an Austin restauranteur and his blond sidekick. "Come party with us," they said.

She got in their car and rode with them to the restauranteur's lakeside house. He showed her his dogs, his boat, his house, his bedroom. He kissed her in his bedroom. His blond friend walked in and started kissing her, too.

"I don't feel good," whined Martin. She wondered if she was going to be raped for a threesome. "I don't feel good."

Martin safely left the house.

In Ricks's thinking, Martin was just "too into it," thinking the customers were her friends, calling them to let them know what nights she was dancing.

Roxy Ricks hated stripping. *It breaks down your soul,* she thought. *It distorts your perception of men and sexual relationships. It's dysfunctional. It's a lower-level vibe that I don't want to bring home.*

"Eric," Martin called as she and Todd Brunner were in the throes of sex.

Acting as though he didn't hear, Brunner kept pushing his body against hers, until he climaxed. He rolled over, then looked back at Martin. "What did you say? Did you say what I think you said?"

"I. . . ." Eric had been Martin's previous lover. She had been thinking about him, but not in sexual terms. She'd just been thinking about how weird she thought he was.

It wasn't all that unusual for Martin to think about things other than sex while making love. Sometimes she just got bored.


Martin eventually took herself off antidepressants and stopped going to the psychiatrist. In 1993, while still living with Todd Brunner, she also stopped dancing.

She loved dancing, but she hated dancing topless, she claimed. She decided to concentrate on college. Her modus operandi had been to attend Austin Community College for a semester, drop out a semester. Attend. Drop out. Or drop half the classes.

But by July 1994, Martin had visions of modeling dancing in her head. That month Martin returned to the Yellow Rose to earn a quick $2,000 so that she could fly to California for a modeling contest. Overnight, she dreamed, she'd be a super rich super model.

Almost overnight Martin made the $2,000. In August she boarded a jet bound for Orange County, California, where she and 150 other girls with megamodel dreams checked into the

Red Lion Hotel in Costa Mesa. The prize they fought for was the opportunity to model in a swimwear magazine.

Martin stood in the hotel lobby people watching. She'd been to San Francisco before, but never to Southern California. A dark, handsome man in a good suit walked up to her.

"Are you here to model?" he asked.

"Yeah," she said, her Oklahoma accent thick.

"I'm a photographer. What's your name?" Soon he asked her if she wanted to go to a club with him. "We can talk about taking some pictures."

"Yeah," she agreed, jumping at the chance.

They drove in his rent-a-car to a local nightclub. As music throbbed, as he bought her a few drinks, he asked her what pictures she had taken. "Would you show me your portfolio? I can come up to your room—"

"I'll get my portfolio and bring it down to you in the lounge," Stephanie answered.

They returned to the hotel.

"Oh, this is wonderful," he said, flipping through her book.

Martin smiled. "I just got here, you know. And I don't know much about what goes on. What kind of—are you gonna take pictures of us when we go to the beach or what, you know?"

The modeling contestants were scheduled for runway and beach photo sessions.

"I do videos," he answered. "Adult videos."

Stephanie Martin laughed. "Oh, no. That's not what I came out here for."

Martin returned to Texas, even more depressed. "They wanted tall, full-figured women," she said. "I'm too short and too petite. And I'm not full-figured." She laughed at herself.

"I'm not into modeling, anyway. It's a joke. You have to pay your way until you suddenly make it big. And I realized I'm not really into it. I want to do something that matters. Modeling is fictitious to me, you know." Martin laughed again.

She entered a contest to be photographed for the annual Yellow Rose calendar, an unpaid modeling job.

She was named one of the winners of the contest.

Mark Daughn, a judge for the contest and the calendar photographer, was a bit leery of using Martin since she was untried. But she showed up on time, and unlike many dancers, she showed up sober and rested. She easily climbed onto the pontoon boat that raced them across Lake Travis to the shoot.

It had rained that morning, and as they rushed across the lake, dark clouds were moving back in. They had to hurry. Three girls, the photographer, a videographer, and several more were on board. Daughn had an advertising mission. He wanted to turn the Rose from a blue-collar club into a white-collar one.

Martin was the prettiest girl there, and she wasn't acting like a prima donna. Daughn eased her into the waters of Pace Bend Park and she took off her top. He floated his camera just above the water. Click. Stephanie Martin would be the cover shot for the 1995 Yellow Rose calendar.

# Fourteen

Martin peered over her customer's head and watched the center stage. Serena was dancing, and Martin couldn't take her eyes off her. Martin almost couldn't do the lap dance she was in the very midst of doing for watching Serena. She did one more tilt of her breasts near the customer's face, let him whisper a touch to her thighs, then took his $20 and walked over to the bar. Her crush on Serena was costing Stephanie Martin a portion of her income.

When young, well-toned women swirled their naked breasts and bare bottoms right in front of her hazel eyes, Stephanie Martin couldn't help but get turned on. Martin reached for a drink.

"Why don't you come out and party with us tonight?" Amber walked up and touched Martin's shoulder with a slow, light stroke. "On the boat. There's a nice moon. Nice breeze. The light on the water. A few drinks . . . maybe . . ." She caressed Martin's arm.

Stephanie Martin knew that what she had once thought was a simple party on a houseboat was really an orgy of girls. She glanced at her near empty drink. She toiled in her mind. *Maybe I should just get drunk and go.*

She gaped at Serena. *She's so beautiful. She has so much sex appeal. She can dance so good.* "No, thanks," said Martin. "Todd's waiting for me."

She walked up to Yellow Rose customer Jon Noyes and began to dance in his lap. *Nice-looking,* thought Martin. *Stock-broker.* She recalled having met him a year or more earlier, taken a tour of his apartment, and pecked him on the cheek.

"Want to go to breakfast?" he asked. He was funny, and he tipped well.

She wondered if she wasn't interested in sex with men, or simply not interested in sex with Todd. She got in her car and followed Noyes to breakfast, then got in his car and rode over to Lake Austin to look at his boat. It was three in the morning. He grabbed her and kissed her.

Martin pushed him away. *God,* she thought, *he might rape me.*

He tried again to kiss her.

"Stop. Stop." Martin wasn't interested at all. "I didn't come out here to have sex."

They talked until Noyes took her back to her car.


By October, Martin was again enrolled at Austin Community College but still dancing at the Rose. It was a packed Friday night, and she glanced around the room, cigarette smoke choking the air. Martin didn't notice. All she saw was the mesmerizing hazel-green eyes that lingered on her.

The man with the eyes motioned her over to his table. Softly, in the din of the music, he said, "Can I buy you a drink?"

Martin sat down as the customer kept his eyes steady on her eyes.

He asked her about herself . . . and he listened.

She asked him if she could dance.

"I'd really just like to listen to you," he said, slipping her $50.

She insisted that she dance. Still gazing into her eyes, he lightly touched her shoulders and her hips, gentlemanly, assuredly.

"Tell me about you," she begged.

"Oh, nothing. I work for the government."

"Yeah?"

"It's a very secret job."

"What?"

He shook his head. "Let me get you another drink?" He ignaled the waitress.

Martin talked him into drinking a B-52 with her. "Now tell ne what you do," she begged.

His beeper went off. He looked down. "Excuse me," he said. 'It's Fred. I've gotta go make a phone call."

He disappeared. Martin waited for him. He was worth waitng for. He was confident and comfortable, not macho.

He said he owned a ranch in Montana with 200 horses on t. He told her he traveled a lot. "Sometimes," he said, "I have o kill for my country."

She rubbed his thighs. She just wanted to watch him and isten to him talk. His voice was soothing. She sat in his lap.

"Why not give me your phone number?" he said.

"No," she said, and told him about Brunner.

"I still want you to call me." He scribbled down his phone number and pager number. Three or four hours after she first sat down with him, Will Busenburg left.

Martin wanted to call him, but she didn't. She knew he'd be back. She counted up the money he'd spent on her—$300.


A week and a day later, Stephanie Martin spotted Will Busenburg across the room. He sat in the Rose with four guys, just a half hour from closing time. Martin walked up, smiling.

Busenburg turned to the men. "Okay, you can go now."

They silently got up and left.

"How come, um, they all got up and left, you know?"

"They all owe me a favor." His voice was deep. "I saved their lives on a job."

She left with Busenburg.

Magnolia Cafe was a popular rustic Austin restaurant that

served health-food nuts, junk-food junkies, yuppies, hippies, gays, and straights at every hour of the day and night.

"I love their gingerbread pancakes," Martin exclaimed. It was about 3 A.M. "And their black beans."

A slacker-looking waitperson rushed up and flipped open an order pad.

"The ham and cheese omelette," said Busenburg, "and I want cheese all over it."

"That is so unhealthy," Martin replied. "You do not need to put that cheese all over that omelette." She knew she could sometimes be pushy. "It's already in it." She ordered the gingerbread pancakes.

Over their breakfast, Busenburg slowly said, "My father was a Green Beret who physically and sexually abused me." Tears began to eke from his eyes. "When I was nine years old, he was abusing me, and I shot and killed him in self-defense."

Martin gasped. She thought he looked, at that very moment, like he was reliving the event. "Why are you telling me this? You just met me."

"Because you're different," he answered, gazing into her eyes. "You're different. You're the first girl I've met that I feel I can open up to." He looked away. "After that, they put me in a boys' home. It was so strict, but that's where I learned my manners."

Martin watched him. His posture was perfect and stiff, his manners perfect and precise.

"Then my mom and my sisters abandoned me because I killed my father. They really abandoned me after I went into the boys' home. I always hated my mom because she let my father abuse me. I was suicidal for a year." He started to stir the cheese in his omelette, then stopped.

"That was in Montana." He stared out the window and into the night. "There was this man there. I called him my grandpa, but he wasn't really. He just saw me at the home and thought I was a good worker. So he adopted me and took me on his ranch. He invented the orthopedic hip."

Busenburg said he and his brother-in-law, due to the "grandpa's" influence, started their own orthopedic company. That's why Busenburg was in Austin, to oversee the company. In the basement of Intermedics Orthopedics, they planned their missions.

"He was in the CIA," Busenburg said, still talking about his "grandpa." "He's the one who encouraged me to go into the Army. One day he saw me sharpshooting. He thought I was good at it and suggested that I practice it more. I did, and I worked my way up to Special Forces."

The Special Forces eventually led to the CIA, where he earned his living making hits; $15,000 for an easy target, $25,000 for a tougher one, he told Martin.

Busenburg went silent as he stared out the window at a rotund, old oak tree.

"Will," called Martin. "Will? What are you being so quiet for?"

"I just remembered something." He sat silent again.

"What?"

He didn't talk for the longest while, then finally uttered, "One time, on one of my missions, I had to sit up in the branches of a tree for hours, stalking my target before I had a chance to shoot him."

"Really?" said Martin, breathless.

"That tree," he gestured outside, "reminds me of the tree on that mission."

"How do you do it?"

"I have a sixth sense . . . about other men. That's why I've never gotten killed on my missions. I always know when someone's there." He looked directly into Stephanie Martin's eyes. "I know when someone's behind me. I know when someone is coming. I don't have to hear them, I just know."

Busenburg went silent again.

They walked out to his truck. "It's new," he said.

Martin admired his stereo system.

"I just had it put in." He ducked into his truck and showed her his sawed-off shotgun.

Getting information out of Will Busenburg, she felt, was like squeezing a last dribble from a shampoo bottle, then trying to get that dribble to foam up good. He just waited for her to squeeze, she believed. He was slow, calm, secretive. *Passionate*

She wanted to see him again, and she couldn't wait any longer, despite it being only a few days since their breakfast at Magnolia. Martin paged Busenburg. He didn't answer. She paged him again, but he still didn't answer. She called his phone and left a message.

An hour later, Busenburg strolled into the Rose. "I just got back from a mission," he said.

They got into his truck and drove around Austin, first for something to eat, then easing their way into Round Rock. In the darkness, she showed him her parents' neighborhood.

"Let me show you my houses." He steered his pickup past his mother's home. "I bought it for her." He drove to Brushy Creek, an upper-middle-class neighborhood. He pointed to several homes with For Sale signs in the yards and told Martin he owned those houses and was selling them.

"Let's go inside and look," she said, excited.

"I don't have the keys right now." Busenburg reached over and touched her hair. She seemed so secure. He envied that. But he didn't tell her that. He told her he owned a villa in France and a ranch in Montana.

He wondered about her—about her being with a boyfriend for three years, about her being out with him, Will Busenburg, someone she didn't even know. He didn't want to admit it, but he was a bit frightened of her.

He told her he had a roommate, a Navy SEAL, whom he had met in Somalia during Operation Desert Storm. "We both kind of helped each other out over there. We kind of saved each other's lives."

He talked more about his travels, describing in detail the beauty of the places, how he loved the mountains, the foods he ate. He told her he was twenty-five years old.

He maneuvered his truck back toward Austin, until the couple stopped by Town Lake, a downtown luxury of the Colorado River. The autumn moon shone on the waters. The air was crisp with a fresh north breeze, its winds caressing Stephanie's skin. Will inhaled her sweetness.

*It's like she's come into the world after being bathed in the waters of the gods,* he thought.

They sat down.

*Her skin has eternally kept that sweet beautiful smell.* He watched her smile, the moon in her eyes, the light from her teeth. He watched and glared as others walked up. He wanted them to go away. He didn't want the night to end.

Busenburg drove Martin back to her car. He curled his fingers through her hair and wondered if she was using him to get back at her boyfriend.

Long and sweet, she hugged him good night. He wanted to kiss her, but he feared that if he did, he'd never let her go. Martin let go and waved good night.

Busenburg looked up at the stars, fading with the sunrise, and he prayed. "I know You probably don't remember me." He told God his name. He reminded God that he'd had a rough life and done lots of "bad things." But he asked God for a favor—to see Stephanie Martin a few more times. She made him feel alive, and that was a new feeling.

"What the hell is wrong with me?" he whispered. "I don't even believe that shit anymore." But his soul was still praying.


Will Busenburg thanked God days later as he sat in a Round Rock Chinese restaurant. The food stank, but that didn't matter. Busenburg was once again fixed into the eyes of Stephanie Martin. *Amen.* His pager went off—his mother calling. *Shit.*

The couple soon stood in Fran Wallen's house, presenting her with a birthday cake.

Martin looked around the room. On the TV sat a photo of Will in a military uniform.

"That's me when I was in the Army, Special Forces," he said. "Not the CIA."

They drove over to his Aubry Hills apartment. Chris Hatton was there playing Nintendo and drinking. To Martin, he looked depressed. She moved toward the back of the apartment and to Busenburg's bedroom.

She thumbed through Busenburg's collection of Anne Rice books. "I like her, too." They both liked the musical group Enigma. He had Disney's *The Lion King* video.

Will Busenburg seemed like everything Stephanie Martin had ever hoped for—the perfect mix of masculine and feminine. She kissed him.

Four dates and two weeks into October, Martin sat at the computer in the south Austin home she shared with Todd Brunner. Brunner eased up behind her, wrapped his arms around Martin, and slipped a spoonful of ice cream between her lips.

"I'm leaving tomorrow," she said, the ice cream still wet on her tongue.

"What?" said Brunner, readying the next bite.

"I'm leaving you tomorrow." She saw Will in her mind and his dreamy hazel-green eyes that paid attention to her every move. "You know, I've been feeling so dependent on you, and I want to be independent. I want to get my own apartment and be alone for a while."

"Oh, yeah, right, Stephanie," said Brunner. "You're leaving me." His tone was mocking. "You're gonna tell me tomorrow this is a joke." Brunner set down the ice cream. "I'm going to bed."

The following morning, he asked Martin, "You were joking last night, right?"

"No," she said softly. "I'm really, uh, gonna move out."

She began packing that day while he was at work. When

Brunner came home that evening, he was crying. "I don't understand. Where's this coming from?"

"I went to L.A., Todd, thinking I was going to get a high-paying job and be independent. And then I came back, and I've been feeling, uh, kinda unsettled. . . ." She never once mentioned Will Busenburg, but never once did Will Busenburg leave her thoughts.

The following day, Martin drove her Nissan Stanza over to the Aubry Hills Apartments and told Busenburg she had left Brunner. She and Busenburg made love.

Martin moved in with Roxy Ricks and Roxy's boyfriend, Colby Ford.


A couple of days later, Will Busenburg gentlemanly opened the door for Stephanie Martin to enter the apartment he shared with Chris Hatton. Hatton sat in the living room drinking and watching a video.

Busenburg glanced over. "Oh, you're watching that thing again."

Martin asked, "What is it?" She saw uniformed men in hats walking across a stage receiving a piece of paper.

"That's when I made it into the Navy SEALS," said Hatton.

"So . . . why do you watch it all the time?"

He took a swallow of his drink. "Because that's what I always wanted to do, and I'm mad that I went AWOL and gave it all up." He took another swallow.

She thought about how Busenburg said he killed people—sharpshooting or with his hands. She looked around the room and noticed a dartboard on the wall and knife holes in the Sheetrock. "So . . . how do you make your hits?"

Hatton looked up at her. "I drown 'em."

# Fifteen

It was the last few days of October 1994, and Martin sat across from Busenburg. Again he had that faraway look in his eyes.

"I have this friend," he said. "And he went on a hit in Colombia and got captured by drug lords."

Martin moved closer with curiosity.

"He saved my life once, so I owe him. So I'm gonna take my own money and get him out."

"Really," breathed Martin. "How?"

"It's gonna cost me three or four million dollars. That's just about all the money I have. After that, I'll only have about a million left."

Busenburg had just spent hundreds of dollars on Martin, driving her to Houston, taking her to the Renaissance Festival, buying her gifts for her apartment, checking them into a nice hotel.

"When?" she said. "When are you going to do this?"

In less than a week, he told her, he had to leave on his rescue mission.

Martin reached over and kissed Busenburg for luck.

They drove from Houston to San Antonio, to play like kids at the Fiesta Texas amusement park. As Martin sped Busenburg's truck down Interstate-10, Enigma blasted on the radio. Lightning flashed across their windshield. The rain beat in time to the music. Will Busenburg kissed Stephanie Martin all over her body.

She pulled the truck over to the side of the highway, switched off the engine, and switched herself on. They made love by the side of the interstate. Her sex drive was back full-speed.

"They say they're full," Busenburg announced as he reached into his truck and pulled out a card, and as Martin sat in the driveway of a very nice San Antonio hotel. "But I'll get them to give us a room," he promised. "Just wait."

Ten minutes later, Busenburg was back. "The CIA got us a room. I just gave the clerk my number to call."

Martin glowed. That night she stripped by the hotel pool and dove in, nude.

"I wish I could let my guard down like you do and feel free," said Busenburg. They went inside and made love.

Halloween night, 1994, Will Busenburg, Stephanie Martin, Roxy Ricks, Colby Ford, and another couple drove to Austin's Sixth Street to party and parade. In the crush of tens of thousands of ghouls and Satans, Busenburg was dressed as the Grim Reaper. Stephanie Martin was too, with deathly white makeup.

With the music of the clubs falling like candy into the streets, Busenburg and Martin swallowed a hit of Ecstasy. Then he told Martin that when he turned thirty years old he was going to inherit $30 million from his "grandpa."

As beer sloshed and the throngs thickened, Busenburg squeezed up next to Colby Ford. "You know what I do for a living?" he said. "I kill people."

Colby Ford walked away. He didn't buy one word of Will Busenburg's stories. He didn't like Busenburg one iota.

At 3 A.M., a group of boys grabbed at Martin and Ricks.

"Will! Will!" screamed Ricks. "Come get them!"

Busenburg rushed up, glared in their faces, then pushed them back. "You guys better move on."

They did.

Martin smiled, impressed, again. She heard Busenburg say,

"I could kill them all if I wanted." To her, he looked serious. "Oh, c'mon, Will. They're just guys drunk. It's no big deal."

Two days later, Martin didn't get a response when she paged Busenburg.

"Oh, gosh," she said, panicked. "He's had to go early on his mission."

"It's going to be all right, Stephanie," Roxy said, as she watched Martin pace.

"This is so nerve-wracking," Martin cried. "I don't know if he's okay, you know."

"It's going to be all right. He'll be back."

The next two days dragged by like years. Stephanie Martin couldn't eat; she couldn't sleep; she couldn't study.

The phone rang in Roxy's apartment. Roxy answered it and yelled, "Stephanie, it's Will."

Martin raced for the phone. "Will, Will," she gasped, "are you okay?"

Calmly he responded, "Everything went fine."

A roar like a jet engine groaned over the phone line. "You're—you're still in the plane because I—I can hear it," she anxiously stuttered.

"Yeah," he answered. "I have a phone. I'll be back in a few hours. I can't talk to you about the details right now because there's a lot of people around."

"Okay," she said, "I'll be waiting." It was 11 P.M.

Will Busenburg knocked on Roxy Ricks's door at 2 A.M. Stephanie Martin threw it open and fell into his arms.

"There was a time," he whispered, "when I almost didn't think I was going to make it, but your love pulled me through."

She squeezed him tighter.

"Now that I've got you in my life"—his soft breath caressed her skin—"I don't think I can do this anymore. I don't want to not come back."

Stephanie pulled him into the apartment and finally stood

back to look at her lover. Black greasepaint was smudged beneath his eyes. A black beret topped his head. A black sweater, black army pants with a black belt ready for bullets, and black boots completed the outfit.

Roxy and Colby sat on the couch staring.

Busenburg told them he had parachuted into a Colombian drug lord's backyard while men and women skinny-dipped in the pool. "I had to kill them all," he said.

"There were people naked in the pool and you had to kill them?" Ricks quizzed.

"Well, yeah. I have to do that sort of thing," Busenburg responded nonchalantly. "If I didn't, I would have got hurt."

Later, when Stephanie and Will were by themselves, he told her, "All my life, I've been alone. All my life, people have hurt me. Since I've met you, I have reason to live."

Tears came to their eyes.

"Before I met you, I had no conscience about killing. I just blocked it out. That was part of my job. It was for my country. But since I've been with you, my feelings have come back. I have nightmares about the men I've killed. I'm letting myself love again. Because of you, Steph, I want to get out of the CIA."

Martin reached over to touch him.

The CIA wouldn't let him go, he told Martin countless times, because he "knew too much." They'd have him killed or thrown in prison, rather than let him go, he said.


Robert Martin sat at the dining table and listened to his daughter's stories about Will Busenburg. "Stephanie, something's wrong," he warned.

Stephanie Martin kept talking, trying to convince her parents that Will Busenburg was indeed a CIA Special Forces operative.

"This guy is really telling some stories out in left field, Stephanie." Martin's blood pulsed angrily through his veins. "I don't think he's going to inherit all of that. I don't think he's been to Montana and owns this ranch."

His daughter talked on.

Robert Martin saw that Stephanie and Will Busenburg were two intertwined personalities. "Stephie," said Martin, seething, "Will Busenburg is a double-f liar."

"No, he's not!"

"There's no question in my mind." Robert Martin's voice boiled over. "He is way out in left field! No way is this guy real! Can't be!"

It was another night of arguing in the Martin home.

"You need to meet Will, Mother," Stephanie pleaded.

Just over one week into November, Martin moved into the Villas of La Costa Apartments, a complex with two swimming pools, tennis courts, and a sand volleyball court.

Will Busenburg phoned. "It's a good thing you and Lynn didn't stay here last night," he said. Lynn was Lynn Carroll, a study partner of Stephanie's from Austin Community College.

"Why?"

"Come over. I don't want to talk on the phone."

Martin jumped into her Stanza and raced north to Busenburg's apartment. She walked in, greeted by hugs and kisses. Busenburg sat her down.

"Two men who were sent to kill me came to the apartment last night. I sensed them at the door." He talked again about his sixth sense, the sense that made him the best in the business, the sense that had awarded him with more than 300 confirmed kills.

"So I was waiting for them. They picked the lock, and as they entered the apartment, I caught one by the throat and killed him while I hit the other in the nose and killed him."

"Will, oh, my God," gasped Martin. "What'd you do then?"

"I picked them up and threw them in my truck. I drove them to Georgetown, to the house of the man that sent them, and set them on his doorstep with a note."

"What'd it say?" she begged.

"If you send anyone else to kill me, I will kill you and your family."

"Oh, wow," she said, and hugged him.

Martin confessed to Busenburg that she wanted to go on one of his missions with him. She wanted to ride on the plane and parachute down. She wondered what it was like to kill someone. She was curious and in awe of the act.

"Does it make you feel like God? Or powerful?"


Martin entered Busenburg's apartment. Will was still at work, but he'd given her his key. She walked over to the bar that separated the kitchen from the living room and noticed two bank deposits on the counter, each made out to Busenburg's account, each for $15,000, each the price of a hit.

*Wow, he really is telling me the truth,* thought Martin.


Everything Roxy Ricks said, Will Busenburg had to top. She had a pet lizard and a pet miniature Doberman. Busenburg said he had an eight-foot lizard and a full-size Doberman and the lizard ate the Doberman.

"Well, where did you have this big lizard? Where did you keep this big thing?" she asked.

"I have this awesome house, and it has this big terrarium room with waterfalls and trees."

Ricks warily looked over at Martin. She believed it was stupid of Stephanie to believe "some guy in a titty bar" telling her this stuff. Roxy Ricks didn't forget for one moment that Will Busenburg lived in a little dinky apartment.

He told her he was premed at Montana State. He wore a Montana State sweatshirt. Roxy couldn't stop believing that Martin was gullible.

Crying, Busenburg phoned Martin. "Come over here now," he pleaded. When she walked into his place, Busenburg wept, "Hold me."

"Will, what's the matter?" she said, stroking his hair.

"My grandmother died." Will and his grandmother used to dance the waltz together, he said. He could still smell the bacon she cooked for him every morning, he said.

Martin wrapped her arms around him and held him like a little boy.

He inhaled within her hugs for a moment, then jerked himself back into military mode. He always did that, talked about one of his missions after fearing he'd acted too sentimental.

Busenburg hadn't spent much money on Martin since they'd gone to San Antonio. "If you have millions of dollars," she purred, "let's just get up and go on vacation to Cancun or something."

Upset, Busenburg replied, "I want you to love me for me and not my money. Other people in my life have wanted to be around me because I have money. But when I met you, I knew you were different. And I want you to love me for myself and not my money." He looked down. "After I know you love me, I'll spoil you."

Martin hugged him tightly.

The next day, Busenburg presented her with a new VCR.

The day after that, while sitting in class at ACC, Martin flipped on the calculator she'd borrowed from Busenburg, and a message flashed across the tiny screen: "Stephanie, if I ever leave for a mission and I don't come back, I want you to know that you were the love of my life, that you saved me from myself, and we'll be together in the next life."

During Thanksgiving weekend, Busenburg was off with his family, but he left his truck with Martin. She took the opportunity to search it. Beneath the seat, she found papers about military forts and maneuvers and information on karate and boot camp.

Less than a week into December 1994, Busenburg told Martin that Chris Hatton planned to leave the United States and join the French assassins.

"What's that?" she said.

Navy SEALS sometimes resorted to working for the French assassins, he explained. "A black market sort of thing. So I have to train him to kill on land."

The following day Busenburg showed up at Martin's apartment. He and Hatton, he said, had gone to Houston to do a hit. "Chris did the job sloppy," Busenburg reported. "He was loud and overexcited the whole time." He shook his head. "Chris was just too into the killing and the thrill of it. He doesn't take it serious enough. He's going to make a terrible hit man."

Friday, December 9, 1994, the day after the reported hit, Busenburg and Martin went to the Intermedics Orthopedics Christmas party at Austin's Stouffer Hotel. There she once again met Fran Wallen, Busenburg's mother.

Wallen recounted to Martin tales of abuse perpetrated against the children by their father. Will nervously paced around the room as she spoke, watching his mother and girlfriend as he paced.

Then he pointed toward a man. "He's following me," he said. "I recognize him from the CIA branch in Austin."

"I love you," Stephanie told him later that night.

"When you say that," said Busenburg, "the room spins. I've never been happier. You're all my dreams come true."

# Sixteen

Saturday, December 10, 1994, Martin and Busenburg drove to the tiny town of Jarrell, a flat, tornado-prone farming community north of Austin, not far from the Copperas Cove home of Chris Hatton's grandparents.

Will introduced Stephanie to a dark-haired, bearded man with a slight resemblance to Will. "He's my uncle," said Busenburg. He was really Busenburg's supposedly dead father. After they talked for a few minutes, Busenburg jumped up and said they had to go.

They left with Will's "nephew," who was really his stepbrother, who they were going to entertain over the weekend. Entertain him, they did.

Martin rubbed the seeds from the marijuana before filling her pipe and passing it over to Busenburg. His "nephew" watched. Busenburg was nervous about it. Martin wasn't. She smoked weed about twice a week. He rarely smoked it, telling her that it interfered with his CIA work.

But after seeing Raymond Busenburg, Will needed something to relax him. His stomach queased into the tight knots of anxiety that sent him flying to the toilet and the Maalox.

The next day, he lay in Stephanie's bed as she tenderly stroked his forehead. "I think you need to go to the doctor."

Tears spilled from Will's eyes. "I'm dying."

"What?"

"I was in Somalia for Operation Desert Storm, and I got

into some chemical warfare. About a year ago, I found out that it got into my system, and I'm dying."

"Oh, Will! Why didn't you tell me?"

He wept more and clutched at his stomach.

She started crying.

"I just couldn't," he answered.

"How long do you have?"

"Ten years. But I might be gone in five."

"Oh, God," she wailed. "I can't believe this. We just met, and we're so in love. And now you tell me you're dying of a disease, and you have ten years to live. Oh, God." She leaned her head down to his belly and wept.

The next night, Martin sneaked into her apartment at 3 A.M. to surprise Busenburg with an early return from work. She expected him to be up waiting for her, as usual. He wasn't. She tiptoed to her bedroom door and heard moaning from the room. She stopped and listened.

"Please stop," Busenburg cried in his sleep. "No, no. Don't hit me again."

Stephanie slipped into the bedroom.

Busenburg tossed and twisted in the bed.

She walked closer.

"No!" he screamed, bolting upright.

"Will, Will. What's wrong? It's me, Stephanie."

Sweating and red-faced, he stared at Martin.

She slid into bed beside him, easing him down. He shook in her arms.

"My dad tied me up and sexually abused me," said Busenburg. His breath raced as he recited his dream. "Then he hit me over and over again. The tactics my dad learned as a Green Beret, he used on us kids. My dad was a coke addict."


Will Busenburg and Stephanie Martin sat in a busy restaurant eating dinner when Busenburg's pager went off. "It's Fred," he said, and got up to return the call.

When Busenburg sat back down in the booth, carefully placing his napkin in his lap, keeping his elbows off the table, and sitting erectly, he said, "Fred has a plan for how I can get out of the CIA permanently."

Martin leaned in close to listen.

Busenburg spoke softly. "I'll go on a mission, out of the country, fake my death, and be listed as dead in action." He reached over to touch Stephanie's hand. "But this is the bad part. To do it, we'll have to kill someone else to put in my place, someone that looks like me."

"When?" whispered Steph. "When will it happen?"

"It'll go down in about a week."

Martin suddenly understood why God had brought Will Busenburg into her life and why she dreamed of working in the health care field—to help find a cure for Busenburg's disease. It was all part of Jesus' divine plan, she thought.

"I want more information on your disease," Martin said. "I want to talk to your doctor."

"My doctor is private," said Busenburg. "He's with the Army."

She begged him to call the doctor. Busenburg finally gave in, made a call in front of Martin, and asked for "the paperwork on the disease" to be sent to him.

"Can I talk to him?" pleaded Stephanie. "Can I talk to him?"

"Okay, okay, thank you, Doctor," said Busenburg, and he slammed down the receiver. "He had to go," he said to Martin.

The night was chilly and filled with the white Christmas lights of downtown Austin and the multicolored chaser lights of central Austin. Stephanie Martin and Will Busenburg cruised the Capital City to look at them all. Reindeer, wreaths, and Santas crossed light poles and wires from one house to the next, from one block to the next.

The couple, giggling, decided to drive over to Austin's east side and see if "they" put up lights, too. "They" meant the minorities living on Austin's east side.

Busenburg eased his truck along Twelfth Street, his mind wrapped in the fantasy lights and the belief that Martin was being stalked by an African-American man.

He thought about the words of comfort he'd spoken to her. "Don't worry," he had told her, fuming. "You're with me now. And I can take care of anybody that comes near you. I'll kill anybody that tries to hurt you." His words tightened like a ribbon around him as a black man suddenly crossed the street and passed through the dead aim of Busenburg's headlights. "If that black guy was coming after you, I would kill him right now."

Martin slipped her hand along her boyfriend's thigh.


Music reverberated in the Yellow Rose as Stephanie Martin danced onstage. Suddenly she felt a pull on the back of her thigh. She seductively reached down, as if it were part of her act. Pain shot through her leg. Martin had pulled a hamstring while stripping.

Like the EMS worker he had been, Busenburg carried her to his truck and drove her the five minutes to his apartment. He lifted her up the steps and tenderly laid her down, then ran a hot bath full of bubbles and herbs. He placed her in the tub and massaged his hands along her leg.

The next night, Busenburg and Martin drove through the city when his pager went off. "It's Fred," he said, "telling me to be ready to fly out on the mission." It was the mission to fake Busenburg's death. But within hours, Busenburg walked into Martin's apartment. "The helicopter didn't show," he sighed. "It's delayed until the first of January."


The Martin family packed for San Angelo to see the grand-parents for Christmas. Stephanie was supposed to go with

hem, but she told her parents she had to finish Christmas shopping. She said she'd drive out by herself in a couple of days.
Will Busenburg said he didn't want her to drive by herself; he
would take her.

In San Angelo for Christmas, the Martins met for the first
time their daughter's love of her life. Stephanie and Will arrived
in the evening, just as the family had finished dinner and were
keeping Stephanie's and Will's suppers warm.

Will Busenburg shook Sandra Martin's hand and, while still
holding her hand, looked straight into her eyes, locking their
gazes. It was almost as if he were thinking: if I look right in
your eyes, I can really know you. Sandra Martin liked him
immediately.

Will and Stephanie sat down to dinner.

"I think Stephanie is right," said Sandra Martin to her husband as she and Robert sat in another room. "I think Will
seems to be a very nice person."

Will walked into the living room and sat down next to
Stephanie's sister-in-law. With the plinking sound of the Christmas twinkle lights in the background, he told her about his Special Forces work, that he was the heir to the company he worked
for, and that he would inherit the company when he turned thirty.

"Boy, sounds like he's set for life," she later told her mother-
in-law. The younger Mrs. Martin was very impressed.

Stephanie, too, talked about his Special Forces work.

But with her, he said, "Stephanie, let's don't talk about that."
And with all, he refused details.

If they were around Stephanie's mother, Will said,
"Stephanie, we don't want to bore your mother with that. We
don't need to talk about it."

"Well, I don't think it's boring," Mrs. Martin replied. "It
sounds very interesting to me."

He and Stephanie slipped away and into bed. As they made
love, she placed her fingers in his mouth so that his cries of
coming didn't reverberate throughout her grandmother's home.

Awesome, he later told Stephanie. Incredible. Beautiful.

On Christmas Eve morning, Will Busenburg's pager went off. "It's Fred," he whispered. "I have to leave for the mission, tonight."

Martin grabbed her Christmas present to him and pushed it toward him. "To protect you," she said. It was a gold cross.

Telling the rest of the Martin family that he had to leave on business, Busenburg got into his pickup truck and left.

A few days after Christmas, Stephanie Martin rode back from San Angelo with her parents. When they dropped her off at her apartment, Will wasn't there, although he had been staying at Stephanie's to take care of her cat. Although Busenburg wasn't there, a roomful of Christmas presents was.

The Martins were pleased.

When Busenburg arrived at her apartment, Stephanie opened the presents and found a TV, a diamond-and-sapphire necklace, and a dildo. She clanked out her pots and pans. In her one-bedroom apartment, Stephanie Martin cooked up a Christmas dinner for Will Busenburg—turkey, stuffing, green bean casserole, rolls, and cheesecake.

"I've never had a Christmas dinner with someone who loved me like you do," he said. But as Busenburg stroked Martin, he had bad news to break. "I'm bankrupt." His real estate deals had gone sour. Already he'd told her his accountant had stolen his money. "I'm scared you're going to leave me."

"No," she assured him, kissing him. "I don't care about the money. I love you."

"I still have some assets I can sell."

Stephanie Martin wanted to show off her Christmas presents. Just before New Year's, she and Will walked into the Martins' home in Round Rock. Robert Martin knew that the necklace he stared at was high-dollar diamond.

"How did you get through school with a premed degree in such a short time?" Robert Martin asked as they sat in the den.

"Well, I went to school full time through the summers. I

took full loads, as many hours as I could get." Busenburg detailed the hours he had taken. "I've always been very good in math and science. And I took full loads of courses, and I was able to graduate then in three years."

Busenburg's words flowed easily, like spiked eggnog on a cold night.

"I'm planning on going on and completing my medical degree, but I just needed to take a break. Plus, I wanted to come down here and get a firsthand look at the business," he said softly, so softly that Robert often had to ask Will to repeat what he was saying. "I never took summers off or anything. But sometimes I had to be gone for a week or so when my Army duties would necessitate that I be gone."

Robert Martin quickly added in his mind—Will's age, twenty-five, and the time it would have taken Busenburg to complete these accomplishments. To Martin's astonishment, it added up. Busenburg could have done it.

"The ranch my sister lives on is actually owned by me," Busenburg calmly continued. "She and her husband just keep it up for me."

He turned to Robert Martin and talked about how much he loved to hunt, how he loved to shoot skeet. "Stephanie," said Will to Robert, "she doesn't know how to shoot a gun, does she?"

"No," replied Robert. "She's never shot a gun. She doesn't like guns, I guess. I've never let her shoot any because she doesn't want to."

"Do you have an extra shotgun that I could train her on, that I could take her skeet shooting?" Busenburg asked, still casual.

"Yeah, I guess, if you're gonna do that. That'd be good for her to learn at least how to use one, if she ever stays by herself and I give her something."

Busenburg took the shotgun.

"He must be a really smart guy," Robert Martin said to Sandra after Will walked out the door with Stephanie, and the shotgun.

The Martins met Busenburg, perhaps, two more times.

"I'm moving money from one account to another. I have some money in a Swiss bank account that I'm going to be transferring," he said in front of Sandra Martin.

He also told her that he was having money problems, that Chris Hatton wasn't paying his share of the rent, so he was having to pay it all.

On New Year's Eve, Martin and Busenburg moved some of his things out of the Aubry Hills Apartments and over to Fran Wallen's.

Roxy Ricks and Colby Ford planned to go out that night, but they were stuck waiting at their apartment for Martin and Busenburg, as usual.

"Can we come over and borrow some money?" phoned Stephanie.

Roxy and Colby, and several other couples, had been waiting for Martin and Busenburg for two hours. They needed to get down to Sixth Street and find a parking place before the New Year's countdown.

Finally Martin and Busenburg showed.

"Stephanie, you're really late," said Ricks, exasperated. It was 10:30 P.M. "And besides that, I thought Will was a millionaire. Why does he need to borrow money?"

"Something's wrong with my ATM card," he responded.

"Then write a check," said Roxy.

"Something's wrong with . . ."

*This is bullshit,* thought Roxy. Busenburg didn't even need to finish his lie. "Okay, Stephanie, whatever," she said, and handed Martin some money. "He is weird," she said. "I think he's lying, and he gives me the creeps. If you're going to continue to hang out with him, then don't come over here. You're not welcome over here with Will. He is not welcome here."

Martin, upset, walked out the door with her lover.

Ricks turned to her boyfriend. "You know, Will is weird.

There's something off about him. If Stephanie doesn't get away from him, I'm going to see her on the news for killing somebody or something crazy like that. He's going to end up killing somebody and dragging her along with him, and I'm gonna see her on the news."

That damn worry just wouldn't leave her.


New Year's Day, 1995, and Stephanie Martin was the cover girl of the Yellow Rose calendar, a cover girl who was busy trudging up and down the steps of a not-so-spiffy apartment in a not-so-spiffy neighborhood schlepping Will Busenburg's possessions out of his place.

"Steph," Will yelled from his bedroom. "Come here!"

She walked in.

He was breathless and crimson in the face. "Look at this," he said. "Look at it." He shook a small, empty lockbox. "My cashier's check for six thousand dollars is missing. Chris took it. I know he did, that son of a bitch. He's the only one who knew how to get into this box. There's a key to this box." He threw it down. "Let's go. Let's get out of here before I really go off."


Several days later, Todd Brunner stopped by Stephanie Martin's apartment to drop off his dog. Martin was going to dog-sit while Brunner went skiing. She petted the dog as they talked. "Will's roommate has cashed a check that Will made out to someone else. It was for six thousand dollars. Now Will's short on money," she told him.

Around noon on Monday, January 9, 1995, Brunner rang the doorbell at Martin's apartment, ready to pick up his dog. Martin opened the door. As they talked, Todd heard someone moving around inside.

"Is Will here?" he asked, and slightly glanced over Stephanie's shoulder to see in.

"Yes." She mentioned that she'd gotten a new bicycle.

Todd quickly left.

Tuesday, January 10, 1995, around 5 or 6 P.M., Brunner sat in his south Austin home talking on the phone, when another call beeped in. He pressed the flash button. Stephanie Martin was on the other line.

"Can I borrow a tarp?" she asked.

He puffed with frustration. His new girlfriend was waiting on hold.

"I need to borrow your camping tarp to do some painting at Will's apartment."

Brunner didn't have time for this, or Will Busenburg, in particular. "The tarp's up in the attic with all of my other camping supplies and I'm in a hurry to go out for dinner. You can't use it. And I don't want you digging through my stuff, and I don't have time to find it for you."

They hung up.

Thursday, January 12, 1995, the *Austin American-Statesman* ran an inside story: "MAN FOUND MUTILATED, DISPLAYED IN PACE BEND PARK."

The following morning, there was a second story, also on the inside pages: "BODY'S MUTILATION MAKES IDENTIFICATION DIFFICULT, OFFICIALS SAY."

Around 4 P.M., that same day, Friday, January 13, 1995, Todd Brunner returned home from a quick trip to San Antonio. An hour later, Stephanie Martin phoned again.

"I'm at the impound yard and I need to borrow ten dollars to get a truck out of impound. Will's Impact card isn't working."

"Seems Will never has enough money," Brunner retorted. "But, yeah, come on over."

Five minutes later, Martin knocked on Brunner's door. "Will's roommate," she said as they talked at the door, "is really depressed and upset. So Will got him a job with the French assassins. And so he had to move off to France and his truck was impounded."

Todd just slowly nodded and shook his head, all at the same time.

"Will's roommate might have left his billfold in the truck and some of the money that was owed Will might be in the wallet."

Brunner gave her a $20 bill, and she gave him back $7. Stephanie walked away. Todd stood in the door and watched. He saw Will Busenburg's black pickup truck drive away. He thought he saw two people sitting in the truck.

# Seventeen

Saturday, January 14, 1995, between 11:30 P.M. and midnight, the phone rattled the silence in the Round Rock home of Sandra and Robert Martin. Sandra rolled over in their bed and picked up the receiver.

"Mother, I need you to help me."

Sandra Martin bolted upright. *She's been raped,* she thought. "Stephanie, what's the matter?"

"I've been arrested."

"Where are you?"

"I'm in jail."

Sandra girded herself for strength. "What happened, Stephanie?" She could tell someone was there with Stephanie listening to her daughter's every word.

"Will's roommate tried to rape me, and I shot him."

Robert Martin grabbed the phone from his wife. "You haven't signed anything, you haven't said anything, have you?"

"Yeah, I signed a confession."

"You what?" *Oh, Lord, how could she do . . .* "No, Stephanie, what have you done? Stephanie, do not say anything. Just shut up, Stephanie. We'll be down there. Just don't talk anymore to them."

Robert Martin briefly conferred with Sergeant Timothy Gage.

"Oh, God, oh, God," moaned Sandra Martin.

Robert and Sandra Martin didn't know whom to call. They

certainly didn't know any criminal lawyers. They phoned a lawyer from their church for a recommendation.

"Ira Davis," he said.

The sheriffs detectives sat chitchatting in their office with Will Busenburg. He indicated that he thought the human body would burn like paper. He'd just expected that he and Stephanie could easily feed Hatton into the fire. He looked up at the wall and saw an award for rodeo riding. He started talking about rodeoing.

Mancias glanced at Sawa and they stepped outside. "You know," said Mancias, "this guy just doesn't have any remorse."

They mulled over the situation as they waited for search warrants. Martin's and Busenburg's statements were almost identical. To the detectives, that didn't indicate truth-telling; that indicated made-up stories that had been rehearsed.

*He's just a cold-blooded killer*, thought Mancias.

With his chief, Mancias climbed into his vehicle and navigated the Saturday-night drunken streets of Austin to Judge Carrie Key's home for her to sign her name on the search and arrest warrants.

She initialed Mancias's signature, and Mancias and his chief returned to TCSO headquarters. It was 12:20 A.M. Mancias still hadn't gotten any sleep, so he didn't notice until he was back at headquarters that Judge Key hadn't signed the warrants; she'd only initialed his signature.

They drove back to the judge's house. At 12:55 A.M., Sunday, January 15, Judge Key signed the arrest warrants for William Michael Busenburg and Stephanie Lynn Martin, as well as the search warrants for Busenburg's truck and Martin's apartment.

Once the additional search warrants were in hand, Mancias asked Busenburg if he would ride with him and Sawa to Martin's apartment, to point out the apartment, as well as Hatton's truck. Busenburg agreed. Stephanie Martin also went, riding with Sergeant Gage.

Like Busenburg had said, the apartments were located behind Pappadeaux's restaurant, about two blocks east, across the street from numerous office buildings. It was a strange haven of seeming safety in a neighborhood where one block placed one in the midst of white-collar workers, and another block placed one in the midst of dilapidated frame homes of those struggling to make ends meet.

They drove through the apartment's electric gates. Most of the vehicles in the parking lot were a scale or two above those parked at the Hatton complex. Busenburg pointed to Hatton's pickup

Mancias got out of his sheriffs vehicle to circle around the beat-up pickup, observing its every detail. In the cab of the truck was a wadded and wrinkled blue tarp. In the bed of the truck was a can of lighter fluid and a box of matches.

Mancias walked over to Sergeant Gage's vehicle. He leaned in to talk to Stephanie Martin. "Will you tell me where in your apartment is the shotgun you supposedly used to shoot Chris?"

"It's in my bedroom closet," she replied. "It's on the top shelf, to the left, as you walk into the closet."

Crime Lab Technician Tracy Hill and Deputy Harlan had arrived by then and entered the apartment with Mancias. The living room was rather neat, but Mancias ignored that and strode directly to the bedroom.

The bedroom was a mess with clothes strewn on the floor. Mancias looked exactly where Martin had told him to and he spotted the two shotguns. The detective called for Hill, who photographed the guns before they were removed.

Mancias and Harlan checked the guns' chambers for shells. The gun Harlan took was loaded with 12-gauge rounds. The gun Mancias held, which was a Winchester 12-gauge in a camouflage case, was empty. The gun dripped crystal clear oil, as if it had been freshly cleaned. There were also live rounds of shells in a pouch on the camouflage case. Mancias and Harlan laid the shotguns on Martin's bed for Hill to inventory and collect.

Mancias opened a white chest of drawers. Lined with little girl–like, pink-and-white checked shelf paper, the drawers were filled mostly with clothes, socks, underwear, gym clothes. Inside the third drawer from the top, Mancias spotted Christopher Hatton's California driver's license. Underneath the driver's license were credit cards and paperwork, also belonging to Chris Hatton, and a black wallet.

Mancias called Hill over. She photographed the inside of the drawer before any of the items were touched. He exited the apartment to talk to Sawa. As he did, he noticed a maroon mountain bike on Martin's back patio. "Whose bike?" he asked Busenburg.

"It's Chris's," he answered. "We took it earlier."

Tracy Hill walked up to Sergeant Gage's vehicle. She peered in at Stephanie Martin. "Where are the clothes that you were wearing when you shot Chris?"

Martin looked puzzled, as if she couldn't remember.

"They must have been bloody," said Gage to Martin.

"No, they weren't," she answered.

A bit later, Gage was advised that Martin's father was trying to reach him. Sergeant Gage phoned Robert Martin, who asked to speak to his daughter. Gage overheard talk about an attorney.

Sawa turned to Busenburg. "Will you take me to where you and Stephanie took the mattress and box springs?" He was referring to the bloody mattress and box springs from Chris Hatton's bed.

Busenburg agreed. The two drove back up Interstate-35 to Round Rock. At the Creeks Apartments on Palm Valley Boulevard, they circled through the complex and stopped at a Dumpster near the apartment rental office. That, said Busenburg, was where they dumped the bloody bedding. Sawa looked but he found nothing.

He and Busenburg returned to Austin and the apartment Busenburg shared with Martin. There Mancias took Busenburg

Christopher Michael Hatton, 20, two years before his
murder. (*Photo courtesy Holly Frischkorn*)

A teenage Chris Hatton at a Frischkorn family reunion in Iowa. *(Photo courtesy Holly Frischkorn)*

Hatton and Lisa Pc at her senior prom 1993. *(Photo courtesy Lisa Pace)*

Hatton mugging in an Austin, Texas sporting goods store. (*Photo courtesy Holly Frischkorn*)

Stephanie Martin at five. (*Photo courtesy Sandra Martin*)

Fifth-grader Stephanie Martin celebrating her cat's birthday. (*Photo courtesy Sandra Martin*)

While in junior high school, Martin attended church camp.
(*Photo courtesy Roxy Ricks*)

Martin with her mother Sandra (*left*), father Robert and
grandmother at her high school graduation in Round Rock,
Texas in 1990.    (*Photo courtesy Sandra Martin*)

At eighteen, Martin was a topless dancer at the Yellow Rose,
one of Austin, Texas's most popular strip clubs.
(*Photo courtesy Mark Daughn*)

The Yellow Rose used Martin's photo on the cover of its
1995 calendar. *(Photo courtesy Mark Daughn)*

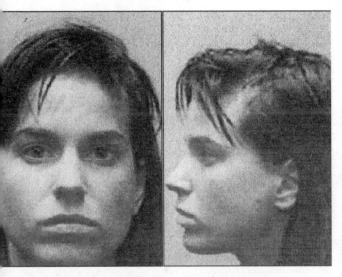

Martin was arrested for the murder of Chris Hatton on January 14, 1995, three days after his body was found. (*Photo courtesy Travis County, Texas Sheriffs Office*)

William Busenburg was Hatton's
roommate and Martin's boyfriend.

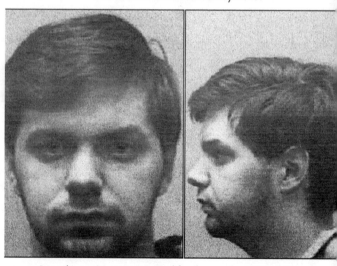

Busenburg, 21, was arrested for the murder of Chris Hatton
on January 14, 1995.
(*Photo courtesy Travis County, Texas Sheriffs Office*)

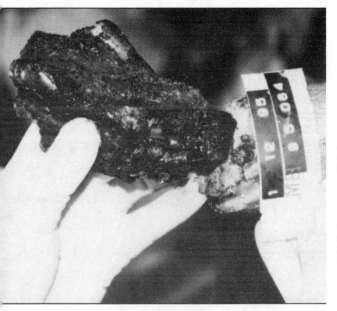

Hatton's hands had been severed from his arms and burned.
(*Photo courtesy Travis County, Texas Sheriffs Office*)

A portion of Hatton's burned t-shirt.
(*Photo courtesy Travis County, Texas Sheriffs Office*)

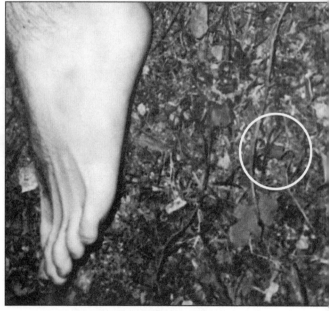

A piece of melted blue plastic near Hatton's unburned bare
feet came from the tarp used to transport his body.
(*Photo courtesy Travis County, Texas Sheriffs Office*)

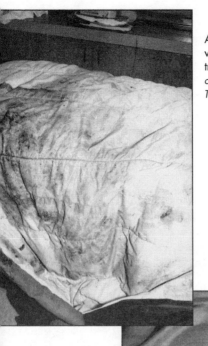

A bloody sleeping bag was found in a nearby trash barrel. *(Photo courtesy Travis County, Texas Sheriffs Office)*

The ID tag in the sleeping bag helped police identify Hatton's body. *(Photo courtesy Travis County, Texas Sheriffs Office)*

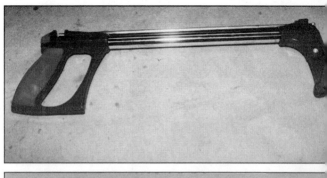

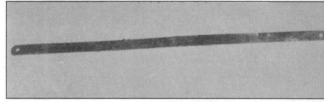

Used to cut off his hands, the hacksaw's blade was found under Hatton's body.
(*Photo courtesy Travis County, Texas Sheriffs Office*)

Cleansing powder and heavy-duty plastic bags used to clean up after the murder were found in Hatton's apartment.
(*Photo courtesy Travis County, Texas Sheriffs Office*)

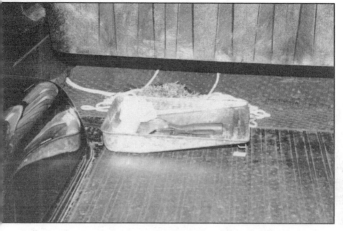

Roller and pan used to paint over the bloody apartment walls
were found in Busenburg's truck.
(*Photo courtesy Travis County, Texas Sheriffs Office*)

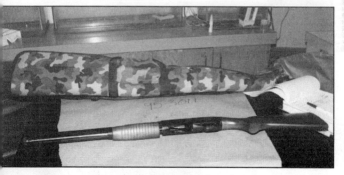

Shotgun used to murder Hatton was found in Martin's
bedroom closet.
(*Photo courtesy Travis County, Texas Sheriffs Office*)

Prosecutor Frank Bryan.

Prosecutor Allison Wetzel.

Christopher Gunter, attorney for William Busenburg.

Ira Davis, attorney for Stephanie Martin.

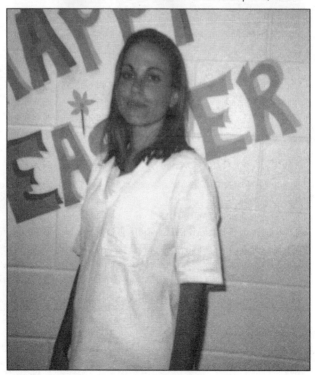

Martin at the Hobby Unit prison in Marlin, Texas on April 9, 2000.

Round Rock, Texas ROTC members carry the coffin of Christopher Michael Hatton.
*(Photo courtesy Round Rock Leader/Mark Prochnow)*

into custody. Gage took Martin into custody. The two officers left with their suspects while Sawa stayed behind.

At 2:50 A.M., on Sunday, January 15, 1995, Busenburg and Martin were booked for murder. Their clothes were collected and turned over to Mancias. Busenburg and Martin were handed jail jumpsuits.

To all the men within eyeshot, Martin looked stunning—even in baggy, ugly jail clothes.

On that night, Robert and Sandra Martin didn't get to see how their daughter looked in jailhouse clothes. They weren't allowed to see her.

Attorney Ira Davis walked into a closet-size interview room and sat down across from Stephanie Martin. She saw that he was nice-looking with a nice smile, curly hair, and a dark, bushy moustache. He looked like he had money and style.

She told him the same story she'd told the detectives.

"We can't fight this case if you're lying to me," said Davis.

"Oh, no, no, no," Martin replied.

The attorney leaned back in his chair and stared at the wall to think. They had a chance, he believed. He could maybe walk her if he could verify or justify the rape. *But burning the body and covering up the crime scene, that could be a problem. We'll have to put that all on Will.*

Davis turned toward his client. Her dark hair was stringy and her eyes were red.

"Be quiet," he said. "Don't talk to anyone but your attorney. Don't even talk to your parents. If you do, they could be used as witnesses against you. I'll explain the same thing to your parents. Now don't talk to anyone."

Two hours after walking into the interview room, Davis stepped out to sit down with Mr. and Mrs. Martin. "If she talks to you," he said, "you can be used as witnesses against her. So don't discuss her case with her.

Mancias and Gage returned to Stephanie Martin's apartment. Sawa told Mancias that Hill had found receipts in the kitchen trash for firewood purchased from an Albertsons grocery store on Highway 183 on Friday, January 6, days before the body was burned.

She'd also located an EZ Pawn ticket showing that Chris Hatton had pawned some jewelry on Friday, January 13, 1995, two days after his dead body had been found. Lying on the kitchen table was the title to Hatton's truck.

Mancias handed Busenburg's and Martin's clothes to Hill for inventory. She promised to process them at seven that Sunday evening.

Mancias and Gage finally called it quits for the day. After more than fifty nonstop hours on duty, they headed home.

On Sunday morning, Robert Martin called a friend from his Sunday school and asked him to take over the class, which Martin normally taught. "We have a very serious family crisis," he said. The Martin pastor was called.

Stephanie Martin was busy on the phone, too. Around 10 or 11 A.M., she placed a collect call to Todd Brunner. "I've been arrested for murder," she said. Martin explained to him how Busenburg wouldn't ask Chris for the money, referring to the check she had previously told Todd that Chris had taken from Will.

"So I went over to his apartment and asked him to give some of Will's money back. But when I got there, he was drunk. He was abusive. He was obsessed with me. He blamed me for Will and him not being friends anymore. He attacked me. He tried to rape me. There was a gun in the apartment, and I shot him."

"Why didn't you call the police?" asked Brunner, dumb-founded.

"After it happened, there was no phone in the apartment, and I couldn't call. So I, uh, just sat in the corner of the apart-ment for a while. I was crying, and I was hysterical. I left there and called Will. Will told me that we needed to cover it up because I'm a dancer and that the police wouldn't believe me. We took the body to Paleface Park."

Freaked, Todd realized he knew about this case. A friend had told him about it. "I don't want to talk about this," he said. Brunner hung up the phone.

As soon as Round Rock Baptist Church said its closing prayer that morning, its pastor drove to the spick-and-span home of Sandra and Robert Martin.

"We've had some things—not just like this—but we've had things happen before in our church and people want to handle things in different ways. Do you want this kept quiet? Or do you want the church to know about it?"

"We want them to know," said Robert, the Sunday-school teacher and church secretary.

"We're going to be having prayer meeting, do you want me to bring this up?"

"Yes. If we ever needed prayer, we need it now."


That same day, Detective Mark Sawa drove to Round Rock to knock on door after door at the Creeks Apartments, search-ing for someone who had seen the bloody mattress and box spring in the Dumpster. No one had.

He drove to the dump yard of Longhorn Disposal, the com-pany that handled the Creekside garbage. But that, too, led nowhere.

Holly Frischkorn got on the phone that night and called her Round Rock PD chief and captain at their homes. "Please get me some help," she pleaded.

They refused her request citing that they weren't responsible,

since her emotional trauma hadn't happened in the line of
Round Rock Police Department duties.

"Please," she begged, "get me some kind of counseling.
Help me. I'm having a really hard time with this."

Again they refused her.

Holly Frischkorn killed the pain with constant shots of
Demerol, which she was already taking for a work-related injury. Without realizing, she increased the number of shots. Anything to kill the pain. She sat in her chair, zoned out on
Demerol.

On Monday, January 16, 1995, Sawa and Mancias returned
to Round Rock and the Longhorn dump.

"Oh, I'd say by now that that mattress and box spring are
covered by eighty tons of trash," said the dump's operations
manager, Sam Montgomery. He pointed to the Austin Community Landfill.

They dismally stared out at the endless mountains of garbage, at least six stories high. They watched trucks dump their
trash and earthmovers immediately drag the garbage away and
compact it. Sawa and Mancias turned around and walked back
to their vehicle.

At the Yellow Rose, club manager, Ken Myers, looked at his
records. "Stephanie danced for an hour and a half on Wednesday, January fourth, and for five hours on Monday, January
second," he told the detectives. "The dancers have flexible
hours that they set themselves."

The officers left, but as they walked out of the dark, smoky,
loud bar, they noticed a topless Stephanie Martin on the cover
of the 1995 Yellow Rose calendar. A man couldn't help but
notice it; she looked beautiful.

Back at TCSO headquarters, Mancias prepared a photo
lineup of Martin and Busenburg. Sawa got on the phone and
called EZ Pawn. They drove up to the store at 5 P.M., ducked
under its sky-blue canopy, and walked in.

"Do you remember buying anything on Friday from a male subject who identified himself as Chris Hatton?" said Sawa to pawn employee Damon Cotter.

"Yeah, I did," answered Cotter. "It was a ring."

Sawa was known for his almost photographic memory. He handed Cotter the photo lineups created by Mancias. Cotter couldn't identify either.

Manager Judy Willis, though, promised the detectives that she would get the purchased ring and turn it over to the officers. She gave them a video surveillance tape recorded on January 13, 1995.

Mancias and Sawa headed south to Bernie's Wrecker. Employee Lisa Gonzales remembered Hatton's beat-up brown truck and the couple that had retrieved it days before.

"It was around four o'clock," she said. "He was a white man with a U.S. Navy military ID. And he had a white woman with him who was wearing black-framed prescription glasses."

She looked at the photo lineups. She couldn't identify either Busenburg or Martin.

"But I remember that he didn't have enough money. I gave him directions to the Seven-Eleven at Slaughter and Manchaca. They came back awhile later, and I gave them their truck."

Sawa talked to Aubry Hills apartment manager Dawn Trevino, Glenn Conway, and Lisa Pace.

*Bad breakup. Crazed girlfriend,* thought Lisa Pace as she sat down in Sawa's office. *I'm glad they've already apprehended these people because I probably would be a prime suspect.*

"Do you think Chris would have tried to sexually assault Stephanie Martin?" Sawa asked her.

She looked at the cop. She remembered how she had had to pursue intercourse with Chris. "No."

She thought about Chris's strong legs, his sweet smile, his brown eyes, how he and she could just look at each other across a room and have to run to the bedroom.

"Look at the guy. Look how cute he is. Do you think he would have had a problem getting laid? No. He could go into any bar and pick up a girl. Do you think if he wanted sex that he couldn't have called me at any moment and that I wouldn't have *run* over?" She said run as if it were an exclamation mark. "That is the most ridiculous thing I've ever heard."

"If he was going to sexually assault her, would it be likely that he'd be wearing his underwear?"

"What?" *He probably would have been talking with her, drinking with her, getting her into a position where he could control things.* "No, I don't think so," she finally answered.

"What were his sleeping habits?"

"He slept so soundly that I could get up and drive to the grocery store and stay out for several hours without Chris ever waking up."

She also told Sawa that Hatton slept on his back.

Sawa knew that fit the scenario. "What did he wear to bed?"

"He always wore underwear to bed, at least. He never slept nude." Even after they'd had sex, Chris Hatton raced out of bed to put his underwear back on and then got back in bed. "If it was really hot, he slept only in his underwear. If it was cold or cool outside, he slept with sweatpants and a T-shirt on, sometimes shorts and a T-shirt."

"How long have you known Will? Did you know Stephanie? What do you think about Will and his character?" Sawa asked.

"I wasn't friends with Will or best friends or anything like that. We were just acquaintances—seeing him around at school and ROTC. I didn't care for him. I didn't like the way he acted. He gave me a weird feeling." She really felt that he gave off weird vibes. "He was obnoxious. He was rude."

She remembered the way he walked into the room, the way he presented himself, she didn't even like that. She told the detective that one day she went over to Chris's apartment and as she stood inside, she glanced out toward the patio. She saw a lump there, a piece of carpet over the lump, splattered blood, and feathers.

"What the hell is that?" she had said to Chris as she had walked toward the patio.

"Don't go out there," he had ordered.

Chris had explained that it was a dead bird, which he had been feeding and was getting on the tame side. "Then Will shot it with a shotgun." He had left the blood and mess there on the patio.

"Then why don't you clean it up?" Pace had asked.

Chris had changed the subject, obviously not wanting to talk about it further.

Lisa Pace looked up at Detective Sawa, her eyes tired from too many days of tears. "Will would talk about how he hated blacks and how he thought the Ku Klux Klan was great."

"When was the last time you saw or spoke with Chris Hatton?"

"Either the fifth or sixth of January," she said. "Chris asked me about our furniture."

"Did he mention any problems he was having?"

"No." She looked down.

Before Lisa left Sawa's office, he asked her to identify the bicycle, a silver necklace, a school ring, a gold ring, and six watches. "What's the deal with all these watches?" he said.

Pace couldn't help but laugh. That was Chris. And it was either laugh or cry as she stared at a photograph of a gold ring with three diamonds. It was the gold ring she'd given Chris for Christmas in 1992, the day he'd asked her to marry him.

What rang in Sawa's mind after Lisa left was her statement, "I always considered Will to be violent."

The phone rang on Sawa's desk.

"My name is William Earls," said the caller. "I regularly go to the Yellow Rose to have a drink and relax, and I got acquainted with Stephanie Martin. She told me some things that I think I probably need to discuss with an investigator."

"Um-mm," said Sawa as he took notes.

"But I probably need to talk to Stephanie first. I don't want anybody to get into trouble."

William Earls hung up.

* * *

The room was silent at sheriffs department headquarters as
detectives sat in front of a TV watching the EZ Pawn video.
In Sergeant Tim Gage's eyes, Stephanie Martin and Will Busenburg were dancing around the pawnshop like lovebirds looking
for a wedding ring. *Unbelievable,* he thought.

On the scratchy, black-and-white video that flashed like a
bad movie, Martin and Busenburg casually strolled into the
store. He was wearing light-colored clothes and a baseball cap;
she was wearing her dark-framed eyeglasses and her hair pulled
back into a ponytail.

He stood calmly at the counter. She drifted from jewelry case
to jewelry case, studying the contents, and once pulled Busenburg over to look at an item. She crossed and uncrossed her
arms, ducked her head as if trying not to be seen, and
watched—and appeared to laugh at—another customer. He still
stood calmly.

After the pawn deal was closed and just before the couple
was handed the cash, Martin turned to Busenburg, wrapped her
arms around his waist, and gave him a good, long, hard hug.


The phone rang in Roxy Ricks's apartment.

"What is Stephanie's last name?" said the caller.

"Martin."

"Well, you need to turn the news on."

Ricks turned on the TV. "Oh, shit." There was Stephanie,
under arrest for murder. She dropped the phone. She couldn't
believe it. "Oh, my, god."

Her disbelief was so strong that she picked up the phone
again and called and called Stephanie. It didn't soak into her
head that her best friend was in jail and couldn't be reached at
her apartment. She left message after message.

"Stephanie, pick up the phone. You need to call me back.
Something weird's going on. There must be a mistake."

* * *

On Tuesday, January 17, 1995, Robert Martin opened the
*Austin American-Statesman* newspaper. The lead story on page
one of the city and state section scrolled across the entire width
of the newspaper: "FRIENDS ARRESTED IN KILLING, MUTILA-
TION."

Three photographs centered the story: a respectful military
head shot of Hatton; a mug shot of Busenburg; and a frowning,
blank-eyed mug shot of Stephanie Martin.

He skimmed down the page. "Stephanie Lynn Martin,
22, . . ." His daughter's name was the first three words of paragraph two. ". . . and William Michael Busenburg, 22; . . ."

Martin reread: "William Michael Busenburg, 22." He
fumed. The boy had lied. He was three years younger than what
he had told the Martin family.

Robert Martin continued to read. In paragraph three, he saw,
"Martin, a dancer at the Yellow Rose . . ." He stopped. He read
it again. And again. This was not the start of a good new year.
He'd just learned that his daughter was a topless dancer. But
at that point, after learning that his daughter had confessed to
murder, nothing could bother him. He was too numb.

Charges were filed that day against Stephanie Martin and
Will Busenburg.

Stephanie Martin looked up from her shackles and smiled
over at Roxy Ricks, who was in the courtroom for moral support. Everyone knew Martin was soon going to be released on
bond.

Martin watched the judge's face as he was shown the photographs of Hatton's burned and mutilated body. Ricks wanted
to see the photographs, too. She wanted to see what her best
friend had done. The judge slammed down his gavel. Bond was
set for Busenburg and Martin at $100,000 each. Martin
wouldn't be going home with her family.

Sandra Martin's scowl was as hard as an iron frying pan.
Robert Martin ducked his head as if in prayer. He hated to

admit it, but he was embarrassed by the whole ridiculous nightmare. Ira Davis gathered Stephanie's stunned supporters and rushed them out the back way so that they could escape the media glare.

As he did, Sandra Martin flashed her eyes at the cameras. "Exotic dancer"—the word shook furiously in her brain. That's all she believed the media was interested in.

# Eighteen

The Martins walked into the Del Valle county jail facility. A tiny, poor suburb southeast of Austin, Del Valle was not a community the prosperous family from Round Rock frequented, or expected to frequent.

Separated by a window, Sandra and Robert Martin sat across from their daughter. In her jail clothes, Stephanie was hunched in a small, hard, straight-back chair, her knees curled up to her chest, her arms wrapped around her legs, sobbing and shaking.

To her parents, she looked like she'd been through hell. This was not the life expected for a Christian girl from white, upper-middle-class, well-educated Round Rock.

Sandra and Robert Martin were literally a good sight for Stephanie. Days before, Stephanie had had to remove her contact lenses and since then had been without any sort of seeing aid. At Del Valle, her parents were allowed to give her her eyeglasses.

Robert Martin wondered, *What's happened? How can you be confessing to being raped by this man? You don't even hardly know him.* But Robert Martin wasn't about to ask any direct questions. There were officers standing nearby. He thought that perhaps a hidden tape recorder was recording their every word.

Mrs. Martin wanted to hold Stephanie, but her daughter was behind that window, and she couldn't do a darn thing for her child. She reached for the telephone as she watched Stephanie through the glass partition. "We love you. We're here for you. Your lawyer will be here for you. We'll get through this."


*I feel completely like shit,* Lisa Pace thought as she awoke on Wednesday, January 18, 1995—the day of Christopher Michael Hatton's memorial service. *But I'm going to put on some makeup, and I'm going to fix my hair, and I'm going to look nice.*

Lisa Pace drove herself to the funeral home, arriving early, when only family was there. She noticed that Chris's brother, Brian, wore a new suit. "You look really good."

"Thanks," said Brian, shy and embarrassed like his brother.

Pace reached for a doughnut and took a bite. *This doesn't taste like a doughnut. I don't feel like I'm eating a doughnut.* She threw it away.

"You know who did all of this?" Chris's grandmother whispered in her thick Eastern European accent. "Holly. Holly's so nice. She got this coffee and doughnuts for everybody. And she took Brian and got him a suit to wear. Doesn't he look nice?"

"Yeah, he looks really nice," said Lisa. "Everything looks really nice." But Pace was ticked. She was ticked at Bill Hatton. Sitting on top of Chris's casket was a large photograph of Chris. The photograph's frame had an enormous crack in it. It ticked Pace off that Bill Hatton had brought a photo with a huge crack in the frame, that he hadn't asked her if she had any nice photographs of Chris in day-to-day life, with friends and family.

Officers from the Round Rock Police Department began to arrive for Holly and officers from the Travis County Sheriffs Office were there for Bill.

Lisa Pace hugged and kissed Glenn Conway hello.

Conway couldn't believe he was at a funeral for his best friend. He pushed Lisa back and focused on a dot in the future, forcing himself to be ice cold, displaying no talk and no show of emotion.

Pace walked over and hugged more people, forcing herself

to keep busy so that she wouldn't fall apart. She helped Jim Fletcher, Holly's fiancé, select Chris's favorite songs to play during the service—"The Dance" by Garth Brooks, "Stand by Me," and "Sweet Home Alabama."

Chris's grandfather took Lisa by the shoulders. "You're part of the family. You're going to sit over here with us." She sat with Holly and Brian; Bill sat a row away.

As guests left, Lisa Pace watched their faces and thought about how much Chris was loved. Tears flooded her face. She thought about how much he was going to be missed. She looked at Holly and saw her makeup had run down her cheeks. *Great, I thought I'd make myself feel better by wearing makeup, and that's probably what I look like.* Pace's laughter was a mere distraction from the agony in the casket.

She looked back at it one more time.

A devout Christian, Lynn Carroll, Stephanie's Austin Community College study partner, never dreamed she'd be sitting across from a homicide investigator talking about a friend accused of murder on the same day of the murder victim's memorial service.

"I met Stephanie Martin around the first of September 1994," said Carroll to Detective Mancias. "We met in an intro to chemistry class. At first we were only acquaintances and talked only in class. But around the end of October, we started talking more. We were both going through some personal problems."

Carroll's face was tight with anxiety. "She took me out to lunch sometime around October 25, 1994. She told me she was moving out because her relationship with her boyfriend was going nowhere and she had met someone else that she was interested in. That person was Will Busenburg. . . .

"The day she took me out to lunch, she told me about Will . . . that Will was in the CIA and frequently left the country to do government jobs. She told me that she had met Will for the first time at the Yellow Rose, where she danced. She also told me that Will was twenty-four, originally from Montana, had a premed degree, and was a millionaire. She told me that he killed people—terrorists and drug dealers—in other countries for the U.S. government and was paid millions to do it.

"She also told me that Will had part ownership in Intermedics Orthopedics and was going to inherit thirty million dollars when he turned thirty. A week or two went by before we spoke again outside the classroom. We were going to have a chemistry test and we decided to study together." Carroll, petite and pretty, looked down.

"We decided to study over at Roxy's. This was the first time I met Will Busenburg. The next time I saw him was at Stephanie's apartment a couple of weeks later. Stephanie and I were studying for another chemistry test. We stayed up late and decided to go to bed and study some more the next morning.

"However, Stephanie was rather afraid to stay there alone because she said some guy had been calling her. She decided we would stay at Will's apartment that night. Will had no objections. Truthfully, I felt safer at Will's, also. That night was the first night I met Chris Hatton."

As she spoke, tears for Chris Hatton were still wet on the faces of police officers, friends, and family.

"He seemed like a quiet, nice, friendly guy. The four of us —me, Will, Stephanie, and Chris—stayed up and watched *Sleepless in Seattle*. The next morning, Stephanie, Will, and I went back to Stephanie's apartment."

She and Martin met several other times to study, usually with Carroll staying for only a couple of hours, then leaving for her own home, she told Mancias.

"I rarely saw Will these nights since he worked until eleven P.M. At some point during these few weeks, Stephanie began to tell me about things that Chris had done or had been doing.

She told me he was always very depressed when she and Will would go over to Will's apartment.

"She told me he would stand around cussing and yelling about what a rotten world he lived in and would throw knives at a target in the living room. She told me Chris had warned Will about her, saying that Will should stay away from her because she was only after his money.

"Stephanie was always excited when she would tell me about Will's adventures he had while working for the CIA," said Carroll. "She would tell me the same stories that he had supposedly relayed to her about killing people. She told me that she wanted to go along with Will when he did something local—a killing—and she told me, 'I want to pull the trigger.' "

"Those were her exact words?"

"Yes. I thought she was joking because she was always laughing when she talked about Will and all the people he had supposedly killed."

Carroll wanted to stop but knew she couldn't.

"Somewhere during this time frame, Stephanie started to tell me that Chris was stealing money from Will. She told me that Will would give Chris money to pay the rent or utility bills and Chris would spend it on something else instead and then come back and tell Will about it, laughing all the while. She told me Chris was irresponsible and couldn't keep a job. She began to tell me that he should be 'put out of his misery.' "

"Is that an exact quote?"

"Yes. She told me that he didn't deserve to live. He was expendable. I told her and Will to get him some help if he was so depressed, and they kept saying, 'Oh, we will.' She told me Will was going to sit down and have a talk with Chris.

"One night, when Stephanie and I were at the apartment studying, she told me she and Will had been riding around the night before in east Austin looking, and I'm quoting, 'for the nigger who had been calling her.' When they couldn't find him, they were going, and I'm quoting again—I don't talk like this—they were going to 'kill a nigger in east Austin.' And she wanted to 'watch their face' as Will killed them or she wanted to 'pull the trigger herself.' "

"She actually said that?"

"Yes, she did." Carroll said that Martin kept talking about Busenburg and the CIA, adding more to the tale every day. "She told me he had told her about this abusive, alcoholic, and drug-dependent father. She told me that Will had said his father used to beat him and his brothers and sisters and sexually assaulted Will."

Carroll then reiterated the story about Will killing his father, about going to the boys' home, about joining the military and becoming a sharpshooter. "That was how he was able to join the CIA. She told me that she had seen Will being followed, while she was with him, by the bad guys in the CIA."

Busenburg and Carroll rarely talked, she said, but he did tell her some guys were after him. And whenever Stephanie talked of the CIA around Will and I, Will would just shake his head up and down and agree with whatever she said. However, there were times when Stephanie would start talking about the CIA that Will would just look sharply at her and say, 'We don't have to talk about that right now.' Needless to say," said Carroll, "they were very convincing, and I was very scared."

"When was the last time you saw Chris?"

"Somewhere around December thirteenth. Stephanie and I were studying for the chemistry final and, again, we ended up staying the night over at Will and Chris's. I do remember that Will kept a shotgun in his room in a dark-green case. He also kept a shotgun under the seat of his truck. At some time during the night, Will, Stephanie, and I were awakened—

"We were all sleeping in Will's bed—to shouts coming from the living room and a loud pounding on the floor. Chris was in the living room yelling at the neighbor downstairs and pounding on the floor with something very heavy. He was yelling because the downstairs neighbor was playing his radio too loud. He was yelling"—she looked down—" 'turn your god-damn radio down, you fucking nigger!'

"Stephanie and I were alarmed until Will said, 'Oh, that was just Chris showing off for y'all. He gets mad when the guy downstairs has his radio on too loud.' I told Will and Stephanie that they needed to get Chris some help. They said they would. I even offered to talk to him."

The next morning, said Carroll, she got up and went into the bathroom across from Chris's room to get ready to go to school, and she saw Chris. "His door was open, and I saw that he was uncovered and wearing only a T-shirt and boxer shorts. I also saw a bunch of gifts on the dining table addressed to members of his family. Stephanie told me later that Chris had bought those gifts with Will's money, money intended for the rent. She also told me Chris had bought some clothes for himself.

"When Will and Stephanie and I would talk about Chris's condition, they would tell me he was suicidal because he started keeping a gun by his bed. They even told me that he had bought the gifts for his family as a good-bye gesture."

Just before Christmas, said Carroll, Martin told her about the check she and Busenburg claimed Hatton had stolen. "When I asked Will why he didn't just move out or stop paying the bills, he would just say, 'Because Chris is my friend.' "

"When was the last time you saw Stephanie?"

"On January sixth, she called me at home to tell me this was the last day she was going to have her ex-boyfriend's dog. . . . She wanted me to come to her apartment, but I told her I was too tired. So, she said that she and Will would come out to my house and bring the dog. She said they wanted to 'take a walk.' I said okay. Stephanie had never been out to my house before."

Around 5 P.M., said Carroll, Martin phoned and said they were going to pick up Busenburg's mother at the airport at 6:30 P.M. They would then drop his mother off, close to the airport, and then come out to Carroll's house.

"I told her not to worry about coming. It would be too dark by the time they got there. She told me that that was okay, we could take a walk in the dark. She kept saying they were going to come out so that we could take the dog 'for a walk.' They didn't arrive at my house until around nine P.M. And needless to say, it was late and we did not take a walk.

"They made up some excuse for being so late. They did not stay long. Before they left, however, they looked up Chinese restaurants in the phone book because they were going to order takeout to take back to Chris. They said they were being nice to him so that they could get their money.

"Outside," said Carroll, "I asked them what they were going to do to him, and they just said they were going to get their money."

Mancias was so impressed with Carroll that he let her type up her own statement. Besides, she was a faster and better typist than he was.

A headline ran that day in the *Dallas Morning News*—"PAIR CHARGED IN MURDER, MUTILATION OF EX-CLASSMATE."

Sandra Martin looked at her daughter. "Stephanie, people are thinking you murdered him." Her words were slow and deliberate.

"Mother, no one could believe I would murder someone."

"Yes, Stephanie. They are believing it."

"Mother, you don't understand. Will can't go to prison. If he went to prison, he would die."

Mrs. Martin knew Stephanie was referring to Will's incurable, deadly disease. Stephanie had already had her parents call Will's mother to see if she could get him something to help his stomach.

Sandra Martin remembered how Stephanie had told her that Will Busenburg was everything she'd ever dreamed—caring, gentle, loving. "If he asked me to marry him today, I would do it." He was perfect. "Plus, he needs me. He's had such a bad life."

She shook her head and sighed the frustrated sigh that only a mother can do.

Jon Noyes sat across from Detective Tommy Wooley and thought about the dances Stephanie Martin had danced in his lap, the kisses she'd placed on his skin.

"I only had about three total meetings with her," said Noyes. "All of them were while she was working at the Yellow Rose. During this time, she called me at my house a few times.

"The last time I spoke to her was last August, when I ran into her at the Yellow Rose. She was always nice and friendly. But she seemed to always have some emotional problems and seemed depressed. She told me once that she was on antidepressants."

They had some long conversations, said Noyes, and the last time he saw her was in late August, at the Rose. "This is when she told me she had met this guy who had been a hit man for the CIA, and that he had taken her to his house one night after work and he had showed her weapons and explained to her how he had killed people all over the world.

"She was very taken by this. She seemed impressed, as if this was some excitement that needed to be brought out in her. During the course of the conversation, she told me that she really wanted to kill someone. When she told me this, I asked her what she meant by this, and she said that she wanted someone to come into her house so she could blow his head off."

Noyes added, "I never really thought anything of it at the time . . . until I saw it in the newspaper yesterday. I didn't even know Stephanie's last name until I saw her photo in the paper."

Every time the Martins turned on the television or flipped open the newspaper, they saw the same thing about their daughter—Stephanie Martin, the topless dancer at the Yellow Rose; Stephanie Martin, the exotic dancer at the Yellow Rose; Stephanie Martin, the stripper at the Yellow Rose.

It irritated the hell out of the Martins that their daughter was portrayed as nothing but a stripper. "What does that have to do with what happened?" ranted Robert Martin. "Nothing."

# Nineteen

From county jail, Stephanie Martin finally phoned Roxy Ricks.

"Stephanie, what the hell's going on?"

Martin relayed the rape and self-defense murder story.

"That sucks," said Roxy, "but I'm sure you're gonna get out."

"Yeah, in about a week. A week or two, I'll be out. Then I'll tell you all the rest, and I'll explain it. This will blow over. It's no big deal."

Roxy Ricks didn't really believe her friend had murdered Chris Hatton. But something inside of her just knew that Stephanie Martin had cut off Chris Hatton's hands.

Ricks stared through the glass partition at the Del Valle jail facility that separated her from Stephanie. There was a glare that hampered her view, so she leaned to the left and tried for a better angle.

"It was all Will's idea to cut Chris's hands off," said Martin.

Roxy nodded. She remembered that Busenburg had read *Gorky Park,* a story where hands were cut off and teeth knocked out to hide the identities of victims.

Martin tapped nervously on the window and looked away. "I cut off his hands."

Roxy looked up, despair wrinkling her face. "But, Stephanie, why? Why'd you do that?" As much as Ricks desperately yearned to deny it, she couldn't anymore—her best friend had a dark side. "I heard that Chris's head had been cut off," she said.

"No," answered Martin. "I shot him at such a range that his head was blown off."


The next day, Gary Thompson, Hatton's supervisor at Capitol Beverage and the man who had provided the cops with Hatton's Social Security number, met Detective Mancias, in person, for the first time.

"Over the last few months," said Thompson, "I became close with Chris to the point that he would come and visit me at my home. During this time, I never knew Chris to complain about his work. He was a good worker and was very reliable and he never missed a day of work.

"Chris was a quiet person, very quiet, but at the same time he was very well liked by his fellow workers and myself. I never knew Chris to be one that drank a lot or even to get drunk. I never heard him talk openly about being with women or make sexual remarks.

"Chris opened up to me and he told me about prior troubles in his life involving the death of his father and the trouble with his mother. I remember when Chris mentioned to me that he had moved into an apartment with someone, but he never told me who. At first Chris would tell me about him and his roommate and everything sounded as though things were good for him.

"But about three weeks ago, Chris began to mention to me that his roommate had begun to start dating a topless dancer and he was beginning to act 'weird.' "

"You mean the roommate or Chris?"

"The roommate. Chris also mentioned to me that his roommate was coming and going out of the apartment, but hadn't moved out. About that same time, Chris began to mention to me that there was some girl that was calling him and hassling him.

"Chris never did tell me why the girl was bothering him or who she was. Also around this time, Chris told me that he no longer had a phone, therefore for me to call him on his pager."

Thompson wiped his brow; he had cared for Chris.

"The last time I spoke with Chris was when he called me at home from one of the stores and told me that he was running a little late."

"When was the last time he worked?"

"Sunday, the eighth of January, when he checked out with another manager around nine-thirty P.M. On Wednesday, the eleventh, I was at work when the sales manager, David Miller, called me around noon and told me that Chris hadn't shown up to work. I began to page Chris on his pager, but I never heard from him. When I got home that evening, I called Chris some more on his pager again, but again he didn't return the calls."

Thompson looked around. The room seemed awful hot for January.

"By this time, I began to feel that something was wrong, because this wasn't like Chris. On Thursday, when Chris didn't show up to work, again I really felt that something was wrong. It wasn't until I read or saw the news, and they gave a physical description, that I began to believe that the person who was found dead might be Chris.

"On Friday, I continued to call him throughout the day, but I never got a call from him. That evening, when I got home around five P.M., I was still feeling that something was wrong with Chris. After a while, I went out driving around by myself in order to think. A while later, I saw some Round Rock police officers at a convenience store, and I decided to stop and talk to them."

Thompson asked them if they knew where Holly Frischkorn was working.


At 7:30 that evening, Mancias sat down with June Conway, while Sawa sat down with her son Glenn. Once again, they told the detectives about Chris's concern that Busenburg was dealing drugs and Chris's lack of trust of Busenburg's topless-dancing girlfriend.

June Conway specifically noted, "After reading in the newspapers the accusations Stephanie Martin said about the sexual advances Chris had allegedly done, I am not able to believe that. I have known Chris for eight years, and he never made any type of advances on my fifteen-year-old daughter. I would even trust him enough that he would stay at my house alone with my daughter while I was out of the house."

Night after night, Glenn Conway Jr. was having nightmares of Chris standing at the sliding glass doors to the backyard and Chris trying to get into the house. Glenn always woke before he could get to the door and give Chris a welcoming hug and a "hello, brother."

Conway kept that all inside as he talked to Sawa. "I never really considered Will a friend mostly due to the fact that he had a tendency to be both a liar and self-centered."


The following day, Friday, January 20, 1995, Mancias talked with witness after witness.

Jennifer Luengas was another chemistry class study partner of Martin's. She, too, had met Busenburg and had heard the many stories about the CIA and millions of dollars.

"It was during this time," said Luengas, "that Stephanie began to tell me about Will's roommate. She described him—I believe his name was Chris—as one who was emotionally disturbed. Stephanie would tell me that she didn't like Chris and on numerous occasions she would call him an 'asshole.' Stephanie also told me that Chris was being a 'leech' and that Will was paying all the bills.

"Once while I was with Stephanie in the rear parking lot of the Riverside campus [of Austin Community College], she took out a large rifle-type gun. The gun was underneath the seat area of the truck, which was Will's truck. She told me that she had gotten stopped by a cop and that she was worried about going to jail, because she didn't have a permit for it.

"When Stephanie talked about her and Will, she told me how even though she had had a previous relationship that was bad, she felt different about Will. Stephanie told me that when Will and her would make love, it was the first time that she really enjoyed making love to another [person]. Stephanie once made the comment that 'he needs me as much as I need him.' "

"I'm calling," said Shawn Murphy, a coworker of Hatton's, "because I keep seeing in the news that Stephanie Martin is accusing Chris of attempting to sexually assault her. I want to let you know that he was a shy and nice guy.

"I've gone out with him to the Post Oak"—a local country bar—"and the whole time we were there he drank maybe two beers. He's not the type that would provoke anger out of any-one."

"Chris was shy, nice, and sweet," Karen Remmert, another coworker of Hatton's, said to Mancias over the phone. "I recall that at our Christmas party, a bunch of us decided to go to the Lumberyard and continue partying. Chris went. He just kind of stood in the background alone. He was being quiet."

"Did he get drunk?"

"No. He even turned down drinks when people offered them to him."

"Was he the type of person who made sexual advances?"

"No. I know another female employee who liked Chris. She eventually quit trying to get his attention because he was so shy and hardly ever made any conversation."

Roxy Ricks warily sat down with Mancias. She was predis-posed to hate cops due to her father's deadly run-in with the law.

"Were you ever involved in any black magic with Stephanie?"

"Black magic?" She laughed as though it was a ludicrous question. "No."

Mancias watched her. Tiny, pretty, sweet smile, she looked more like an earth mother than a topless dancer. He asked her again about black magic.

"No," she said, "I'm sorry, but no." Ricks felt like the cop didn't believe her, and she was irritated.

"Did Martin dabble in the occult?"

"No." She also felt like he was harping on the subject. Martin had told her that she used to go sit in a cemetery and play with a Ouija board. But that had been during her senior year in high school, after she'd left Oklahoma and Roxy.

"I went to see her on Wednesday," said Ricks. "She told me it was all Will's idea to cut off Chris's hands and cover everything up and not call the police."

She told Mancias about Todd Brunner and that Martin had tried to borrow a tarp from him.

"Even though I know Stephanie shot someone, I don't believe she acted alone. Stephanie was very naive, gullible, and easily influenced. Stephanie was also a very trusting person, and easily manipulated. When I last spoke to Stephanie, she told me that she did everything Will told her to do. She also told me that she felt bad about being manipulated by someone who wasn't who he claimed to be."

Ricks's boyfriend, Colby Ford, sat down across from Mancias. "When I met Will and as I talked to him, I knew he wasn't nothing but a liar."

Ford was an average-height, nice-looking, dark-headed young man who loved motorcycles. "I feel that Stephanie was so gullible that she would try to protect Will. I feel that Will killed Chris and that somehow Stephanie is covering up for him.

"After Stephanie got arrested, she called Roxy and I at home. Roxy told me that Stephanie said not to say anything bad about

Will, in reference to him working for the CIA, because it would just incriminate her."

Mancias typed up the young man's statement, Ford signed it, and finally Detective Manuel Mancias left for a weekend off.

Ricks told Ford. "When Stephanie gets out on bond, she can stay with us. No problem."

"No," he answered. "She's not staying here. Nuh-huh. She's crazy. She's a murderer."

"No, she's not. You don't understand."

With the speed of the pulsating music, rumors flew through the Yellow Rose, Sugar's, and every other topless club in the Austin area.

Martin and Busenburg had hung Hatton up by his ankles, bartenders said. The murder and mutilation were a Satanic ritual, bouncers said. "I don't know if I want to talk to you," a customer said to Roxy Ricks as she tried to dance. "You may be one of those crazy dancer girls."

But the most frightening rumor the dancers spilled, and their customers drank up, was that Martin had cut off Hatton's penis. "Your friend's crazy!"

Stephanie Martin was a part of Roxy Ricks. She was her other half. Roxy walked out the doors of the strip joint and didn't walk back in for a month. She also walked out of her classes at the University of Texas. She just couldn't concentrate with Martin filling her mind. Roxy needed time to resolve for herself Stephanie's crime.

Sunday, January 22, 1995, Raymond Busenburg picked up his son's personal items from the Travis County Sheriffs Office. Those items included some of Chris Hatton's belongings: his Navy identification card, Social Security card, a temporary Texas driver's license, a Visa card, Exxon card, and a Sears card.

On Monday Detective Manuel Mancias sat down with Brian Hatton, who was the spitting image of his older brother, with the same sweet smile.

"We moved down from Alabama because our mom had a drinking problem," said Brian, his accent thick and slow. "My brother and I were pretty close and we would do things together even after he moved out into his own apartment."

"Did your brother drink much?"

Brian shook his head. "As far as I know, he's never been drunk. I believe that he didn't like drinking a lot because of the problem my mom had with her drinking."

Like everyone else before him, Brian Hatton told Mancias of the problems Hatton had been having with Will Busenburg and Stephanie Martin. "He thought she was kind of weird."

"When was the last time you saw Chris?"

"Tuesday, the tenth of January, around eight-thirty P.M. He called my uncle at the house and he told him that he had broke down in his new truck. Chris told us that he was broken down at the car wash in Round Rock and he needed us to go pick him up. My uncle Bill and I then drove to the car wash and helped him start his truck. It turned out that he needed a new battery, which he bought at the Auto Zone in Round Rock.

"After he bought the battery and started his truck, my brother said he was going to go meet with the person who had sold him the truck in order to sign some papers over. Before Chris left, he told us that he would come to our apartment on Wednesday so he could show us his new truck closer.

"The following day, my uncle paged him throughout the day, but he never called or came by."

Brian seemed like a good kid.

Long, tall Bill Hatton sat down across from Mancias. Hatton told Mancias about his nephew's problems in the Navy, the DUI, the discharge.

"On Christmas Eve, I went to Mike's apartment in order to pick him up and take him with us to my parents' home." At that time, Christopher Michael told his uncle about the troubles with his roommate, whom Chris never mentioned by name.

"Mike told me that his roommate dated strippers and that two strippers had stayed overnight with his roommate one day."

"When was the last time you saw Chris?"

Like Brian, Hatton related the tenth of January, when Chris's truck died. "When he got his truck started, he told me that he was going to his friend Glenn's house and talk to him about getting the brakes on his truck fixed. When Mike left the car wash, which was about seven P.M., this would be the last time that I would see him."

After a week of trying to reach William Earls, Detective Mark Sawa finally made contact with the Yellow Rose patron. The forty-two-year-old fan of Stephanie Martin's wasn't as talkative as he had been a week earlier.

"I heard Stephanie was arrested for murder and I wrote her a letter while she was in Del Valle," said Earls. "Stephanie called me while she was in jail on the evening of January 22, 1995." Sawa glanced over at a calendar. January 22 meant Earls had heard from Martin just the day before.

"I spoke with her and gave her my support."

"Did she tell you anything?"

"She didn't discuss any aspects of the murder case with me."

"I think she was involved with this guy; she was getting raped; and she did kill him," Robert Martin heard his attorney tell him. "The confession was real."

"No way," Robert Martin bit back. He glared into Ira Davis's moustachioed face. "That is so far off base," Martin fired.

Six months before, Stephanie Martin had walked the Martin neighborhood for three hours, knocking door-to-door, trying to learn why the family cat had cuts all over it. His daughter was a protector, not a killer. "I know my daughter. She did *not* have a relationship with this man. She did *not* get raped. And this is a cover-up."

Robert Martin was as hot and relentless as the West Texas wind. "She's never even fired a BB gun, and you're gonna tell me she goes in there and she's being raped and she knows where the gun's at and she gets the gun out of where it's at and she . . . first of all, you've gotta tell her how to pull the trigger or cock it. She doesn't know any of this stuff. It's a bunch of bullcrap. It's BS. It's a cover. You'd better start looking and checking."

Ira Davis hired private investigator Drew McAngus, a devout, born-again Christian. Maybe he could relate to Stephanie Martin in a way Davis couldn't, thought the attorney.


Mancias reached over his desk and took a 1994 weekly pocket calendar from the hand of Realtor Marion Marshall.

"It belongs to Stephanie Martin," said Marshall, sitting down. "About one or two weeks prior to November eighth, I showed Martin several apartments . . . and one of those was at the Villa La Costa." And that, she explained, was how she came into possession of Martin's calendar—Martin had left it in the Realtor's car.

After Martin had moved into the Villa La Costa on November 8, 1994, Marshall had tried time and again to return the calendar. "I left several messages for her, but she never returned the calls. When I saw the news and heard about Martin, I decided to turn the calendar over to you, in case it was important."

Marshall shifted in her chair. "One time, while I was showing her an apartment, a conversation about safety came up. She made the comment that she had a gun and that she wouldn't have a problem shooting someone if she had to. I thought the comment was somewhat out of place, especially while she was trying to rent an apartment."


On Thursday, January 26, 1995, a "wholly destitute" William Busenburg received a court-appointed attorney, Christopher

Gunter, the same attorney the court appointed to represent serial killer Kenneth McDuff, a man who would be put to death.

Mancias learned that the corrections officer who had removed Busenburg's clothing in the wee hours of Sunday, January 15, 1995, had remembered seeing some of Hatton's credit cards and ID mixed in with Busenburg's possessions.

Mancias called Ray Busenburg. It took a while for Mancias to reach Raymond Busenburg, who then hesitantly denied having any of Chris Hatton's possessions.

"If you locate something later, would you please contact me?" said Mancias.

Mancias called Will Busenburg's new attorney, Chris Gunter, and explained the situation to him.

Not long thereafter, Gunter phoned Mancias. "Mr. Busenburg has all the items but the Sears credit card. You can meet Mr. Busenburg at my office tomorrow at five P.M., and he'll turn everything over to you."


"I have some information about Will Busenburg you might need to know," Beckwith Steiner, an assistant manager at Cinemark Movies, where Busenburg had once worked, told Mancias on the phone.

Mancias invited the man to TCSO headquarters to talk.

After Will left the company, said Steiner, he still dropped by to watch movies. "It was during this same time that Will introduced me to his girlfriend. I don't remember the girl's name," said Steiner, "but I recognized her as being the same girl that got arrested with Will.

"When Will introduced me to his girlfriend, he told me that she worked as a dancer at the Yellow Rose." Busenburg, he said, invited him several times to the Rose with the intention of introducing Steiner to some dancers. Steiner always declined. "I'm not into that type of entertainment."

On Friday, January 13, 1995, said Steiner, around 9 P.M., Busenburg and his girlfriend came to the theater. "Will asked me if our company had any theaters in Colorado. I told him that I didn't think so, but that I would look at our company list." He looked, and told Will there weren't any, said Steiner.

"Will then told me that he and his girlfriend were thinking about moving out of state and that they were thinking about moving to Colorado." They talked more, said Steiner. "And it was then that I mentioned to him that my truck had broke down. Will then told me that he had an older truck that he was thinking about selling. I told him that I already had a car lined up."

Busenburg told Steiner that he needed some cash and asked if Steiner knew anyone who wanted to buy a VCR or TV. "I told him that I did need a VCR, but I didn't have any money." Busenburg asked Steiner to contact him if he ran across anyone who wanted to buy the items.

"After Will left that night, I didn't see him again until I saw him on the news a few days later. I didn't think anything about my conversation with Will the last time I spoke to him, until I received a phone call from his mother, Fran, at my work. I didn't speak to her directly because she had left a message for me to call her. When I called her later, she told me that Will wanted to speak with me and if it would be okay for him to call collect. I was sort of stunned by the fact that he wanted to speak to me, but I told her that it would be all right. I have yet to hear from him."

The *Round Rock Leader* ran a story headlined: "FOSTER FAMILIES RECALL BUSENBURG." In the story, *Round Rock Leader* publisher Ken Long, Busenburg's foster parent just prior to the Children's Home, said he remembered Busenburg as being manipulative.

" 'He orchestrated everything for his benefit," Long said. . . . 'He took over everything,' including his son's room and his daughter's television set."

Long added, " 'If anything, we knew some of what his home

life was like, but we would never have thought he was capable of this.' "

Busenburg's Children's Home houseparents were kinder in their words to the *Leader*. " 'I think what has happened is really tragic,' Kay Williams said. 'We still care about Will.' "

On January 27, 1995, Detective Mancias and Sergeant Gage drove the few blocks from TCSO to Chris Gunter's office, a quaint old house within walking distance of the courthouse. At 5 P.M., they collected Chris Hatton's credit cards and ID from Raymond Busenburg.

# Twenty

"So were you shocked when you heard the news?" Stephanie Martin wrote a letter to Lynn Carroll, as she sat in the county jail. "They've really painted a nice picture of me and Will, haven't they?" It was the first few days of February, and she was writing Carroll an eight-page letter. "Well, I know you've only known me for a short time, but I'd hope you realize I could never murder anyone intentionally. Neither could Will.

"Surprise, surprise, he's not really in the CIA or the Army or anything! He completely fooled me, and you too! He's never hurt anyone and he never could!" Martin wrote that Busenburg knew some karate, that his father abused Busenburg and the entire family, "and I don't know what exactly happened to his dad.

"He's only 21 years old! Isn't that crazy? He was so insecure and felt like nobody when he met me, so he decided to create a big story about himself, not knowing he would see me again. So, then he digs his own grave, watches everything he says, and is stressed out all the time, because he had fallen in love with me, and didn't want me to know he was a nobody! Isn't that sad? My mom and dad say he's crazy and that I should hate him, but I just can't."

Martin wrote Carroll about Hatton allegedly taking Busenburg's money, and she slowly began her story about going to see Hatton about the money.

"You remember how we would make jokes about Will killing

Chris to put him out of his misery? Well, Will wouldn't hurt a flea." But Hatton, wrote Martin, had tried to rape her. "So I manipulated him into thinking I would be with him, something I can't believe I actually had the capability to do in total fear. Then I got on top of him, he looked delirious and confused, so I grabbed his gun, cocked it, and shot him.

"It was dark in the room, so I couldn't see where I had shot him. I almost fainted after I shot him. I sort of blacked out. I was in shock. I couldn't believe I had shot him without even hesitating."

She had waited for someone to come, she said. When no one did, she phoned Busenburg. Later they burned the body, she wrote. "Well, Will had really never done anything like that, he probably read it in a book! Neither one of us used our brains in the whole situation."

She pointed out, "Oh, and we did not mutilate his body, that was an extra the media threw in. . . . I told the detectives what happened, they believed me, so I thought." Three days later, she said, she and Busenburg were facing a murder charge.

"Anyway, my parents got me a lawyer, he was really expensive. Will had to have a court-appointed attorney since his mom and uncle don't have much money."

Martin still didn't know that Will's "uncle" was his father.

"I feel very bad for Will. He has been charged with murder and he doesn't deserve it. And I don't deserve it. It should be involuntary manslaughter. But, see the bad thing about this case is that people only 'see' the burned body after the incident. They focus on that only and assume that Will and I are morbid human beings."

Martin wanted to know if Carroll thought she was a murderer. "Well, I hope not. My lawyer may ask you to tell the court how believable Will was, and how I looked up to him and trusted him. And how he was unstable and could easily make a bad decision in this incident—covering up the shooting.

"I know you don't know me that well . . . but I may need your help. But I don't want to push you. My trial won't be for months. I'll be out on bail in a few weeks. My dad had to take out loans. They had to raise $40,000 for the attorney, and $15,000 for my bail."

Martin wrote about how much Busenburg loved her.

"Well, you can write me back if you want. It's your choice. If I never hear from you again, I hope our friendship meant something to you and that you can live your life happy."

Martin signed the letter with a heart for love.

On Tuesday, February 7, 1995, Lynn Carroll phoned Detective Mancias.

"I got a letter from Stephanie," she said. "I don't want to communicate with Stephanie or her family."

"Can I get a copy of the letter?" said Mancias.

Every chance they got, usually once or twice a week, the Martins drove the hour from Round Rock to Del Valle to see Stephanie. Every day they wrote their daughter a letter.

Stephanie wrote letters, too. There wasn't much else to do in county jail other than watch soap operas, make collect phone calls, and write letters.

"Mother," she wrote, "I just sit here and think about my life and what I had compared to 99 percent of the people here. They don't have anybody. They didn't have a good home." Constantly Stephanie told her mother how much she appreciated her family.

She also explained the circumstances of her confession, how she hadn't said a thing until they told her Will said she'd shot Chris.

"Okay, did he try to rape you?" she wrote to her mother that the detectives had asked her. "That's when I said, oh, Will's come up with a story. That's what our story's supposed to be. I'm supposed to say that."

Stephanie Martin told her father that as she and Will Busenburg sat in the detective's car, waiting to be transported to the sheriffs station, she and Will discussed the rape story.

"Stephanie," he said to his daughter, "you're past gullible. Everything you've got is what you deserve because you've gone beyond being comprehensive gullible. I don't know how you could have ever believed that this guy was trying to help you in any way in this process. You're actually helping him. Look at what all you had to do."

At 1 P.M., February 8, 1995, Lynn Carroll dropped by TCSO headquarters. "Stephanie's mother called my home number and asked to talk to me. My father told her that I don't want to speak to them. I still don't believe everything that happened, not the way Stephanie tells it in her letter."

Carroll handed Mancias the original letter. "You can have it," she said.

On Valentine's Day, 1995, Detective Manuel Mancias met with Chuck Register, the TCSO officer who had found Hatton's mutilated corpse—the man who worked at the same Del Valle jail facility as Bill Hatton, the same facility that currently held Stephanie Martin.

A lovelorn Stephanie Martin sat in county jail writing Will Busenburg a letter that same Valentine's Day.

"Tell me if you think like I do," she wrote. "I go to sleep and have nice dreams about you and forget about the reality that you're away from me and locked up in a hellhole. Then I hear, 'Wake-up call ladies, come and get chow!' I then wake up to the reality that I'm in jail and the huge difficult road that lies ahead of us. When I think about our hearing and our trial, I get butterflies in my stomach and I feel sick.

"Did you know that we are going to be at different trials? I don't know if I like that or dislike it. I really don't want to see you in the courtroom and not be able to touch you, wondering if we're going to be taken away from each other forever. That's a morbid thought, isn't it? I'm sorry.

"If we were together today I would make love with you on a bed of roses. This is the first Valentine's day you've ever had someone to love and love you, and yet we can't be together. I can't explain to you how sorry I am."

Martin said she had to think positive thoughts and enumerated the positive—they would be able to see each other, she would get out on bail, they could hear each other's voices, they could hold each other.

"God brought us together and he will bring us back together, I just know it. Life isn't this unjust. We'll make it through this together."

Her parents' home, she wrote, would be hers and Will's home. "I love you forever, Steph."

Her parents sat across the glass partition pleading with Stephanie. "What he told you, it's not true." He had ulcers, said her mother, but no incurable, deadly disease.

"But, Mother, he had no reason to lie to me."

He didn't kill his father, said Mrs. Martin, he's alive and living in Jarrell. He didn't inherit millions, she told her daughter, he got his money from a back injury he suffered. There was no $6,000 check. There was a $5,700 check to GMAC.

Attorney Ira Davis and private investigator Drew McAngus walked into the Del Valle jail facility on February 17, 1995. Davis was his thin, dapper self. McAngus was a former deputy sheriff dressed in cowboy clothes replete with silver belt buckle. Slightly overweight, with a drawl and a pickup truck, he was the stereotypical Texan.

He was also a Christian Texan who continually and fervently searched for ways to witness to others, including taking mission trips to Romania and Mexico. McAngus had prayed for discernment the entire time he had driven his pickup truck to Del Valle. His job, he believed, was not to decide guilt or innocence, but to be a finder of facts.

He'd studied the Busenburg and Martin statements, and

talked to friends of Busenburg's and Martin's. He'd done some background work on Busenburg and talked with Martin's father to get background on Stephanie.

Robert Martin and McAngus had met at Stephanie's apartment, where McAngus had looked around for anything that might help his seeking of the facts. He had punched the button on Stephanie's caller ID and had written down every single phone call. He hadn't known why he had done that; he just knew he had.

Later, he had crisscrossed the numbers to learn who had phoned his client and from where. His discerning gut had told him that he and Davis didn't have the entire story.

All of that led him to Stephanie Martin's new home at the Del Valle jail where on that mid-February day, McAngus sat down for the first time with his client, the slim, young stripper from the Christian family in Round Rock.

McAngus pulled out his notepad. Davis sat nearby, planning on just listening and letting the hired investigator do all the questioning.

"We may be here for thirty minutes or four hours. Whatever it takes, we need to get as specific details as we can." He wanted as much minute-by-minute detail as possible—from the day before the crime to the day after the crime—to later compare to the evidence. He knew if there was a gap in Stephanie Martin's story, there would be a reason for that gap.

Stephanie began to speak. As she did, in his thin script, McAngus began to take notes. Martin took a while to get her thoughts together, but McAngus just concentrated on his notes.

Her story was still consistent with her statement. Drew McAngus still believed there was more. He pondered the way she told him that she'd shot Hatton and then had called Busenburg to come get her at the Aubry Hills Apartments.

"Stephanie, where did you call him from?"

"Oh, it was a phone in the apartment."

"Stephanie," his voice was slow and deliberate, "that's impossible."

McAngus knew that there was a phone call to her own apartment at approximately the same time she claimed that she'd called Busenburg. But he knew that call hadn't come from the Hatton apartment. The crisscrossing he'd done showed the call had come from a phone near the swimming pool and laundry room of the Aubry Hills Apartments.

"Oh, it was the phone out at the bus stop out on Lamar," she replied.

Again he told her she was wrong.

She said it was the phone at a nearby convenience store.

He told her it wasn't. McAngus now knew why he had written down those phone calls. He looked his client straight in the face. His lips barely moved as he spoke, "Stephanie, you don't know what phone this call was made from, do you?"

Stephanie Martin froze.

McAngus watched her. He believed she was stumped and startled by the question. He saw it on her face. Drew McAngus stared his client square in her hazel-green eyes. "Stephanie, when did you leave your first love?"

The room went quiet. Davis looked up. McAngus still stared at his client's eyes. She stared back. Drew McAngus, the witnessing Christian, was talking about her love for Jesus Christ. Martin began to cry. Tears the size of an Oklahoma thunderstorm began falling in the Texas jailhouse.

"Drew, you're a Christian, aren't you?" she said.

"Yes."

"Oh, my gosh. I've been praying about this."

"Stephanie, whether you want to tell us the truth, God knows the truth. And from knowing your background and your history, I understand that you had a relationship with Him at one time, but you've left your first love."

"I've been praying that God would intervene. Maybe this is it."

"I'm not God. I'm really a nobody. I'm a little peon who knows the Lord. You know, Stephanie, it's time that the truth comes out. And if what you're telling is the truth, great. Stick to it. If it isn't, then we need to know this."

She broke down. Martin told McAngus that Will Busenburg had shot Chris Hatton and Will Busenburg had been the one to make the phone call from the Aubry Hills Apartments complex.

When she told about deciding to burn the body and cut off the hands of Chris Hatton, to McAngus, Martin seemed uneasy, perhaps embarrassed.

Stephanie Martin's change in confession came so rapidly that Drew McAngus hadn't had time to write down another word. He had only half a page of notes. He sensed a peace in Stephanie Martin and believed it was the relief one felt after confessing to the Lord and asking His forgiveness.

Three or four hours after they had walked into the Del Valle interview room, Stephanie Martin was led back to her cell, and Ira Davis and Drew McAngus left.

"I can't believe what just happened," said Davis to McAngus. "This was unbelievable."

McAngus smiled. He believed it was a witnessing time for Jesus to attorney Ira Davis, too.

There was still one heavy question puzzling the mind of McAngus, and that one question absolutely would not leave his thoughts.

*If this new story is true, then why in the world did she go in there and sign a confession saying she did it. How in the world could Busenburg have that kind of control over her to get her to do that?*

He had to do more research on Busenburg. He found a pattern of grandiose ideas and blatant lies.

*Still,* he wondered, *can somebody really have that kind of control over you? Yes,* he thought. *Historically, there's been people that could do that.*

Charismatic people. People with charming personalities. Like Charles Manson.

Drew McAngus believed it was possible. He knew; he taught

police officers about abnormal personalities. He wanted to talk
to Busenburg. But Busenburg wasn't talking; *it's as though,*
thought McAngus, *he had something to hide.*

Robert Martin answered the phone. It was Ira Davis.

"I guess you do know your daughter better than I do," he
said.

"Why?"

"You were right. She's changed her story. She told me today
that she wasn't being raped. That it was all a cover-up. He told
her to say it."

Martin hung up the phone. The call that was supposed to
make him feel better only made him feel worse.

# Twenty-one

"I wanted to tell the truth," Stephanie told her mother. "I didn't know if I should call Ira or tell Dad. I kept wanting to say I've been telling a lie this whole time about this. I didn't shoot Chris Hatton. I didn't know what to do. I knew when this investigator came with Ira that I was going to tell him."

Stephanie Martin wasn't the type of person who could sit silently with her thoughts and feelings. She was a woman of talk and action. Ira Davis had told her time and again to sit and be quiet, but it was like telling a chicken not to cluck.

On Friday, February 24, 1995, Stephanie Martin sat in the Del Valle jail battling her urge to cluck. She had too many questions that she couldn't stand to go unanswered, so she wrote Will Busenburg a half-page letter, telling him she hadn't written lately due to her lawyer's advice. But, she said, she'd "been doing a lot of thinking and praying about what has happened, and I've asked clergy people and God for guidance. I do not understand all this. If you truly love me, why have you allowed me to be so involved in this, and why have you let this go on so long. How can you let people think these horrible things about me? I can't see that your love really runs deep for me if you allow this to keep going. Please think about this Will, and pray for guidance. Love, Stephanie."

For Stephanie Martin, it was a very short, to-the-point letter. Four days later, she wrote Busenburg again.

"Hi love. Yes, my lawyer will not let me write. And yes, he

has all your letters. There are very important reasons why we are doing this. Please hold yourself together, I know you are feeling a lot of pain right now, along with loneliness and confusion. But Will, this is the way it has to be. You must do the right thing, for both of us."

Half a page down, she wrote, "I will definitely be calling counselors from Riverbend [Church] to come see you as often as possible. I will pray for you every single day. Please open up to your family and to counselors about your abuse, because I truly believe that is the cause of all of this nightmare for you. I will be going to my mom's by the end of this week, my parents probably won't want you to call for awhile, we need a little time to have peace and forget about this for awhile. Will, please talk to someone. I can't stand to think of you in such pain. Remember I do love you, and I always will."

On March 1, 1995, Stephanie Martin shuffled into the courtroom for another bond hearing. Martin wanted to glance up from her shackles and chains to look at Will Busenburg, but she didn't dare. If she did, she might start weeping on the spot. She would want to reach out from her chains and touch her skin to his.

He'd already written her about how his bond had been raised to $250,000 and how he was hopeless, scared, and panicked. She still had hopes that her father was going to get her home by paying fifteen percent on a $130,000 bond.

Martin glanced over at the Hatton family. She thought she was going to faint under the heat of their glares. She looked at the judge and saw it in his eyes. Her bond, like Busenburg's, was $250,000.

Stephanie Martin wrote her mother a birthday letter on March 6, 1995. She wanted to give her mother the best gift a daughter could give from jail.

"You've been extremely strong and supportive through all this. I don't want you to *ever* think you did something wrong as parents. I take full responsibility for my actions and for the irrational decisions I made. I've been the biggest fool and the biggest idiot," she wrote.

"When I left Todd, I was weak and still dependent on others. I thought by leaving him and moving in with Roxy I would become more independent, instead I went right into a relationship with Will. Will made me feel alive and satisfied. I was infatuated with him because I thought he was dangerous, heroic, powerful, intelligent, and still a little boy that desperately needed me."

She explained how he lured her with his lies.

"I don't know if Will loves me or not, maybe he really tried in his own strange way. But he's definitely manipulative and self-pitying in a major way. I am certain he's got a personality disorder and cannot rationalize Chris's death and how he got me involved in it. I don't know if he realizes Chris and me are the victims in this, he may think he is the victim and now I have deserted him."

Again she talked about Busenburg's lies to her.

"[Will] said [Chris] should pay with his life for stealing from Will and betraying him after he had helped him. Well then I said, you and Chris go camping and have a boys night together and maybe Chris will break down and tell you he stole the check. Will also had another plan to drug Chris and make him pass out, so we could come in like spies and find the money on him or in his room. I even somewhat committed murder in my heart, because I knew that the sleeping pills could kill Chris but I didn't care. I even prepared myself that it might happen, and I still didn't care."

She explained that she was home at her apartment when Busenburg, she said, shot Hatton.

"When we were arrested, he told me I better take the rap for him, and he stared at me the whole time we were on our way to the sheriffs station. . . . I shouldn't have done those things to the body, they were grotesque. Just know that I did whatever Will wanted me to do and I did everything possible for him to not get caught. I didn't want or think of those things, like burning the body and getting rid of the hands. Sorry I wasn't stronger and got away from him. And I'm sorry I lied for him to everyone. I have messed up my good life for someone who wasn't even real. I hope that you are able to live somewhat of a normal life during this. I truly am sorry."

Martin wished her mother a happy birthday and said, "I've given up on Todd, he doesn't want my troubles to interfere with his life. Here were his exact words to me on the phone last. 'I stuck with you when you were depressed. How much do I owe you now? I don't have time for your troubles and I can't support you through this. I can't have my name tarnished by you and your murder charge. Everyone tells me to stay away from you.' Well, that's all I need to get the hint. Me calling him only hurts me more than before I called him. He's still selfish and uncompassionate. I'm better off forgetting him. I'll just visit Sheba [the dog] every once in a while if I get out on bail."

Detective Mancias took a sworn affidavit on March 7, 1995, from Valerie Denise Cornnor, a former cellmate of Martin's. "About a week after I was locked up with Stephanie, she told me that she had shot and killed a guy named Chris."

Cornnor was in Del Valle on a check forgery charge.

"About a week or two later, we got a new roommate named Nicole Foltz. When Nicole came into our cell, Stephanie told her the same story that she told me about Chris trying to rape and kill her."

Cornnor said Stephanie left the cell in mid-February and returned crying. She had gathered up some letters from Will and left again. When Martin returned to the cell, she was still crying. "She began to tell me that her lawyer had brought the truth out of her."

Cornnor asked Martin, "What's the truth?"

"I really didn't shoot Chris. Will did."

Martin explained the circumstances of the shooting to Corn-

ior. According to Cornnor, Martin said, "Will told me that he
put two pillows over the barrel of the gun so no one would
hear it."

Cornnor told Mancias, "Stephanie said the next day they
went back to the apartment about eleven A.M. and they took
Chris and hung him by his feet in the bathtub, to let all of his
blood go out of his body. . . . I asked Stephanie what he looked
like and she said that the top part of his head was gone, like
from right underneath his nose on up. I asked her if it made
her sick and she said no."

Cornnor talked about how Busenburg and Martin burned the
body. "Stephanie said that later in the week they went to see if
Chris's body and truck were still there, and Chris's body was but
that the truck wasn't." They then got the truck out of impound.
"And when they got the truck back," said Cornnor, "Chris's body
parts were still there. So they went to the campground and put
his arms and legs into a Dumpster at a little store."

The inmate wound down her statement. "I haven't seen
Stephanie for about a week now because I got moved to a different cell after she and I got into an argument and I slapped her.

"When I made the decision to speak with the detective about
what Stephanie told me, the thought of a favor from the sheriffs
or district attorney's office never came to my mind. I don't
expect to receive a favor because of the information which I
gave. I decided to speak with the police because I feel that
what Stephanie and Will did to Chris is a horrible crime and
both of them need to be punished."

Martin wrote on March 9, 1995, a 5 $^1/_2$ page letter to Busenburg professing, again, her undying love for him.

The following month, Stephanie Martin sat down and took
a polygraph test, without the presence of district attorneys or
deputy sheriffs.

"Did you kill Chris Hatton?" said polygrapher Doug Farris.

"No," she answered.

242*Suzy Spencer*

Stephanie Lynn Martin passed the test.

Ira Davis contacted the District Attorney's Office and offered to have Martin take a polygraph test for them. He also contacted the press.

On April 24, 1995, the *Round Rock Leader* ran the headline "WOMAN CHARGED WITH MURDER RECANTS CONFESSION."

" 'She is denying shooting him,' said Ira Davis, Martin's attorney. 'It's the truth.' "

Chris Gunter responded to Davis's statement. " 'If that's what she's saying, we dispute that'. . . . 'Mr. Busenburg did not participate in the killing of Christopher Hatton.' "


On May 9, 1995, prosecutor Frank Bryan met with Lynn Carroll. "Stephanie talked about violence and death all the time," she told Bryan. "One time, at the kitchen table at Stephanie's, Will told her that the next time he went on a mission, she could go watch. Then Stephanie said, at the kitchen table, he's going to let me pull the trigger. She said that three or four times."

Detective Mancias and Frank Bryan drove to the Travis County jail on Friday, June 2, 1995, at 3 P.M., to meet Mac "Chubby" Opara, an inmate buddy of Will Busenburg.

"Meeting with us will in no way help your pending case," Bryan emphasized to Opara. "We're here to only discuss the Busenburg case."

Opara answered, "I'm only talking with you because I feel it's the right thing to do."

A native of Nigeria, Opara had come to the United States he said, to attend college. Then he split with his wife, left her and the kids, and said, "I'll be back." After eventually making his way to Austin, he was picked up on an assault charge.

"That's when I met Will. We were thrown in the same tank. He started to talk to me about his case. He told me that he had shot his best friend, a guy named Chris, with a pump shotgun. He said he shot him because he thought that Chris was trying

to take Stephanie away from him. He said he told the girl to
stay away from Chris.

"He said he went to Chris's apartment to see if Stephanie
was there with Chris. But when he got there, Chris was asleep
in the bed, facedown. He said he shot him with a pump shotgun
that belonged to Chris."

Mancias thought back to the guns he had found in Stephanie
Martin's apartment. They were the same kind of Remington
that was issued to sheriffs deputies.

"Will said Stephanie wasn't there when he shot Chris. He
said he called her after he shot him and had her come over to
the apartment. When she got there, he said, she tried to leave,
but he stopped her and asked her to help him. Will also said
that Stephanie was the one that told him to cut off the hands
so that nobody could identify the body. So, Will cut them off."

"Did Busenburg say how he killed Chris?"

"Once in the face, point-blank range. He said his face was
blown off."

"Did he say where the gun was before he shot Chris?"

"He told me it was either in the apartment or Will's truck."
He shook his head. "I can't remember which one he said. But
he told me that Stephanie had gotten an attorney and that she
has to tell the truth now. He said that he first told Stephanie to
tell the cops that Chris had tried to rape her and that would make
it look like self-defense. He said, 'I can't believe this thing happened. I can't believe I killed my best friend behind a bitch.' "

"Did you hear about the case through the media before, or
even after, you met Busenburg?" said Mancias.

"No."

Mancias and Bryan walked out the door, Bryan dwelling on
Opara's words—Busenburg cut off Hatton's hands. That's one
thing that Stephanie Martin had never denied doing. It was the
one part of her story that had never changed.

"I'll let you know if I want an affidavit from him," said
Bryan.

# Twenty-two

Six months after the murder of Christopher Michael Hatton, the Round Rock Police Department decided that Corporal Holly Frischkorn did, indeed, need psychological testing.

They decided that after she had sent thank-you gifts of engraved gold pens to the TCSO detectives who were working on Chris's case.

However, even after the Round Rock Police Department tested her, even after they deemed her unfit for duty, they never provided her with counseling.

Without realizing it, Holly Frischkorn was suicidal over the death of her ex-nephew. She knew she had a trial to get through, so suicide wasn't an option but Demerol was. She gave herself another shot, and once again zoned out in her chair for the night.

Eventually, due to Michael's death, Holly Frischkorn lost her job with the Round Rock Police Department. Since she was five years old, she had dreamed of being a cop.


On July 3, 1995, Mac Opara wrote Will Busenburg a letter telling Will that the DA, Will's arresting officer, and a private investigator had been to see him. He said they "called me out to help the innocent girl out. . . ." He told Busenburg that the Martin family was "begging" him to make a statement for Martin to "help her out of the death penalty."

What Opara failed to tell Busenburg was that the prosecutorial team had sat down with Opara at Opara's request.

Still, he assured Busenburg that he, Mac Opara, was not an informant, despite the officers of the court offering him "all kinds" of deals.

In truth, no deal of any sort was offered to Opara.

Opara "bluntly" had told the investigators that he had only ninety days to his discharge, he wrote Busenburg. "So they said how about money. I told them that I am not a poor black man."

No money had been offered him, either.

Opara told Busenburg that he had even slammed his hand on the table to emphasize that he could not be bought, and that that slam on the table had scared Frank Bryan.

Busenburg answered Opara's letter on July 6, 1995. He wrote that it was "pretty shitty" that the DA and all of Stephanie's attorneys came to Opara. He expressed his astonishment that Martin was trying to place the murder on him. "Teach me to love someone again. How can anyone be so cold?"

He added, ". . . to think this is a girl I was going to marry. Makes me sick." Busenburg wrote that he would never have been in jail and Hatton would still be alive if it weren't for "Stephanie killing him. . . ." Busenburg inserted the word "asking" just before "killing."

Later Busenburg asked Opara when he might be able to talk to Opara's attorney. He was considering getting a new attorney since he had phoned Chris Gunter after receiving Opara's letter. According to Busenburg, Gunter had refused his call.

Busenburg closed the letter with various German phrases and "Remember: Anger is the wind that blows out the candle of the mind."


At 8:45 A.M., on Friday, July 28, 1995, Detective Mancias drove in the opposite direction of Austin's rush hour traffic.

Mancias was headed south, then east, to Del Valle to pick up Stephanie Martin.

The day was already steamy with Texas heat and humidity, and Martin was nervous. She was scheduled for her second polygraph test, this one arranged by prosecutor Frank Bryan, at the encouragement of Ira Davis.

Mancias escorted the thinning young woman in her orange jailhouse jumpsuit to the Texas Department of Public Safety (DPS) office. They met briefly at 9:05 A.M. with attorney David B. Fannin, an associate of Davis's and cocounsel for Martin.

Mancias stepped a few feet away to give attorney and client time to talk. Sergeant Peter Heller, the polygrapher, arrived.

The four chatted and Fannin left, as he wasn't allowed to attend.

There were three chairs in the polygraph suite. Martin was motioned to one of them. She sat down, with the other two chairs less than two feet away.

Heller read Martin her rights. She initialed each line, indicating she clearly understood her rights, then signed the document. Signing away her rights was becoming "old hat" to Martin.

Heller read her a consent form so that he could give her the polygraph test. She signed it, too, with Mancias witnessing her signature. Mancias went to the next room to observe through a one-way mirror and listen through a speaker.

Heller explained the polygraph test to Martin and discussed her case. From that conversation, Heller told her, they would both create several yes/no questions that she would answer during the polygraph.

Martin recounted the same story she'd told everyone since the day she'd retracted her confession to the private investigator Drew McAngus—she'd only heard about Chris's murder, then helped cover it up. "I didn't have anything to do with the shooting."

They formulated ten questions, six control questions that would illicit a lying response, and four relevant questions. The responses to the relevant questions, Heller would compare to the control questions.

At 10:45 A.M., about an hour and fifteen minutes after Heller and Martin had sat down together, Martin was hooked up to the polygraph machine. She felt the humidity of the day in her jail clothes and the air-conditioned cold of the room on her skin.

"Before 1995, have you ever lied to protect someone from going to jail?"

"No."

"Prior to this year, have you ever lied to cover up for a crime?"

"No."

Those were control questions.

"Were you physically present when Chris was shot?"

"No."

"Did you personally shoot Chris?"

"No."

Heller kept his eyes on the polygraph printout, marking it as she answered. "Did you see Chris get shot?"

"No."

"Did you pull the trigger of the gun that was used to shoot Chris?"

"No."

Martin's fingertips were sweating and her blood pressure was rising. She was asked the questions three times, with a minute or two break between each series of questions. For the third round of questions, Heller told her that the order of the questions would change, some questions she would hear twice, some she wouldn't hear at all.

"Did you personally shoot Chris?"

"No."

Heller unhooked Martin from the polygraph machine at 11:10 A.M. In his office, he scored the results.

"Deceptive," Heller told Mancias.

The DPS officer knew he was required to let Martin explain the reason for the failed test. He walked back into the polygraph suite.

"You failed the test," said Heller.

"That's impossible because I told the truth. I didn't shoot him and I wasn't there."

He asked her more questions, question after question.

Martin felt intimidated and confused. She felt like he hated her. She said she'd left something out—that she had "intentionally planned to kill Chris." Hatton was to die from an overdose of sleeping pills, which Busenburg was to slip to Hatton. It was supposed to look like suicide.

"I never planned on Chris to die by being shot," she said.

Heller listened and took notes.

Mancias watched again through the mirror.

"We went and got some sleeping pills," said Martin. That was at a Randalls grocery store on FM 2222, a road that wound from near her apartment, which was just blocks from Interstate-35, through the flats of central Austin, around the hills of west Austin, and finally out toward Lake Travis, the dump site for the body.

But that was about five days before the murder, and the sleeping pills she and Busenburg purchased as they stood side by side in the grocery store line were Sleepinal. The plan, she said, was to kill Chris and steal the money that Will believed was in the apartment.

"We went to Chris's apartment," she continued. They slipped him the pills. "But that plan did not work when we tried it." Not at all. "He didn't even go to sleep."

The Sunday prior to the murder, they went to Albertsons grocery store on Highway 183, the main thoroughfare that separated the Aubry Hills Apartments from the Yellow Rose. At Albertsons, Martin and Busenburg bought a different brand of sleeping pills, Unisom, plus more Sleepinal. They went to the Hatton apartment in two vehicles.

"Why two vehicles?" asked Heller.

"Just in case Chris looked outside." They didn't want him to become suspicious if he saw her sitting in Busenburg's truck, she explained. "I was to wait outside for thirty minutes. Then Will was going to come out and talk to me." She drove around for about thirty minutes and waited for Busenburg to come out and tell her that Hatton was "dead or out."

After two hours and no word from Busenburg, Martin feared her lover had been killed. Busenburg, she said, had previously told her that there might be a struggle.

"I got out of my car. I went up to the apartment."

Heller noted that that contradicted her earlier statement to him when she had said she never left her vehicle.

"I looked through the window." She said she leaned close and listened for any noises inside. She went back to her car, and she drove around the complex. She saw Will, and he said, "I just shot Chris."

Later that night, they went back to the apartment, stole a camera, a Walkman, and some jewelry. "This was to get even," she told Heller. She added that she and Busenburg talked about pawning the goods in order to have money to leave the state.

While inside the apartment, they rolled up the body in a comforter, put the body in the bathroom, and left. They didn't return until the next day.

When they did return, Will convinced her that they had to take the body out and burn and mutilate it because "that's the way they did it in the CIA." She agreed, and they took the body to Pace Bend Park. There, she poured lighter fluid on the body and cut off the hands because "Will told me to." She was convinced by Busenburg that this was part of a government killing.

Stephanie Martin still denied that she shot Chris Hatton.

Detective Mancias came in and pulled a chair up close to Martin so that they sat almost knee to knee. "Are you absolutely sure that this is what happened?" he asked kindly.

She watched him from behind her eyeglasses. She could almost feel his calm pulse, he sat so close. "Yeah," she answered, and physically backed away a bit.

Mancias noted her movement.

"What I told Sergeant Heller was the truth."

He steadied his stare on her body. Her legs were crossed. Her arms were crossed. The more yes/no questions he asked her, the tighter and more defensive her body language became.

He reached over and physically uncrossed Martin's legs, then slipped his knees between her knees so that she could no longer hide behind her wrapped-tight body language.

"Did you kill Chris Hatton?"

Martin never answered his question. She only wept.

Mancias leaned back. To him, that was the same as saying yes.

"I wasn't there," Stephanie Martin wept as Mancias drove her back to county jail. "I'm an awful person for drugging Chris with sleeping pills." *It's hopeless,* she thought.

Ira Davis was enraged. Time and again he'd warned Martin to answer only the polygraph questions and ask for her attorney if the test showed deception.

"Well, I don't remember you telling me that," said Martin.

"Well, you should have known better!"

For months and months, the Martins' attorneys argued what the Martins felt was a solid loophole, that Stephanie Martin had been denied an attorney on the night of her confession and arrest. After months and months, the judge disagreed. Martin had asked for her father, not an attorney. No rights had been violated.

On August 1, 1995, Will Busenburg sat down with a bag of Chee-tos, his prison sustenance, and wrote Mac Opara another letter. Busenburg said he was trying to get his court dates reset until mid-October: "May Buddha walk with you through all hardships and keep you healthy and fit."

By August, Stephanie Martin was in love with another inmate.

On Friday, September 1, 1995, Busenburg wrote Opara to

tell him he had converted back to Christianity. "Pretty cool huh?" By September, Will Busenburg was lusting over another woman.


About a year after Chris Hatton's death, Lisa Pace phoned Brian Hatton, then living in Alabama. She asked Brian to take a photograph of Chris's headstone and mail the photo to her.

He couldn't do that, he said. There was no headstone; the family, he said, hadn't been able to afford one. When he turned eighteen, Brian was going to get some money from an insurance policy Chris had left him. With that money, he said, he was going to buy his brother a headstone.

About that same time, Holly Frischkorn and her therapist finally realized that Holly was abusing Demerol. Realizing this was not what her nephew Michael would have wanted, Frischkorn cleaned herself up.

Lisa Pace received subpoenas for court appearances. After every subpoena, just days before the scheduled court date, she received a follow-up letter or phone call telling her the court date had been moved or cancelled.

Her frustration grew as she heard conversations regarding the prosecutors' and deputies' quandary over who actually pulled the trigger, Will or Stephanie.

On Wednesday, January 24, 1996, the pretrial hearings finally began. Detective Manuel Mancias was the sole witness. He testified to the basic facts of finding the body and searching the Aubry Hills Apartments. The defense attorneys began laying out their plan to insinuate that the officers had made an illegal entry and search of the apartment.

On February 6, 1996, Detective Mancias was back in court again testifying about the basic facts, and again the defense attorneys tried to hint that the search of Chris Hatton's apartment was illegal.

On February 20, 1996, Detective Mancias didn't have to show up for court. Instead, prosecutors and defense lawyers questioned Detectives Richard Hale and Bruce Harlan, the officers who initially took Busenburg and Martin into custody. Later in the day, Sergeant Timothy Gage took the stand. Like Mancias, he was grilled about the search of the apartment.

Finally apartment manager Dawn Trevino was brought to the stand. They quizzed her about the lease.

"I thought under the terms of the lease, the standard lease, that when a person gives motive of intent to terminate or move out, vacate, whatever, that they have to give you their new address, their forwarding address so you know where to send the deposit to," said Chris Gunter.

"If they want their deposit back, that's correct," answered Trevino.

"[Will Busenburg] had not given you any notice—"

"No."

"—of any new address, had he?"

"No."

"Fact is, he was still responsible for the rent, was he not?"

"Yes, he was, under the lease."

"You bet. And in fact, had Christopher Hatton walked [away from] the lease, you would have and could have gone after Will Busenburg for the rent, couldn't you?"

"Could have, yes," said Trevino.

"All right. Just because Chris Hatton told you [Busenburg] moved out—and by the way, he didn't give you any of the circumstances about why he moved out, or where he moved, anything like that, did he?"

"No, he didn't."

". . . On January fourteenth, William Busenburg had a completely legal interest, enforceable legal interest in that apartment, did he not?"

"Yes, I guess so."

"All right. Had you received any complaints in, let's say, the week before January fourteenth, about any unusual or strange goings-on in [that] apartment?"

"None that I recall," answered Trevino.

"Any reports about gunshots being heard in that apartment?" said Gunter.

"No."

"Any reports about screams coming from that apartment?"

"No."

"Any reports—"

"I think she's stated that she didn't hear anything," said Judge Mike Lynch, "so that includes screams and gunshots, doesn't it?"

# Twenty-three

On March 12, 1996, Chris Hatton's grandparents, William Crutcher Hatton and his wife, Elsa, filed a Victim Information Sheet, a form enumerating the sufferings experienced by the family of the murder victim.

Mrs. Hatton wrote that she had not been harmed "in money ways. But in sorrow and pain of losing our beautiful grandson. My health must also pay the price of this great loss!"

Mr. Hatton wrote that he had suffered loss of sleep, had experienced nightmares, depression, lack of concentration, anxiety, job stress, anger, and that his family was no longer as close as it had been.

He stated that he had suffered monetary loss. Prior to Chris's murder, said Mr. Hatton, he had been teaching college courses in business management and psychology at the Gatesville units of the Texas prison system. He had to quit the job, he said, because "I cannot support the criminal in education when at any moment there may appear in my class one of the murderers that took my grandson's life!"

He also wrote of the devastation experienced by Brian Hatton: "The impact of this crime on my other grandson, Brian Hatton, has caused depression, fear, anxiety, poor grades at school and he had to return to Alabama. . . . This kind of impact on children is not acceptable in America. It's time the criminal pays and not the victims of the crime. The criminal seems to gain celebrity status and the victim is forgotten. We cannot let this happen in our society today. This must change and the criminal must pay in full!!"

On March 15, 1996, Detective Mancias and three other officers drove north on Interstate 35 to the small community of Jarrell and the home of Raymond Busenburg. They were there to search for jewelry Will Busenburg and Stephanie Martin had purchased with Chris Hatton's Kay Jewelers credit card.

"Our records show that the items were released to you," Mancias said, as he stood in Busenburg's doorway.

"What items are you talking about?" Busenburg replied.

"A gold necklace with a gold cross, a single earring with a diamond in it, and a men's Paul Buguette watch."

Busenburg walked into a bedroom, dug through a few boxes, scavenged through a jewelry box, then handed Mancias an earring and a cross. He said he couldn't recall where the watch was. "My wife can probably remember. But my phone's out."

Mancias handed him a TCSO cell phone.

After hanging up, Busenburg reported that Fran Wallen had the watch. "She wanted it because she said she'd given it to Will. I don't know of any other watch in the house that belonged to him."

Mancias wrote out a receipt for the two items. As Busenburg accepted it in his hand, he looked up and said, "When's my son's case going to court? He's taken me off his visiting list."

An hour and a half later, Mancias rang the doorbell at the Martin home in Round Rock. "I'm looking for a ladies' emerald ring and a ladies' Movado watch," he explained to Sandra Martin.

"I only know of one watch and ring that Stephanie has," Martin said in her slow, deliberate, west Texas drawl. "I did get them, but they were given to Stephanie for Christmas."

Mancias handed Martin a consent to search form.

Sandra Martin almost signed it, then hesitated, backed away, and walked into her house. Moments later Robert Martin stood in the doorway.

Again Mancias explained what he needed.

"I'd prefer you get a search warrant before coming into my home," said Robert Martin.

"I have a search warrant." Mancias handed it to Martin.

Soon Sandra Martin walked out of a first-floor bedroom and gave the detective a ring and Movado watch.

Ten days later, Mancias walked into Kay Jewelers in Highland Mall, a mall located only moments from Stephanie Martin's apartment. He handed a photo lineup to manager Larry Maxwell.

"It's been over a year since they were in the store," said Maxwell. Still, he managed to narrow his choices of Will Busenburg to two, then one. The photo he picked wasn't Busenburg. The photo he almost picked was.

He then narrowed his choices of Martin to two, then one. Again the photo he chose wasn't Martin. The one he almost chose was.

By April 10, 1996, the bluebonnets were in full bloom in Texas as defense attorneys and prosecutors gathered in District Judge Mike Lynch's court for the fifth and final pretrial hearing. It was to be an unusual day.

Texas DPS polygrapher Peter Heller took the stand. The Martin team did not want to hear this testimony—not when the expensive private polygraph test that Robert Martin had paid for was not being admitted alongside the state's test.

"Let me direct your attention back to July 28, 1995," said prosecutor Frank Bryan. Bryan was a thin, bespectacled, wavy-haired brunet with Republican leanings and political aspirations. "On that day, did you administer a polygraph test to a person named Stephanie Martin?"

"Yes," said Heller, "I did."

Slowly, awkwardly, and appearing unprepared for his testimony, Sergeant Heller led the precisely prepared prosecutor through July 28, until Bryan asked Heller to enumerate the relevant questions that the polygrapher had asked Stephanie Martin.

"Were you physically present when Chris was shot?" answered Heller. "Did you personally shoot Chris? Did you see Chris get shot? Did you ever pull the trigger of the gun that was used to shoot Chris?"

"All right. What happened when you administered the test using those questions?"

"Using those questions—came out with deceptive response, or a deceptive test."

Heller went on to recount Martin's explanation for her failure of the polygraph test. "She stated that she got out of her vehicle, went up to the apartment, which was contrary to what she had said earlier—she had said she had never left her vehicle—and looked through the window."

She said she saw Busenburg, Heller reported, who told her he'd shot Chris. Later that night they returned to the apartment and stole some of Hatton's possessions, said the officer. "And this was to get even, she said."

He went through the decision by Martin and Busenburg to burn the body. He emphasized, "She never did admit shooting the victim, or—she did admit the plan was to kill him. She had been convinced by Will that he was a member of the CIA and that this was part of some government killing. After talking with you, with assistant district attorney, I—we ended the interview."

Ira Davis stared hard at the state's witness. "I couldn't help but notice earlier, before we started this pretrial, that you were having a conversation with a woman that I've identified as Holly Frischkorn, I believe." His gaze didn't leave Heller's face.

"That's correct," Heller replied, unperturbed.

"Can you tell me what your relationship with her is?"

He explained that he once patrolled the county Round Rock

was in and knew Frischkorn from her Round Rock police duties.

"So you were aware of the facts of this case prior to doing the polygraph exam?"

"No," the sergeant answered. He said he'd heard that the victim was a relative of a Round Rock officer. "That's all I knew. I didn't know it was her until about two months ago. My captain said something about some pretrial case and said, 'That's something you worked on.' And I said, 'How did you know that?' And he said through—Holly had called or talked to him. That's all I knew."

"It's your testimony that you had no idea who Chris Hatton was prior to doing the polygraph?"

"No, I didn't," Heller stated simply.

Davis wouldn't let it go. He grilled the state's witness, trying over and over to prove prejudice. He never outright proved anything.

"How many questions did you ask during the examination?"

"Ten."

Davis seemed less concerned about the actual polygraph test than he did about the conversation that ensued after Heller had scored the test.

"So you go back in. What's the first thing you say [to Stephanie Martin]?"

"We have to explain. I have to tell her the results."

"I understand you have to tell her—is the first thing you did when you went back in, wad up the piece of paper, throw it on the floor, and accuse her of being a liar?"

"No."

"Well, what's the first question you asked her when you went back in?"

"I have no idea."

"You didn't write that down?" said Davis, acting appalled. He knew that in front of a jury, it would be the DPS officer's word against the former stripper's.

"I don't write down what I say or do when I walk back in. It changes from person to person," said Heller.

It would also be the word of a DPS officer who had been seen earlier talking to the deceased's mother figure, Holly Frischkorn.

"And you didn't observe Sergeant Mancias or Investigator Mancias making any notes in the interrogation of her after the exam, did you?"

"I don't know. He's behind—in the observation room."

Davis looked straight at the officer. "Are you telling us, Sergeant Heller, that he never came back in there and asked any questions at all during the time you interrogated her after the test?"

"I don't know."

"You don't remember that?" said Davis, incredulous.

"I don't remember."

"You don't remember both of you questioning her?"

"It's not uncommon," said Heller, "but I don't remember it."

Davis battered Heller with questions until the attorney steadied his blue eyes on the DPS witness. "How many times did you accuse her of being a liar?"

"I don't know."

"You did accuse her of being a liar?"

"I'm sure."

"And more than once?"

"I have no idea," Heller calmly responded.

Davis paused for a moment. "Okay," he said softly. "Did she indicate to you that she passed a polygraph examination on these things?"

"I believe she said she took one. I don't know if I ever—I think I did know that she passed one. That's correct."

Davis stifled a snicker that was about to ooze out of him. He pictured his words, as if they were the glint of a new knife. "Is that when you told her that she must have passed that because her attorney paid off the polygraph examiner to pass her?" Davis was referring to himself.

"I don't remember saying that."

"You don't recall saying that at all?"

"No."

"That wouldn't be an interrogation technique or question you might ask somebody to rattle them?"

"No."

"You wouldn't—"

"However, she—the indication here is that Doug Farris gave the test. And I might have made the comment that that wouldn't be the first time that we have overturned his cases."

"Maybe you said something more along the lines that wouldn't be the first time that an attorney had paid him—"

"Objection," yelled Frank Bryan. "Asked and answered. Irrelevant."

"Sustained," said Judge Lynch.

The judge turned to look at Chris Gunter, Busenburg's attorney who had been waiting and listening patiently.

"Mr. Gunter," said Judge Lynch, "do you have any questions?"

"Just a couple of brief questions, Judge."

Bryan glanced at Gunter, then stared at His Honor. "Judge," said Bryan, "I'm going to object to any questions by Mr. Gunter. His client has no standing in this matter."

"Overruled," said Lynch. "Ask your questions at this time."

Gunter was a somewhat small man with thinning blond hair and bright-blue eyes that could pierce like a laser. "Sometimes," said Gunter, "I see in polygraph reports where the answer is deceptive. Other times I see it's inconclusive. What was your judgment about her answers?"

Heller again replied deceptive.

Gunter asked Heller if he was satisfied with Martin's explanation for her deceptive rating.

"Oh, yes. Yes," said Heller.

Gunter wanted to know if that explanation explained away her deception on the question "Did you shoot Chris?"

"To that question, no. Nothing she said changes that."

"Or how about to the question 'Were you physically present when Chris was shot?' " said Gunter.

"Objection," called Frank Bryan. "Relevance."

The judge disagreed.

The polygrapher stated again that Martin changed her story to say she had been at the apartment, listening at the window.

"Did she say she was in the apartment?" said Gunter.

"No. She never would say that she was in it at the time of the shooting."

"And the question 'Did you see Chris get shot?' A no answer to that. Was that ever explained by her—"

"No."

"—afterward?"

"No, it was not," said Heller.

"And the final question, 'Did you pull the trigger of the gun that shot Chris?' A no answer to that. Did she give any satisfactory explanation of that?"

"No."

"That's all I have," said Gunter. "Thank you."


The state was about to do something unusual.

Travis County Assistant District Attorney Allison Wetzel stood, her red hair in strong curls. She was a prosecutor who wanted to pursue the strongest case. Frank Bryan was a prosecutor who wanted to pursue the truth.

"State calls Frank Bryan," said Wetzel.

Judge Lynch looked over at the defense table. "Any objection. . . ."

Frank Bryan interrupted, stating that Ira Davis had talked about calling the prosecutor as a witness. ". . . And I think Ms. Wetzel and I decided it would just be better for me to go ahead and take the stand."

Seeker of truth may have been Bryan's reputation in the District Attorney's Office. But with defense attorneys, he was renowned for being black and white, right and wrong, no in-betweens.

Still, he was taking the stand to determine whether the state had made a deal with Stephanie Martin, a deal that Ira Davis worried that the state was reneging on.

Bryan stated under oath that in June 1995, as chief prosecutor in the 167th District Court, he had been assigned to the Stephanie Martin and William Busenburg case. As such, on June 29, 1995, he had interviewed Martin at the Travis County jail.

"And I assume that you and Mr. Davis had had some kind of discussion before you all made arrangement to go to the jail and interview Ms. Martin," said Wetzel.

They did, answered Bryan, probably more than one discussion.

Wetzel asked if he and Davis had gone over any ground rules.

"I did." Bryan explained that, in front of Davis, he had told Martin that her answers to his questions could not be used against her when they went to trial, since he was not giving her her Miranda warnings. "I explained, however, that if she got up on the witness stand in the trial and told something inconsistent with, or in some way different than what she was telling there in the jail, that I could impeach her with that."

"And did you explain what it meant to impeach her?"

He did, he said.

Wetzel asked Bryan to summarize what Martin had told him, and Ira Davis objected on the grounds of irrelevancy.

"I think it is relevant to motions that are on file with the court," argued Chris Gunter, Busenburg's attorney.

The judge overruled "for purposes of this hearing."

Bryan said that he had had two interviews on two different occasions with Stephanie Martin, each interview lasting a couple of hours. Bryan stated that Martin had told him basically the same story she had told polygrapher Heller—she absolutely was not present when Chris Hatton was murdered.

Wetzel asked if Bryan had discussed with Davis and Martin the possibility of Martin submitting to a DPS polygraph test.

They did, he said.

"And did she indicate in the interview at the jail that she had already passed one polygraph?"

"She did," said Bryan.

"Do you recall ever having a discussion with Ira Davis that these statements that Ms. Martin was making could not be used against her for any purpose?"

"No, I don't recall that. Mr. Davis mentioned to me before court today something to the effect that he thought these discussions were in the process of plea discussions. And he also mentioned to me that he'd mentioned that during the interview at the jail with Stephanie Martin."

Bryan professed that he didn't recall that. "He may have and I can't say he didn't. But it was my understanding that the ground rules were what she said could be used as impeachment."

"Did you ever agree with Mr. Davis that this was a conversation that was in the nature of a plea discussion?" Wetzel asked.

"No."

"In fact, did you ever offer Stephanie Martin any punishment in exchange for a guilty plea?"

"No."

"What was the purpose of having these discussions with Stephanie Martin?"

The truth, said Bryan, had been the purpose—to determine whether or not he believed her new story. The interview had been intended to help him decide what to do next if he did, indeed, believe Martin's new scenario, he explained.

"Did you consider this part of the investigation of the murder?"

"Yes."

"Did you expect that Stephanie Martin would fail the poly-
raph at DPS?"

"No. Well, I need to add to that answer. My personal opinion
f her story that she told me in the jail was that I didn't believe
verything she told me at the jail, no. And then I understood
aat she was going to take a polygraph on the issue of whether
r not she was the shooter. And I guess I need to correct my
arlier answer. I expected her to give that same version that
he had told me at the jail to the polygraph examiner."

After the witness was passed, Ira Davis looked at Frank
ryan and asked the prosecutor whether he recalled meeting
vith Will Busenburg's former cellmate—the cellmate, re-
ninded Davis, who had heard Busenburg claim responsibility
or killing Chris Hatton. Davis was referring to Mac Opara,
vithout mentioning Opara by name.

Bryan said he recalled the meeting.

"And subsequent to that, you and I entered into discussion
bout Ms. Martin's version of those events. Is that true?"

"Yes."

"Okay," said Davis. "And I indicated to you that her story
night be quite in line with the discussion in that letter."

"You told me that she wasn't the shooter, right."

"Professionally and personally, is it your belief that when a
lefense attorney approaches you and asks you, 'Can we talk?
Aaybe there's some way to work this out,' that that is that
lefense attorney's way of indicating to you that he's attempting
o begin the plea negotiations?"

"If he said those words, yes."

Davis asked Bryan if he recalled Davis's precise words when
ae broached the subject of plea negotiations.

"I'm nearly one hundred percent certain you didn't say,
Maybe we can work this out.' "

"Okay." Davis didn't respond to the prosecutor's cattiness.

Bryan didn't give the lawyer a chance to respond. Bryan
oushed on, despite no question being asked. "I don't recall

us—you ever saying those words to me in this particular case.
And no, I don't recall the exact words."

"To be more precise," Davis finally said, "probably I have
on more than one occasion indicated to you that we could enter
into plea negotiations over a particular term of years. I have
indicated a number of times a term of years that would be
acceptable, haven't I?"

"Yes."

"So you would certainly consider that a form of plea negotiations—very rudimentary?"

"Right," said Bryan, returning to only answering the question asked.

"And those discussions have gone on between us for some
time now."

"Right."

". . . What was your opinion," Davis asked, "of where we
were going when I entered into these discussion with you concerning possibly interviewing [Stephanie Martin] and her taking the polygraph examination?"

"Well," said Bryan, "I certainly believed you were trying to
convince me that she was not the shooter."

"Towards what purpose?"

"Well . . ." Bryan didn't answer.

"Negotiating a resolution of this case?"

"Yeah, in a broad sense, that's true."

"You took copious notes of the interviews in the jail," said
Davis.

"I did."

"And do you have those notes with you?"

"They are in my trial notebook, and you all have had discovery of all of those notes."

Davis flipped his gaze over to the judge. "Well," he said,
"I beg to disagree on that, Your Honor." Davis groused that
he hadn't been given any copious notes, and even if he were
to be given the prosecutor's notes, they would be so lengthy

hat he wouldn't have time to go through them prior to cross-
xamination.

The notes had been available to the defenses, claimed Bryan.

"For the record," Chris Gunter interrupted, "today is the first
lay that I have learned that the district attorney had had two
wo-hour interviews with defendant Martin. Today is the first
ime that I have heard anything about any copious notes of
hose interviews."

Judge Lynch tried to soothe all sides and move on.

Bryan, still sitting in the witness chair, requested that he be
ble to ask Davis a question.

"It's a reversal of roles, but I'd be happy to answer his ques-
ion," Davis replied.

"Go ahead," said the judge.

"Are you saying that [the notes are not] in the binder you
ave looked at?"

Davis said that the notes he had looked at were not typed.
Then he confessed, "The last I looked at your binder was some
ime long before this pretrial."

Davis proceeded on and urged the prosecutor to recollect
hat he, Davis, had said that the Martin interview was pursuant
o plea negotiations. They disputed the point back and forth,
with Bryan still stating that he didn't recall. Davis emphasized
hat he and Bryan had had additional discussions about the
case and that Bryan had indicated that he had reservations
about Martin's story.

"That's true," said Bryan.

"And you asked that before we proceed any further, sort of
along those lines that we were talking, that she agree to submit
to a polygraph examination. You told me that she would need
to pass a polygraph. Is that what you told me?" said Davis.

"I don't remember saying it that way, and I don't remember
whose original idea it was. But we did talk about her taking a
polygraph."

"You don't recall saying that she would need to pass a polygraph on this story?"

"Well," said Bryan, "need to pass it for what?"

"That's exactly my point," Davis grumbled.

It might have persuaded him to try Busenburg first, rather than Martin, said Bryan.

"And . . . it never flashed at any time across your mind what was going on here were negotiations between you and a defense attorney on a resolution of this matter?"

"No, I—"

And Davis and Bryan continued to bicker until Davis finally passed the witness.

"I have some questions, Judge," said Chris Gunter.

"Your Honor," pleaded Wetzel, "I don't know what the relevance of Mr. Gunter's questions is."

They argued, and finally Judge Lynch let Gunter cross-examine Assistant District Attorney Frank Bryan.

"One thing that has come out, been pretty clear from Mr Davis's questioning, is that plea discussions had been going on for some time between you and defendant Martin," said Gunter.

"My question," said Gunter, "is I would like to know what the status of the plea negotiation—what has the defendant been wanting? What has defendant Martin been wanting in exchange for her testimony against Will Busenburg?"

"I object to the relevance of that," said Wetzel.

The judge overruled.

"We've never discussed any plea bargain in terms of an exchange for her testimony," said Bryan.

Gunter asked again, "What have they been asking for? What has the defendant Martin been asking for? I am using your own words, Mr. Bryan. You said Mr. Davis asked you—"

"If you would like. A couple of times Mr. Davis has approached me with a number of years. 'What about this?' And I have said no."

"What has he approached you with?"

"Twenty or twenty-five, something like that, TDC [meaning Texas Department of Corrections]."

"In exchange for her testimony against Busenburg?" asked
unter.

"It was never stated that way," Bryan replied. "And I don't
ake plea bargains in exchange for testimony in that way, like
exchange for testifying against a codefendant."

"You don't make that a condition of a plea in a joint defen-
nt case?"

"No. It would be truthful testimony—in exchange for truth-
l testimony," insisted Bryan.

"Okay. That goes without saying. Has defendant Martin been
king for a sentence of twenty to twenty-five years in ex-
ange for her truthful testimony against Busenburg?"

"I don't believe that has ever been mentioned in his—when
e's approached me, Mr. Davis has approached me, it's just
en a term of years. That's my recollection."

"And your testimony," said Gunter, "is the current offer of
e defendant or request of defendant Martin has been for
venty or twenty-five years?"

"I believe it's one of those two. May have been twenty. I'm
ot—twenty or twenty-five. Whatever it was, I said no."

"Have you made any counteroffers?"

"No."

"None?" asked Gunter.

"None," Bryan replied.

"Okay. Well, I have to concur with Mr. Davis then. What
as the purpose of meeting with Stephanie Martin two times
st summer? I mean if it was not in an effort to get her case
solved somehow?"

"It was an effort to find the truth of what happened," said
ryan.

"Okay. And in those two interviews, are you satisfied, based
n your knowledge of the case, that she made inconsistent—or
he made untruthful statements to you?"

"Am I satisfied that she—"

"Well," said Gunter, "let me just be more direct. In your

opinion, was she untruthful with you on matters in both of those interviews?"

"I did not believe everything she said to me, no."

# Twenty-four

On Tuesday, July 23, 1996, prosecutor Frank Bryan met at the Travis County jail with inmate Tonya Williams to discuss Williams's former cellmate, Stephanie Martin.

Williams, who also went by several aliases, said, "Stephanie seemed like a nice person." For the ten days they had been cellmates, just the two of them, Williams explained, they had been separated for only an hour a day—to shower and use the phone.

"One night, though, Stephanie broke down. She cried sometimes. And sometimes she laughed. She said on the day of the murder that Will wasn't feeling like his normal self."

"She said Will was going over to Chris's apartment. And Chris came home while they were both there. She said she left because Will asked her to leave. Then, around twelve or twelve-thirty, Will called Stephanie and asked her to come back to Chris's apartment. She said when she got there Will was pacing up and down, but she could hear Chris snoring."

Bryan thought about the facts he knew: Chris Hatton was at the Conway home at 12:30 A.M. Maybe she'd gotten the time wrong.

"Chris had six hundred dollars," said Williams. "Will needed six hundred dollars."

Bryan knew the figure bantered around was $6,000, one zero off.

"Will was saying, 'Chris has it, and he's not going to give

it to me.' Will said, 'I know how I can get it.' Then he got up, walked into Chris's bedroom, and Stephanie heard a gun go off."

"She said she was in the apartment when the gun went off?" asked Bryan.

"Yeah, she was in the apartment, and she said she was thinking, 'What do I do?' Will came back into the living room. And Will said Stephanie should call her house. That would show that she wasn't there when it happened."

Bryan pondered the situation as he wrote on his legal pad. Williams's story explained the phone call on Martin's caller ID.

"After that," said Williams, "they left the apartment and drove around, thinking about what they should do with the body, and talking about what to tell the police. Later, she said, they went back to the apartment, carried the body from the bedroom to the bathroom. And Stephanie said she stuck her hand in the opening where Chris's head had been to see what it felt like. Then they went to clean the blood up out of the room.

"She said Will went into the room and found between five hundred and six hundred dollars in cash in a box, and he took it. They put the body in a tarp and wrapped it up." She backed up and mentioned that Martin and Busenburg stole a Walkman and a bike.

"They took the body to a park. She said she was saying to Will, 'Let's drop it at the dam.' But Will said, 'No, we have to burn the body.' They carried it out of the truck. Stephanie cut the hands off, they burned the body, and then they were going to pack up their things and leave town.

"But the detectives searched her apartment, she was taken to APD, and she asked for an attorney. She said they planned the story of Stephanie shooting Chris in self-defense. And she's been fighting it ever since. She said she'd changed her story before. She said she trusted me." Tonya smiled. "She said she's being reindicted and getting a light sentence. Stephanie reads true crime stories, but she only reads the real graphic parts."

Tonya Williams also told Frank Bryan about herself that she didn't have a drug problem at that moment, but she used to.

"I don't want my husband to know."

On October 10, 1996, Bryan returned to the Travis County Correction Center. With him were Allison Wetzel, their investigator John Phillips, and attorney Ira Davis—all there to talk to Stephanie Martin.

Bryan and Wetzel were still considering prosecuting Will Busenburg first. The meeting, they believed, was to help them make that decision. The meeting, Martin believed, was to prepare her to testify against her former lover.

"What's your explanation for the receipt found in your apartment for firewood bought at Albertsons on Friday, January sixth, at one-thirty-five A.M.?"

"Um, we didn't go to Albertsons on January sixth," said Martin. "We went to Randalls on January seventh. We bought firewood the week before for the fireplace at Will's mom's, and that had nothing to do with this. . . . I don't remember if I went with him to buy it. I probably did. We stayed overnight there at his mom's.

"Uh-um," she corrected, "I think the night we stayed at his mom's was New Year's Eve. I know we went to Randalls on January seventh. We only bought firewood. . . . I don't know who bought the firewood on January sixth. He could have. Um, I know I didn't."

On Sunday, January 8, said Martin, they went to Levitz Furniture late in the afternoon. "Will had Chris's Levitz card. Will went into the closet and got the box the week before that had all the credit cards." She rattled off the names of the cards: Levitz, Sears, Kay Jewelers, Montgomery Ward, maybe a MasterCard, and Chris's military ID.

"We got to Levitz around five or six in the evening. Will signed the receipt. He used Chris's ID. I saw Will sign the receipt. We, um, picked up some furniture on Wednesday night, three days later. We put the furniture in the back of his truck."

They showed Martin photographs of the furniture, which she identified. "We took the table and chairs with us on Sunday. Will put them together. We picked up the couch on Wednesday." She brushed back her hair.

"Did you talk about why you were using Chris's cards?"

"Will said that Chris had stolen money from him, so Chris deserved it. Will said that Chris was fixin' to move and leave the country and he wouldn't notice. At the time we were using his card, we didn't discuss killing him."

The prosecutors handed Martin a receipt from Montgomery Ward for the purchase of a camera and battery at 12:54 P.M., on Monday, January 9, 1995.

"Can you identify this?"

Martin looked at it. "Yes. I was with him."

"Did you see him sign the receipt?"

"Yes."

"What happened to the camera?"

Martin looked over at Davis. "I don't remember. Maybe we put it in my apartment."

They showed her another receipt for the same day, a little over an hour later—2:13 P.M.—from Kay Jewelers.

"We both shopped around and bought some jewelry." Again she said she saw Busenburg sign the receipt. "He used Chris's ID. We bought an emerald-and-diamond ring, an emerald-and-diamond necklace, a woman's watch, a man's watch, and a diamond stud earring."

They showed her a receipt for a tarp from Academy sporting goods at 8:59 P.M.

"I bought that by myself. Will was working."

They showed her a receipt from January 13, 1995, from Franklin Federal bank. "Did you make a hundred dollar deposit?"

She glanced at Davis. "Uh, I guess so."

"Where was it?"

"On Airport Boulevard going toward Highland Mall."

"Did you drive through or go inside?"

"Uh, I can't remember. Probably drove through."

Busenburg made a deposit, picked up his paycheck on Friday around noon, she said. "I waited in the truck, and he went in and got his check. He called in sick Wednesday, Thursday, and Friday."

They then went to a 7-Eleven where Busenburg checked his balance, Martin said. "We were trying to get money to get his truck out of impound."

Davis listened to the way his client spoke. She continually said he, without clarifying who he was. That concerned him: Would jurors be able to follow Martin? Would she sound like she was implicating herself when a "he" referring to Hatton was really a "he" referring to Busenburg, and vice versa?

Martin continued. She and Busenburg went to Albertsons, she said, still trying to get the money together to get Hatton's truck out of impound, then to Brunner's home. "We got twenty dollars from Todd and got the truck out about four P.M. I was standing next to Will when he signed to get his truck out."

Still a problem with "he," noted Davis.

At 7 P.M., said Martin, she and Busenburg went to the pawn-shop and pawned Chris's ring.

"What kind of ring was it?"

"A wedding ring."

"Did you see Will sign the receipt?"

"Yes."

They went to the Movies 12 on Wells Branch Parkway at 9 P.M., she recounted. "Will told Beck [his ex-boss] that he was planning on moving to Colorado right away. Oh, yeah," she said, with a "this is so stupid" tone to her voice, "Will told me he owned stock in Movies Twelve." Martin got serious. "We were exploring the possibility of going somewhere together. I think Will asked Beck if he wanted to buy some things. We were selling Chris's things and our things."

The prosecutors asked Martin about the hacksaw. They wondered if Busenburg had bought the hacksaw in preparation for the murder.

"Uh"—she glanced over at Davis—"the first time I saw it was when Will got it out of his truck. I wasn't with him when he bought it. I think he had had it for a long time." The day Hatton was killed, she said, Busenburg went to work.

The prosecutors noted that Martin jumped around a lot in her story.

"He said he wanted to do things normal. His body was in the bathtub all day Tuesday, the tenth."

Davis stared at the wall. His client was once again not clarifying who "he" was. That just wouldn't work well in court, he knew.

Martin proceeded. "Will worked that day, all day, from three to eleven. And then he went back to the apartment that night. Will told me, uh, to get back over to Chris's apartment and wash the bottle of Jim Beam and wash the glasses. He called me from work and told me to go get a tarp. We went to the apartments together at eleven-thirty or twelve. And he got some gloves from work."

"What was Will wearing?"

"Um, jeans. Dark clothes. Black tennis shoes."

They moved the body Tuesday night, said Martin. "Before Chris was killed, we talked about the sleeping pill plan."

She was still jumping around.

The prosecutors wanted to zero in. "Is there anything Will did or bought that we can use to prove there was planning or knowledge that the murder was going to happen?"

Martin said they bought sleeping pills at Randalls on Saturday and sleeping pills at Albertsons on Sunday. And on Tuesday, she noted, Busenburg called her from work. "He told me to get garbage bags, carpet cleaner, and paint. I got the"—she shook her head—"paint and garbage bags from my mom's house and carpet cleaner at Chris's apartment."

"What about the phone call from the pay phone at four-forty-nine A.M. on Tuesday morning?" The prosecutors thought about Tonya Williams's statement.

Martin ran her fingers through her hair. She looked at Davis. That phone call could prove her innocence, she believed. "I'd been driving around, and I went back to Chris's apartment, and Will said, 'I just tried to call you.' "

The prosecutors didn't blink.

She explained that when she had talked to the sheriffs detectives on the night she had been picked up and had told them she had called Will from Chris's apartment that she hadn't known where Busenburg had phoned from. "I knew Chris's phone was disconnected." She looked at Davis.

"Did you tell him you wanted to kill someone?"

"No. Of course not. I never said that. I asked Will a couple of times what it was like to kill someone. . . . I wanted to *know* what it was like. I didn't want to do it."

"But did you want to participate?"

"Yeah. I was turned on to the spy thing. I wanted to be involved in a mission."

"Well," Bryan said, "three people said you told them you wanted to kill somebody."

She looked over at Ira Davis. "I did talk about the subject. Will knew I was into it. Mostly, the conversation was me listening to his stories. He knew I was intrigued and impressed."

The first month she was with him, she said, Busenburg told stories about the CIA and going on missions. "After that, he said he wanted to get out of the CIA. He said he had nightmares about the men he killed. Um, he said he, um, wanted out because he had found someone to be in love with."

She looked at Bryan and smiled.

Busenburg, she pointed out, slipped Hatton the sleeping pills. "The plan, uh, was for me to search Chris. Will thought Chris had some money on him or some money in his truck." Busenburg, she noted, had already searched the apartment.

"When did you first discuss this plan? This sleeping pill plan?"

"Friday night. Will said that he would get Chris drunk and sedate him. And that he would put sleeping pills in Chris's drink. I thought Chris was training to be a professional hit man. On Saturday Will said that he would take Chris fishing or camping at Lake Travis."

They went to Randalls grocery, she explained, and got firewood, lighter fluid, and a pack of Sleepinal. They took the pills and crushed them up in a Baggie. "Will went over about eleven. The plan was that Will would ask Chris if he wanted to go camping that night. If Will didn't come back by one, I was supposed to come over."

Busenburg was then to pour Hatton a drink and dump the crushed pills into the drink while Hatton wasn't looking, she said. "The Jim Beam was Chris's." She said she went over to the apartments at 1 A.M. and waited in the parking lot. "At two-fifteen or two-thirty, uh, Will came out and said the sleeping pills weren't working."

Sunday night, she said, the plan was the same, but Hatton never showed. "Will and I went to the apartments in separate cars. Will went in and came right back out and said Chris wasn't there. We waited thirty minutes, then gave up and went back to my apartment." They would try again the next night.

"Will told me that Chris was leaving the country to become a French assassin."

On Monday, she said, they went back to the apartment, in separate cars. She returned to her place at 1 A.M., waited until 2:30 or 3:00, and worried that something had happened to Busenburg.

"How many guns do you have?"

"He gave me a Mossberg shotgun. . . . He had a rifle. I don't think he had another shotgun. He might have."

Frank Bryan watched her. "Well, there were three shotguns at the apartment."

"The small brown one is my father's. There's a Mossberg. And the third one was Chris's."

"Have you ever fired a shotgun before?"

"When I was twelve or thirteen years old, in sixth grade."

"How do you fire it?"

"Just pull back and pull the trigger. Will wanted me to go deer hunting with him so that he could show me what a good shot he was." She noted that Busenburg didn't take the gun with him when he went to Hatton's apartment.

"Was the plan to kill Chris?"

"I said the sleeping pills could kill. And Will said, 'I don't care if they do.' He didn't care because Chris had stolen his money. Chris was crazy and evil. I, um, uh, thought there was a chance that the, um, pills could kill him. But, um, I went along with the plan." She shook her head.

"The first night when the sleeping pills didn't work, Will seemed happy. [On] Monday night, Will came out of the apartment and said he shot him. I think he went into one of his trances. He told me he shot his dad when he was nine years old. He used to say he heard his dad's voice from the grave. And he said, um, Chris reminded him of his dad. He said Chris would be a bad assassin because he was crazy and reckless. I thought Will went crazy, like he thought it was a CIA hit. He said, 'Go get the brown gun.' That was Chris's gun."

They placed all of Chris's credit cards, ID, and watches in a box, she said. "Will told me the watches were his." She looked at Davis. "Will's." On Friday, she said, when they were cleaning up the apartment, Busenburg got the watches and said they would hock the ring.

"When did you first meet Will?"

"On October first, second, or third. I danced. He spent three hundred fifty dollars that first night. He wanted to call me or me to call him. I said, 'I have a boyfriend, and I don't date customers.' The next Friday or Saturday he came back in. He was in the VIP section. And he told the men who were with him that they could go.

"The first night that I met him, he said he worked for the government, the CIA." He had just been on a mission to another country and he was a sniper, said Martin. "He had been in hostage situations and did hits on bad men in other countries."

The second time she saw him, she said, was a Saturday and she went to breakfast with him. "On Wednesday, after that breakfast, I called him and told him to come in. He came in late. He showed me houses that he said he owned. We went back to his apartment, and then I went home."

He bought her a TV, VCR, dinners, and acted as though he had lots of money, said Martin. "He said he had money in Swiss bank accounts. He said he owned houses in Round Rock, California, and Montana. I wondered why he didn't spend more. He said he would spoil me when he knew that I loved him for himself. He told me he was losing his money little by little. He had to support a mission to get a friend out of Colombia, and it cost him millions." She smiled at Bryan.

"He said he had investments in houses that were going bad. And in January he said his accountant ran off with the rest of his money. And he also said he had some money in the bank but that he wouldn't touch it."

"What about the bicycle?"

"The bicycle on my balcony is Chris's bike. . . . Will said, 'I'm gonna steal his bike.' " Busenburg clipped the wires to the bike's lock with pliers and put the bike in the back of the truck, she explained. "Will was doing this to get even with Chris for stealing his money."

"What about the burrito note?" They were referring to the note to Hatton from Busenburg, photographed on Hatton's bar.

"That must have been Sunday night. Will went over there and left Chris a note. I can't remember seeing Will get the food, but, um, he told me he left a note."

To the prosecutors, that seemed incriminating. "Why would you leave a note on the counter?"

"I don't know."

"How did you feel about Will?"

"I was in love. I felt sorry for him. Um, after Chris was killed, we were kind of distant."

"What about the love letters in jail?"

"I was still very much in love."

"What about when you wrote him and said, 'Your crimes were small.' Why did you say that?" The prosecutors had in their minds a letter Martin had written Busenburg where she said, "Don't worry. You won't get in trouble because your crimes were small."

"Well, I knew somebody, um, was reading the letters," she answered. "That's why I said that."

Martin added that she knew that she would do some time. "But I heard that I would get manslaughter."

She said that Busenburg glamorized the missions and killing people for the CIA.

The prosecutor asked Martin about Tonya Williams's statement: Martin placed her hand inside Hatton's head.

"I never said that. Tonya was obsessed with getting out of jail."

They asked her again about the phone call from the Aubry Hills pay phone. And Martin again stated that she wasn't at home when the call came, she was driving around.

"I had been at my apartment from four to four-thirty. And when I got to Chris's apartment, Will said, 'I just tried to call you.' Will wanted me involved, and I wanted to be involved. I thought it was like a game. I was supposed to be there at one to help search Chris."

She got there at one, she said. Busenburg's truck was there, she waited, he didn't come out, she waited until 3 A.M. "I went back to my apartment to see if he had called." Hatton's truck wasn't at the Aubry Hills, she said. "I thought something had happened, that Chris and his Navy SEAL friends had killed Will."

Afraid, she said, she drove around and around, too scared to stop and talk to anyone. She returned to Hatton's apartment. "The lights were off. Maybe the TV was on. It was less light than before."

At 3:30 A.M., she said, she parked the car, left it running, got out and listened at the apartment, went back to the car, and started driving around again. She then went back to her apartment around 4 A.M., she said, and waited until 4:30. She returned at 4:45 to Hatton's apartment and Busenburg said, "I just called you."

"I was screaming and crying. Will hadn't talked about shooting him, but earlier he had joked about shooting Chris to me and Lynn Carroll."

"How did he joke?"

"He said that Chris was worthless and depressed. Maybe he should just take him out in a field and just shoot him."

"Would Chris have let you in his apartment?"

"Yes," she answered. "I saw him about ten times. I never had visited him by myself, but, um, if I had shown up there, he would have been surprised and wondered why I was there. Chris was down on women because his girlfriend had screwed him over."

Tuesday, during the day, said Martin, she was worried about the cops. "I said, 'If they do come to arrest you, I'll say I shot him in self-defense. That he tried to rape me.' " Then, when they sat in the cop car after they were arrested, said Martin, "Will turned around and said, 'You'd better take the rap for this.' "

Again Martin was asked what clothes Busenburg had on.

"He threw them on the floor of my apartment. It was dark outside. I didn't look."

"Did he ever get rid of the clothes?"

"I think they were at the apartment. When he got back, he undressed and took a shower, and he said, 'We have to move the body.' "

They decided to take a break.


Afterward, the district attorneys again showed Martin incriminating receipt after incriminating receipt, including those for the firewood.

Martin explained that they spent New Year's Eve, and January 5 and 6, at Will's mother's home. "I danced that night. He picked me up from work. It was Thursday night, Friday morning. We bought firewood for the fireplace and used it that night. I don't remember if I was with him or not when he bought it. We went to his mom's house because he wanted to be with his dog."

The firewood to burn Hatton's body, said Martin, they purchased on Saturday, January 7. She again explained the camping plan. "I don't know if he was planning to kill him then or not."

She told the prosecutors of Will's mission to Colombia and his phone call from the jet to her. "He told me about the mission in detail."

"Did he ever tell you about the books he read?"

She nodded. "Navy SEAL books. Anne Rice. He talked about his missions all the time. Um," she looked at Davis, "uh, I wanted to go with him to be with him, not to kill anybody." She repeated, "Will joked about killing Chris. He said he was training him to be a hit man. But he said Chris is reckless and talks too much."

They asked her about her drug use.

"I smoked pot a few times. I didn't do coke at all. And I never used drugs at all with Will. Oh, I tried coke when I was eighteen. But I never did drugs while dancing."

Martin glanced over at her attorney, and chose her words very carefully. "I just think I made some irrational decisions in not calling the cops, lying to them, and believing Will."

Stephanie Martin was flirtatious with Frank Bryan. She was charming with Allison Wetzel. Wetzel walked away from the meeting realizing that Stephanie Martin was a likeable person. Wetzel analyzed the situation. There was a con to Martin being likeable. The men on the jury would like her, too.

Busenburg's trial was set for the following month. Chris Gunter had been willing to agree to a tampering with physical evidence charge. The prosecutors had turned that down flat.

Gunter had said that Busenburg wouldn't plead guilty to murder no matter what the sentence. Then the prosecutors had discovered Chris Hatton's credit cards in Busenburg's possession. Theft made Will Busenburg eligible for capital murder.

Suddenly, more and more time served was becoming more and more acceptable to Chris Gunter and Will Busenburg.

# Twenty-five

"Good afternoon," said Judge Mike Lynch. "We are here on the record in Cause Number 96-3350, the State of Texas versus William Busenburg."

It was Wednesday, November 6, 1996, and Stephanie Martin, in her orange jailhouse clothes, had just been led out of the Travis County courtroom. Some people, in that large, chilly, judicial room, didn't want Martin to hear what was about to be said.

Prosecutors Frank Bryan and Allison Wetzel huddled at their table. Will Busenburg, his head bent low, and Chris Gunter spoke quietly.

In the gallery sat Chris Hatton's tired and grief-stricken grandparents and a seething Robert and Sandra Martin. Robert Martin was furious because Ira Davis was honeymooning in Italy while Stephanie Martin sat in jail. Martin had had to pay Davis an additional $25,000 just for the capital murder charge. Robert Martin glanced at David Fannin, Davis's cocounsel.

The docket read that the day was to be Busenburg's plea hearing on Count One, capital murder; Count Two, offense of murder, intentional murder; and Count Three, conspiracy to commit capital murder. Frank Bryan planned to proceed only on Count Two.

"State calls William Busenburg," said Bryan.

In his green jail smock, Busenburg stood, was sworn in, then sat back down at the defense table.

"The state has a motion to amend Count Two of the indict
ment," said Bryan. He wanted the words "and by poisoning
him" added to that murder charge. The amendment had already
been handwritten on the actual indictment. "We would ask the
court to accept that amendment, and I believe it is agreed be
tween the state and the defense."

"All right," said Lynch.

Judge Lynch looked over at Busenburg. "It's . . . my understanding that this is all being done as part of a plea bargain
agreement between you and your attorney and the state, and
that you have no opposition to the amendment. . . .

"Yes, sir." Busenburg's voice was soft.

The judge waived Counts One and Three, then read the indictment. "The grand jury has alleged in Count Two of this
indictment that on the tenth day of January in 1995, here in
Travis County, Texas, that William Busenburg—that's you—did
then and there intentionally and knowingly cause the death of
an individual, namely Christopher Hatton, by shooting him
with a deadly weapon, namely a firearm, and by poisoning him

"That is the state's amended indictment, and the court has
granted—based on the fact that there is no opposition to the
amendment . . . the court has granted the state's motion and
so amended the indictment. Do you understand the indictment
as amended in Count Two?"

"Yes, sir," said Busenburg.

Lynch leaned over his bench for a better stare into the eyes
of Will Busenburg. "Do you have any questions for the court
or for your attorney concerning that?"

"No, sir."

"Then to the charges contained in Count Two of this indictment, let me ask you at this time, how do you plead, guilty or
not guilty?"

"Guilty.

The Hatton family sighed in relief. They wanted this thing
over. They didn't want to suffer a trial.

The judge lifted three pieces of paper and waved them at

Busenburg. The pages were the State's Exhibit 1, Busenburg's waiver of certain rights, his confession, and his written guilty plea. "Have you and your attorney, Mr. Gunter, had a full opportunity to go over this entire document, all three pages?"

"Yes, sir."

Three times the judge asked Busenburg if he fully understood what was happening. Three times Busenburg said, "Yes, sir."

"Did you sign page three freely and voluntarily, indicating that you understood your rights, that you understood the consequences of pleading guilty, and that understanding these things and after a full consultation with counsel, you wanted to waive your rights and plead guilty in this cause?"

"Yes, sir."

Three times the judge asked Busenburg if he was pleading guilty to Count Two. Three times Busenburg said, "Yes, sir."

"You understand, sir, that Count Two is intentional murder. That, in the State of Texas, is a first degree felony. The range of punishment is a minimum of five years to a maximum of ninety-nine years in the penitentiary, or a life sentence. Do you understand that?"

"Yes, sir."

"And you could receive up to a ten-thousand-dollar fine."

"Yes, sir," he answered politely.

Lynch asked Busenburg again if he understood.

"Yes, sir."

The judge emphasized to the young, confessed killer that because Busenburg had used a deadly weapon in the murder of Chris Hatton, the offender would be required to serve one half of his sentence before he could be eligible for parole. There would absolutely be no good-time credit. "Do you understand?"

"Yes, sir."

He told Busenburg that there could be no appeal, either, as a term of the plea bargain. "Do you understand that, Mr. Busenburg?"

"Yes, sir."

Again Judge Lynch made clear that there would be no appeal. And again Busenburg agreed.

"All right." Judge Lynch leaned back in his chair. "The state may proceed at this time."

Slowly and softly Busenburg walked over to the witness stand and stepped into the box.

"State your name," said Frank Bryan.

"William Busenburg."

Busenburg listened as Bryan reread Count Two for Busenburg and the Hattons to relive again—knowingly shooting Chris Hatton and poisoning him. "Is everything stated in Count Two of this indictment true and correct?"

"Yes, sir," Busenburg answered.

"And you are pleading guilty because you are guilty and for no other reason," said Bryan.

"Yes, sir," said Busenburg.

"And your lawyer has been over with you the meaning of being an accomplice or a party as opposed to being a principal in committing an offense," said Bryan. "Is that correct?"

"Are you pleading guilty to Count Two in this indictment as a principal, or as a party?"

"As a party, sir."

"And was another person involved in the commission of this offense with you?"

"Yes, sir."

"Who was that?"

"Stephanie Martin."

Sandra and Robert Martin stiffened.

"The victim," said Frank Bryan, "Christopher Hatton, was shot in the head with a shotgun. Who was it that shot Christopher Hatton in the head with a shotgun?"

"Stephanie Martin."

Sandra and Robert Martin's mouths fell open.

Stephanie Martin turned to the guard in the holding room and asked, "What's happening?"

"You're getting screwed."

Robert Martin now wanted Chris Gunter as his daughter's attorney.

Frank Bryan continued. "[You will testify truthfully to the facts of this murder] leading up to the day of the murder and following the murder. Do you understand that?"

"Yes, sir."

"And that truthful testimony includes your testimony today on the witness stand; it includes your being truthful with me between now and the trial of Stephanie Martin; and all the way up until the time you are sentenced, you must be truthful in order to uphold your part of the plea bargain. Do you understand?"

"Yes, sir."

"Do you also understand," said Frank Bryan, "that if you are not truthful, then you are not upholding your end of the bargain, and the state does not have to uphold its end of the bargain; in other words, when we get to your sentencing, if you have not been truthful to me, I can tell this judge that the defendant has not gone through with his end of the bargain agreement and give you whatever I think is appropriate at this time. Do you understand?"

"Yes, sir."

Bryan presented Busenburg the defendant's written guilty plea and confession, signed by Busenburg.

Busenburg agreed that he had signed it, that he had gone over it with Gunter, and that he understood it.

Bryan asked Busenburg if he understood that he was waiving his right to a jury trial.

"Yes, sir."

The documents were admitted as evidence.

Bryan showed Busenburg a written waiver of appeal, signed by Busenburg and Gunter—State's Exhibit Number 2. "And you understand this is part of the plea bargain, and that I will hold on to this and file this with the court at the time of your sentencing?"

"Yes, sir."

"And you also understand that it is part of the plea bargain agreement that this case will be reset for sentencing at a date after Stephanie Martin's case has been resolved or tried?"

"Yes, sir."

Frank Bryan passed the witness.

Chris Gunter looked at his client. "Will, what is your understanding of what the state's recommendation will be?"

"Forty-year plea bargain."

Judge Lynch turned once again to address the round-faced murderer. "Is it still your desire to persist in your plea of guilty today to the offense of murder?"

"Yes, sir," said Busenburg.

"What is the state's recommendation?" asked Lynch.

"Judge," answered Bryan, "the plea agreement is, the defendant pleads guilty to Count Two of the indictment as amended; he waives appeal on all issues, including all matters raised at pretrial hearings; the defendant agrees to give truthful testimony at the time of his plea and in preparation of the trial of Stephanie Martin; and the defendant agrees that his case will be rested until after the trial of Stephanie Martin. In exchange for those things—"

"Does it also include testimony at the trial?" asked Lynch. "I didn't hear that."

"That's correct. It does," answered Bryan. "Truthful testimony at the trial. . . . It includes truthful testimony from the defendant up until the time that he is sentenced."

"All right," said Lynch.

"And he also agrees that his case will be reset until after [the] trial of Stephanie Martin."

"All right."

"And in return for those things, the state is recommending forty years in the Texas Department of Criminal Justice, and we agree to dismiss the other pending cases, which are third degree felony—a few third degree felonies. I know there's unauthorized use of motor vehicle and theft of firearm. There may be something else—any other pending cases."

"Mr. Busenburg," said Lynch, "is that your understanding of the agreement?"

"Yes, sir," he answered.

"Do you have any questions about it?"

"No, sir."

"And are you willing to accept that if the court is willing to impose that sentence?"

"Yes, sir."

"Then the court finds at this time that based on your testimony, based on State's Exhibit Number One and everything presented to the court this afternoon, that your plea has been freely, knowingly, and voluntarily entered. It also appears to the court that there is evidence to substantiate your guilt. At this time, however, I'm not going to make any further findings or enter any judgment or accept the plea bargain agreement, but I'm going to refer the case to the probation department for their presentence report, and we're going to reset sentencing until after punishment and sentencing after the trial of Stephanie Martin. Is that correct?"

Chris Gunter said it was.

Lynch set a trial date of Thursday, December 19, 1996. "And if the trial of Stephanie Martin has not occurred, then we can reset that probably without a formal hearing. If that case is disposed of earlier, and either side or both sides would like to expedite the hearing in this case, then we can do that also."

Court was recessed.

"This kind of changes a lot of stuff," said David Fannin to Robert and Sandra Martin. "You'd better call Ira next week, and we'd better sit down and talk."

# Twenty-six

On Friday, January 17, 1997, two years and three days after Will Busenburg and Stephanie Martin had been arrested, Frank Bryan, Allison Wetzel, their investigator John Phillips, and Chris Gunter sat down with Busenburg at the Travis County jail.

The prosecutors were there to hear in person, for the first time, Busenburg's side of the story. They were there to prepare for Stephanie Martin's trial. Busenburg was ill, Wetzel was pregnant, and neither one of them wanted to be breathing across from each other in that cramped interview room.

Busenburg lowered his head as he spoke. "I met Stephanie in early October at the Yellow Rose. Chris was with me that night. Stephanie came up and started talking to me. A week later, I saw her again at the Rose. She asked me if I wanted to go to breakfast. We went to the Magnolia Cafe, and after that we were always together."

"What about that first night? What'd you talk about?"

"The first night at the club, Chris and I were kind of playing a game, telling all kinds of wild stories. He said he was a Navy SEAL. I said I was in the CIA. We laid it on pretty thick."

"Had you ever told that story before?"

"No, but Steph was into it. She was excited. She said she liked to wave pistols in her apartment and pretend like she was shooting people. She thought it was neat that I was part of a sniper group."

"How long did you talk?"

"About an hour, an hour and a half. When I saw her about a week later, I had some buddies from work with me. But when we went to breakfast, it was just Stephanie and me." She stayed with him, he said, at his apartment.

"How did Stephanie get along with Chris?"

"She thought he was a hick, that he talked country, acted country." His words fired right out of his mouth. "There was animosity between Stephanie and Chris because he thought she was a gold digger. But it didn't bother him that she was a topless dancer."

The prosecutors knew that contradicted what the Conways would testify to.

Busenburg talked about Hatton's breakup with Lisa Pace and how she came over to the apartment. "She and I were pals in school," he said.

Bryan and Wetzel made note again: That's not what Lisa Pace thought.

Busenburg claimed that he had been the ROTC commander in high school and that Hatton had been depressed about getting discharged from the Navy. "He was a rush junkie," he said. "He was always taking risks. He was drunk all the time."

The Conways and Hattons had given affidavits stating otherwise.

"I had to wake him up in the mornings, and he was hard to wake up. He was always late for work. He drank lots of Jim Beam, but as long as he hit most of his stores, his boss wouldn't notice."

"Why'd you decide to move out?"

"Stephanie said Chris was a bad influence, and I was staying with her most of the time, anyway. I moved my bed to Steph's right before Thanksgiving. By then, I was seeing her every day. I told her the rescue story about getting my buddy out of Colombia."

"Where'd you get your stories?"

"From memories of movies on TV and books."

Busenburg and Wetzel couldn't handle the conversation anymore. He was too ill; she couldn't chance getting ill. A half hour after the conversation began, it ended.

On Wednesday, January 22, 1997, the same group gathered at the county jail, with Busenburg feeling better.

Allison Wetzel pulled out her legal pad. Frank Bryan reached for his lucky Pentel pen. The young Republican didn't believe he could win a case without it. "What did Stephanie say about wanting to be involved in a mission?"

"From the very beginning," Busenburg answered, "she was as excited as she could be. She would get mad at someone and say she wanted to kill him. She would get mad at Chris and say she wanted to kill him. I just started out this mission stuff as a game. I was just trying to impress this girl in a bar. I didn't think it was going to turn into a relationship."

But once it became a relationship, he said, he didn't want to keep talking about the missions. "I tried to avoid talking about it. But she was into it."

Then he emphasized, "Whenever she got mad, she always said, 'I should kill that guy.' A week before the murder, there was a guy at the gas station who wouldn't take her check. She was really angry and talked all night about wanting to kill him."

Busenburg stopped and returned to Martin and Hatton. "At first it was like a joke saying she wanted to kill Chris. Then I got used to hearing her say it."

By January 1995, he told the prosecutors, he was living with Martin, and because of that, he didn't pay any of the rent at Aubry Hills. Hatton, though, phoned Busenburg's mother, he said, and asked her for the rent money.

The week before the murder, he went back to Aubry Hills to get his belongings, he said. "Chris was drunk and in a bad mood, so I left. I went to my mom's." That's when he learned that Hatton had phoned her asking for rent money, he explained. "I got mad about that and told Stephanie. She said, 'We should kill him,'' and she kept saying it over and over again."

He told the prosecutors that he had paid all the Aubry Hills deposits and the first, second, and third months' rent. "Chris had only paid his share twice."

Busenburg explained about the missing check that Martin had claimed was the cause of much of the fuss. "It was for the down payment on my truck," he said.

He said he had purchased a cashier's check to make the down payment, but the dealership had wanted two separate cashier's checks, not one. He returned to the bank, got two new cashier's checks, and the teller returned the original to him, which he placed in his lockbox. "I thought Chris had taken the check."

The prosecutors hadn't been able to find anyone who had actually seen that check.

Busenburg next stated that he and Martin had regularly batted about the pros and cons of various ways to murder Chris Hatton.

"Why did Stephanie want Chris dead?"

"Part of it was the thrill," he answered. "Part of it was the dispute about the money. And the more we talked about it, the more normal it seemed."

"If that's why Stephanie wanted him dead, what about you?"

Busenburg shrugged. "Just meanness."

The prosecutors looked up. Busenburg seemed a bit embarrassed by his comment. The attorneys were beginning to believe his story, the way he implicated himself, the way Martin had refused to implicate herself at all. It made sense to them.

"The plan was that we would poison Chris so that there wouldn't be any mess. We would take him out to a remote area and burn his remains. His body would disappear and people would think that he had joined the Foreign Legion."

The first step they took toward that path was to purchase sleeping pills from two different grocery stores, he said. One store was an Albertsons grocery store, but Busenburg couldn't remember which location. The other store, he said, "was the Randalls by the Yellow Rose on Lamar."

He digressed and emphasized, "When Steph always talked about killing people, it was always about killing men. She never

lked about killing women. Stephanie loves women more than
do."

He moved on and told Bryan and Wetzel that he and Martin
ought kitchen gloves, sleeping pills, lighter fluid, and several
mes they bought firewood. "On Sunday we bought some kind
f poison—either ant, mouse or rat." He was "pretty sure" they'd
ought it at Albertsons. For certain, he knew he made two trips
 the grocery store with Martin and both times he wrote checks.

One of the firewood purchases, said Busenburg, wasn't in-
nded to be used to burn the body. But the other purchases—
vo, in fact—were to be used to burn the body, he said.

The prosecutors looked at the receipts for firewood that sat
efore them, receipts that predated the murder. Inside, Bryan
nd Wetzel nodded; their theory that the murder had been pre-
editated had just been reinforced.

"We used one bundle of wood at my mom's house. That was
ither Friday or Thursday [before the murder]. I'd just gotten
ff work. Stephanie had gone to work. My mother was in Utah.
tephanie met me in Round Rock after she got off from work.
hen we went to have a night by the fire. I got there about
idnight. She got there about one."

Quickly the prosecutors moved on. "Then what happened?"
hey didn't want to think about what "a night by the fire"
ntailed.

"The next morning we woke up and went back to Austin. I
icked my mother up at the airport on Sunday. I got my pay-
heck at work on Friday, January thirteenth."

"Was Stephanie with you when you got your paycheck?"

"Probably." Busenburg said they went to a couple of ATM
nachines on January 13. "She made a deposit of one hun-
lred dollars." He deposited his paycheck and got $170 in
ash. "We went to the Seven-Eleven on Manchaca to check
ny balance. Then we went to the Albertsons on Slaughter to
heck the balance. I remember we went to a lot of different
TM machines."

"Saturday," he said, "I went to the apartment to get my com-

puter desk. I needed Chris's drill, and the door to his room wa
locked. On Sunday I came back and got a drill bit. Stephanie
found a lockbox in Chris's closet."

Chris, he said, had a camera and some of Will's clothes. They
took Hatton's credit cards and went to Levitz, where they used
Hatton's credit card to buy the couch and table and chairs. They
took the table and chairs with them and went back on Wednes
day for the couch. "We knew we were gonna kill Chris when
we used the credit cards."

On their first attempt to kill Hatton, said Busenburg, Mar
tin went over to Hatton's. "She was going to say she wa:
looking for me. I was waiting in the parking lot. The plan
was that Stephanie would wait with Chris and have a drink
She came out about two or three in the morning and said
that she'd put the sleeping pills in his Jim Beam but he didn'
go to sleep."

Bryan and Wetzel made a note: Martin's story had been the
opposite; Busenburg had gone in, while she stayed outside.

Busenburg explained that the couple had broken apart the
capsules. "And she said when he left the room, she put them
in his drink." They thought that would be enough to kill him
said Busenburg. "Then the plan was that she would come and
get me and we'd burn the body. She poured the powder in his
drink when he went to the bathroom."

"On Sunday, we went back to get the computer table. I
was taking it apart, and Stephanie was going through Chris's
stuff. I told her Chris had stolen my check," said Busenburg,
referring to the cashier's check. "I knew the check wa:
worthless."

The prosecutors' hands stopped writing; they were confused
by Busenburg's check story, but they understood the bottom
line: Will Busenburg had never been out $5,700. Busenburg
had only used that check to make Stephanie Martin angry at
Chris Hatton.

"Why did you keep encouraging her in this fantasy?"

"Because I was scared I was gonna lose her. That was her

ttraction to me. I put her on a pedestal. She was pretty, a rich
irl, and too good for me."

He then said they got Hatton's credit limit raised while they
vere at Levitz.

"How'd you do that?"

"We just talked to a salesman at the store."

After the Levitz trip, said Busenburg, he went to the airport
o get his mother, went out to eat, and then drove over to Mar-
in's apartment, got her, and drove out to Lynn Carroll's house.
hey stayed at Carroll's until 9:30 or 10 P.M., then went to
Albertsons. "We bought rat poison and sleeping pills."

"How'd you pay for it?"

"With a check."

"Then what?"

"We went to a Taco Cabana and bought a burrito." They
eturned to Martin's apartment, he explained. "We crushed rat
oison into the burrito. Then I went to Chris's apartment by
myself." Hatton wasn't at home, he said, so Busenburg waited
n hour with the intention of giving the poisoned burrito to his
riend. "Stephanie was at home, and I was going to call her
ifter Chris was dead."

There was a point, he noted, when he thought Martin was
osing her confidence. "After using the credit cards, I knew I
vas going to have to kill him." Busenburg left Hatton's apartment for a couple of hours, then returned, only to find Hatton
till not at home, he said.

"On Monday morning, we went to the mall and went to
Sears, Kay Jewelers, and Montgomery Ward." At Wards, he
mentioned, they purchased a camera and a battery. "That night,
Stephanie dropped me off at work. I worked until eleven and
vent straight over to Chris's." They then went to Hatton's workplace and stole Hatton's bicycle by cutting the lock.

"Why did you steal Chris's bike?"

"Just out of spite."

When Busenburg finally saw Hatton, Hatton wasn't jumpy
or suspicious, said the inmate. "He was extra nice and seemed

to have cooled off from the week before. . . . We sat and had a drink."

Busenburg then returned to Martin's and reported to her Hatton's demeanor. "So Stephanie wanted to do it again." He followed Martin back to Hatton's apartment, he said. "I thought that the food thing would make him throw up."

The prosecutors looked at Busenburg, believing he'd thrown that little tidbit in to make himself look better—as though he thought Hatton had a chance of living if he'd thrown up, despite telling them he knew Hatton was going to die after they used his credit cards.

"On Monday we went to Chris's in two vehicles. We decided Stephanie would go in, because she had a better excuse to show up. She was gonna say she was at work and got bored. I waited outside in the parking lot. Then she came outside about two or three o'clock. She was kinda excited, like she was in shock, and said, 'He's dead. I shot him.' And I said, 'Why?' She said, 'Because I thought it would please you.' "

"Did you hear a shot?"

"No, I didn't. She told me that Chris had gone to bed, but she went into Chris's room and shot him. The only gun in the apartment was Chris's."

The prosecutors asked Busenburg about the various guns.

The 12-gauge Winchester Defender shotgun with the short barrel was Hatton's, he said. The similar 12-gauge but with a pistol grip was his. "The month before, the guy I worked with gave me a loan for it—one hundred fifty dollars. I had a twelve-gauge Mossberg that was at Stephanie's apartment. She owned a twelve-gauge shotgun loaned to her by her dad."

"What'd you do after Stephanie told you she'd killed Chris?"

"I went into the apartment. I flipped on the light. Chris was in bed with the covers thrown off. His arms were in front of him. His legs were up in the air. The top of his head was gone. I couldn't see any blood on Stephanie. I was mad. 'This is not what was supposed to have happened,' I said to Stephanie."

"Could you have shot Chris?"

"I couldn't have done something like that—not while he was asleep. I asked Stephanie, 'Why did you do this?' She started shaking, and she said, 'He's dead. Isn't this what we wanted?' "

# Twenty-seven

Busenburg calmly explained to the prosecutors that he and Martin wrapped Hatton's body in covers and dragged it into the bathroom. Then, said Busenburg, he sent Martin home.

"Why?"

"Maybe to get cleaning supplies." He called her at her apartment and left a message asking her where she was, he said. "She pulled up right when I was talking to the machine. That night was the only remorse by her that I saw. The rest of the week she teased me and said I was a 'puss.' "

The prosecutors thought that over. Sure, it explained the call on Martin's ID, but they still didn't have proof positive as to who dialed that number. "How did she know how to use a gun?"

"I taught her how to use a shotgun with my Mossberg." His shotgun, he pointed out, was bigger than Hatton's. Hatton, he said, always kept a shell loaded in the chamber.

Busenburg explained that as he sat outside of the apartment, he saw the lights go out in Hatton's and thirty minutes later, Martin came out. "I thought about going up. I even started to go up, then I changed my mind.

"On Thursday," he said, "she came up with the whole story about the rape. We thought we had gotten away with it, and she said, 'If we do get caught, we'll say he raped me.'

"The night of the shooting, I cleaned up the apartment for maybe an hour before I called her and said, 'Where the hell are you?' When she came back, she was crying, and I was totally calm. As soon as I saw the body, I knew what had to be done. Later I got antsy, and she was ribbing me about it."

The plan, he said, was to clean the apartment, then move the body. They decided to move the body into the bathtub so that it could drain of blood, he explained.

The following morning, Tuesday, Martin drove back to Hatton's apartment. "I was still in bed." When Martin returned, said Busenburg, she was bubbly and excited and carrying a doughnut box filled with a diamond engagement ring, five watches, a couple of necklaces, a class ring, and Busenburg's camera.

"I think she talked to a friend in Las Vegas. I got dressed and went to work and tried to be normal. I went to see my mom. She could tell that something was wrong. I called Stephanie to tell her to get a tarp."

"How did y'all get rid of the body?"

"I couldn't lift his body alone, so I needed Stephanie's help. We laid the body on the tarp and wrapped it up. She helped carry the body to the truck. She told me she knew of an old deserted campground. We drove around and couldn't find it."

Martin knew of another place, he said. It was Pace Bend Park, so they drove there.

"I backed the truck into the firepit and pulled the body out of the truck. She made the fire. We both put the body on the fire—put the torso on the fire—and kept squirting fire juice over the body.

"She kept asking if she could dissect the body. I said, 'No, we don't have time.' She said, 'The hands are not burning.' " It was important for the hands to burn, he stated, so that the body couldn't be identified.

Busenburg had his hacksaw with him, he told the prosecutors, because a couple of days before the murder, he and Martin had discussed hacksawing the body.

The prosecutors still wondered if Busenburg had bought the hacksaw with the sole intention of cutting up Hatton's body. "Where and when did you buy the hacksaw?"

"Sears. Last August." While watching the fire and body, "I

said, 'Just cut his hands off. We can't have any prints.' She cut off his hands. I sat on a bench and watched.

"The first hand, she had a hard time with it. It took her about four to five minutes to get it off. The second hand, she cut through just like butter."

"Just like butter," the prosecutors repeated in their minds.

"She still kept talking about wanting to do an autopsy. She reached down with plastic gloves and pointed out a certain feature of his brain."

Tonya Williams, the name flashed in Bryan's and Wetzel's thoughts: Martin had pointed to a feature in Hatton's brain. Maybe that's what Stephanie Martin's former cellmate had meant when she said Martin had stuck her hand in Hatton's head.

"Stephanie said some sick prayer over the body and asked me, 'Would it excite you if I had sex with the body?' She wanted to look at his genitals, and she squirted the lighter fluid on his genitals. I thought I heard something in the woods. It spooked me."

They left.

"I followed Stephanie down the road." He was in Hatton's truck. She was in her car. "She was swerving all over the road." They stopped at a gas station, then went to another station and left the truck there, he recalled. Busenburg stuffed everything, including the tarp, in the cab of the truck. By that time, it was five or five-thirty in the morning and still dark, he said. Then he drove them home in her car.

"I called in sick the rest of the week. On Wednesday we went to Levitz and picked up the couch. Her dad came over and helped."

Later that night, said Busenburg, they returned to Hatton's to clean the apartment. "We found blood under the bed and dumped the mattresses." On Thursday, he said, they went back and cleaned for a couple more hours. "Stephanie got some paint from her mother's. We couldn't get the blood out of the carpet. One day during the week, I can't remember which one, we took the day off and didn't go over to the apartment."

"Took the day off." The phrase reverberated in the prosecutors' heads. "Took the day off." Just like it was from a job.

He said they also went to the pawnshop that week.

"Whose idea was that?"

"I'm not sure. The pawn people gave us seventy dollars for one ring. I remember talking to Beck." He meant Beck Steiner, his boss at the movie theater. They talked about leaving town, he said. "He showed us a list of different theaters where I could work. Money wasn't a problem for Stephanie. She could be a stripper anywhere. She could make between three hundred and five hundred dollars in a night.

"We took pictures of cleaning up the apartment." He couldn't remember whether they finished the roll or if the film was left in the camera. "There were a half a dozen rolls of film that I don't think ever got developed." They included his and Martin's trips to Houston and San Antonio, he said. "Pictures of her naked and pictures of me on the couch."

The prosecutors had in their possession topless photos of Martin, photos that were home snapshots, not photos from her Yellow Rose shoot. "What was in the pictures y'all took when you were cleaning up in the apartment?"

"There was one of her on her hands and knees scrubbing Chris's carpet with a brush," Busenburg replied.

"What'd you do with the camera?"

"We took it back to Stephanie's apartment, or maybe we left it in the car. Her father picked up a lot of stuff in the apartment and in her car." He described the camera as a black or gray, long, flat camera.

Busenburg went on to say that he kept all of Martin's letters but one and that he told the police he was born in 1972 because that was the date on his license.

"I tried to sell Chris's truck. I asked Beck if he knew anyone that wanted to buy an old truck, TV, or VCR."

"Did Stephanie know you were out of money?"

"No, she thought I was rich. Otherwise, she wouldn't have stayed around."

"How'd you meet Chris?"

"Through ROTC in ninth or tenth grade. I graduated from Skyview High School in Billings, Montana, in 1992."

"What about any presents you gave her?"

"For Christmas I got her a TV. I put it on my Sears account. I bought her a VCR a couple of weeks before. And I also got her a bong, some perfume, and a vibrator."

"Did you do drugs together?"

"We did Ecstasy a couple of times. She was constantly smoking weed. I smoked it with her a couple of times. She did speed and coke a few times."

Bryan and Wetzel thought about Martin's interview. Her account of drug use was different from Busenburg's. "What was so exciting about Stephanie?"

"I was always a good boy, dated good girls, church girls like Emily Eaves. I'd never been to a strip joint before, until I went there with Chris. He was the one who went to strip clubs. And I was surprised that the girls were pretty. I expected them to be slutty." He repeated for emphasis, "I was surprised that they weren't slutty. Stephanie looked like a pretty cheerleader-type. I gave her everything I had. I paid her rent. I borrowed money to give her gifts."

"What was the attraction? Was it her personality? The way she looked? Was it sex?"

"She was manipulative," Busenburg stated. "She was in control of the whole relationship. It was bizarre and amazing for me to be able to date a dancer. Sex was not the attraction. I would do things to her during sex. And then I would have to force myself to have sex with her. She had a complex about it."

Over and over again, Martin had claimed Busenburg was the best lover she'd ever had. Bryan and Wetzel had read a hundred or more pages of letters between the inmates that touted Martin's sexual joy with Busenburg. They knew them too well. In those letters, Busenburg hadn't complained, either.

"She was a fantasy to me. Chris had told me that dancers

were the hardest people in the world to pick up. Some of them were real aggressive. Some were friendly."

"If it hadn't been for you, would Stephanie have done this?"

"She was involved in some kind of Satanic cult," he answered. "She was in it with some other girlfriend. It might have been Roxy. Lynn thought that Chris was cute. Stephanie got mad at Lynn and said, 'No way. He's white trash.' She told Roxy that she hated Chris and that he was using me. After the murder, she wanted to tell Lynn and Roxy about it, and I told her not to tell anybody. In letters, she hinted about telling the DA about getting the camper from her parents, and her parents said no."

Bryan and Wetzel leaned back in their chairs. There were so many stories that it was hard to sift between manipulation and truth.

"In the police car," Busenburg continued, "after we were arrested, the police left us alone for a couple of minutes."

The prosecutors shook their heads. That was a blatant oversight of police procedure. "What'd y'all talk about?"

"She asked if I was all right and said, 'Remember about the rape.' I said, 'Are you sure?' And she said, 'Yes.' Then at the jail, after we were talked to separately, she said, 'Did you stick with the story?' Then some cop grabbed her and she couldn't say anything else.

"Fletcher Mack, this murderer I met in jail, told me to be careful about what I say because they might be reading my mail. And Chris"—he looked over at his attorney—"Chris Gunter told me not to write to Stephanie, but I kept writing to her."

"Why?"

"Because she was my girlfriend—"

Gunter interrupted. He informed the prosecutors that he had relayed to Ira Davis that there was film in a camera that could have some incriminating photos on it.

The prosecutors looked at him. Gunter was noticeably careful in how he phrased his words. "What did Ira say when you told him that?"

"Ira just said, 'Okay.'"

They turned their attention back to Busenburg.

"Everything we bought with Chris's credit cards was for Stephanie, except for one watch and one earring."

The prosecutors had one last question. They asked again, "Why did you steal his bike?"

Busenburg answered again, "It was just out of meanness. We had tried the sleeping pills the first time, and he didn't fall asleep. And she was so frustrated. I just thought it was something spiteful to do."

Bryan and Wetzel left the county jail. Neither one of them thought Will Busenburg seemed like the type who would, on a whim, shoot Chris Hatton in his own apartment just for the thrill of it. Plan it, yes. Do it on a whim, no.

Stephanie Martin had been running around telling her friends she wanted to know what it felt like to kill someone. . . . That thought wouldn't leave their prosecutorial minds.

The last week of January 1996, Robert Martin sat in Ira Davis's office. "I've been called by the grand jury," he said.

"Get another lawyer," Davis replied. "I can't deal with you. Get another lawyer. Protect yourself."

Davis pointed Martin down the hallway to David Reynolds, a former prosecutor renowned for annoying the DAs with his nit-picking at details.

With Reynolds's help, Martin refused to answer the grand jury's questions. Bryan and Wetzel marched Martin in front of District Judge Wilford Flowers. Flowers ordered the father to testify.

Finally Martin stepped into the grand jury room. To almost every question he was asked, he responded, "I can't answer that question without my lawyer's opinion." Then he got up, walked out of the room, spoke with Reynolds, walked back in, sat back down, and said, "No, I can't answer that question because it might incriminate my daughter's case."

He knew that within the first fifteen minutes he'd antagonized every older person in the room, and there were numerous older people in the room. He knew he was angering the two assistant district attorneys. He knew he looked like he was hiding something.

He was asked about the camera Busenburg and Gunter had mentioned, photographs, and the crime scene.

Martin wanted to answer, "You want to search my house? Go ahead." He said, "No, I can't answer that without my lawyer's opinion."

Forty-five minutes later, Robert Martin walked out of the grand jury room. He turned to his wife. "We just spent five thousand dollars, and all we did was alienate the grand jury, Frank Bryan, and Allison Wetzel. That was wrong." He sighed.

Sandra Martin went through the same process. "I can't answer that question because it might incriminate my daughter's case." She, too, annoyed everyone in the grand jury room.

"This is a big risk," Stephanie Martin's lawyers sternly offered. "Fifty percent chance of capital murder, the way it is right now. Fifty percent at best."

Martin's trial date was just weeks away. Stephanie Martin and her parents knew that the attorneys were telling the truth.

On the table was the offer of a plea bargain—capital murder lowered to first degree murder and fifty years of incarceration— ten years more than what William Busenburg had been offered.

Robert Martin shook his head. "What about conspiracy?"

"Yeah, they'll try us on capital," the attorneys replied. "And if they don't get a conviction, they'll try us on conspiracy to commit capital murder."

"Why don't they just ask for life and we can go to trial and get this over with?" asked Robert Martin. "Where are we going with this?"

"This is not bad. This is only twenty-five years before parole."

"Yeah," Robert moaned facetiously. "What does that mean? Forty years' serving time, maybe. Let's go to trial. We can prove that Will lied. He lied all the time. Nothing about him was real."

"This is why . . ." Stephanie couldn't keep quiet. She'd

made at least half a dozen inconsistent statements. They had the letters she'd sent Busenburg. She'd gotten in trouble at Del Valle time and again—knocking off a sprinkler head, playing a radio, passing notes, holding hands with an inmate. "And this is why. . . ."

"What about the truth?" said Sandra Martin.

"In most trials, the truth never comes out. It's perception."

Stephanie Martin was scared. She'd read in the newspaper too many cases where it'd been his word against her word ending in life sentences. She feared if she went to trial she'd get life.

Her attorneys didn't think it helped matters any that their client was scared. "It's too risky."

Stephanie Lynn Martin pleaded guilty to first degree murder. Ira Davis held his sobbing client as she stood in court and said, "I shot Chris Hatton."


On Tuesday, April 29, 1997, construction noise outside the courtroom muffled the words inside. Stephanie Martin still understood that she had to stand in front of William Hatton, Chris Hatton's grandfather.

Rage flowed from Hatton's hands as he reached for his handwritten statement. He looked at his words. He looked at Martin. "Stephanie Martin, you and your accomplice . . ." But Mr. Hatton's words faltered. He tried again. "You and your accomplice, William M. Busenburg, did murder Christopher Michael Hatton in January 1995. And in your twisted minds, you committed this heinous crime with malice of forethought."

He talked about how his grandson had "stood no chance of defending himself" and how Martin and Busenburg "blew his head off with a 12-gauge shotgun," and "hacked off his hands." Hatton began to weep, his words barely able to flow through his tears.

"You received 50 years. That's not enough for what you have done. You have shown a wanton disregard for a human life and really deserve the death penalty. Were I your judge, you would receive the same death sentence you committed on Christopher Michael Hatton."

Tears flooded Martin's cover girl face as Chris Hatton's grandfather spoke of her "sick mind" and the Ten Commandments—"Thou shalt not kill." His own tears returned. His voice choked and provoked long moments of silence. "You have killed a beloved family member who will not be able to live and propagate the family name." He spoke of his nightmares and monetary loss.

"I cannot express the anger and hate my family has for you . . . I will just say . . . repent your sins. . . . And if and when you come up for parole, there will be a Hatton present . . . to refresh the parole board's mind on the heinous crime of murder you committed and detail how it happened. . . . And may God have mercy on you because the Hatton family doesn't have any."

Martin covered her mouth and was led weeping out of the courtroom. "I'm sorry," she whispered.

After the door closed behind her, Will Busenburg was escorted in. He stood, as always, emotionless.

"Mr. Hatton, do you wish to speak to Mr. Busenburg?"

"No."

Judge Lynch looked taken aback. "Would anyone else like to speak? The Martins, do you have anything to say?"

They sat in stunned silence. *Will, you're the biggest coward, the worst coward, I have ever known,* Sandra Martin thought. *And all of your stories about being such a brave, courageous hero were total lies. And you're letting a girl, Stephanie, take the rap and take the blame for what you have done.*

Sandra or Robert Martin didn't get up and say a word. Sandra Martin recalled her daughter's words to her. "There's always hope, Mother. There's always hope that maybe something will happen, and they'll find out. Maybe Will will talk some time. Maybe . . ."

# RETROSPECTIVE

# Twenty-eight

In the spring of 1999, women in white prison clothes and black boots drove tractors along the edges of a central Texas farm road, while guards on horseback patrolled. This was the Hobby Unit, Stephanie Martin's prison home on the outskirts of Marlin, a tiny farming town just minutes from Waco.

The Hobby Unit consisted of acres of crops and orchards, more acres of industrial-like square buildings, beds of land-scaped flowers, and razor wire fences.

Behind the razor wire, Stephanie Martin sat in an interview room. Thin and tanned from hoeing crops, she picked up the phone and rolled her eyes as she mentioned she'd met earlier in the day with a minister from Round Rock. Martin's makeup was no longer the natural look of the Yellow Rose calendar, but the bright hues of a country church-girl.

She looked through eyeglasses and a glass partition. Martin hadn't spoken face-to-face in more than four years. "The truth," she stated, "never came out when I took that plea 'cause, you know, everything got shut off then. I never got the chance to get up in court and tell what really happened.

"So that was always hard for me, because the prosecutors always thought I was there, always said I was there." She lightly, repeatedly slapped the countertop. Martin was ready to dispute stories.

"I was shocked," she said as she focused her memories on Yellow Rose patron Jon Noyes. "He came forward and made

a statement that I had . . . seen him in the Yellow Rose after
met Will and told him all about Will. I told him that he sai
he was a sniper, and that he was in the CIA, and that, he ha
a rifle in his car, in his truck, and said that was one of th
weapons he used.

"And, [Jon] just listened. He didn't say, oh, oh, he's crazy
or anything, you know. He listened. And, I don't know wha
else I said, but he made a statement saying that I . . . also sai
if someone came into my apartment and tried to burglarize me
I would shoot 'em.

"And I think back to that, and . . . I never said that. And . .
I know I didn't say it in the exact words that he said, but
did . . . say that if someone ever tried to get me, I know Wil
would take care of 'em."

Martin stopped. "I think about that." She brushed her long
brown hair with her hands. "Why . . . would [Jon] come forth
and make a bad statement about me? I didn't do anything to
him. Maybe he was mad because I didn't have sex with him.'
Martin guffawed. "I think that must be it."

Her big, sexy smile was no more. She had a broken, white
Chicklet of a front tooth. Another inmate had socked Martin
in the mouth.

She was embarrassed about her tooth, keeping her hand care
fully over her mouth as she spoke. She turned serious, he
thoughts steadying on the apartment Realtor who had turne
Martin's date book over to the sheriffs department.

"I did have a conversation with her, she said. "And we wer
walking by . . . the fence, the security fence around the apart
ments. She says that I said, 'I don't really need a security fenc
because I have a boyfriend' "—Martin chuckled—" 'becaus
I have a boyfriend that would shoot anybody that came near—
tried to burglarize me.' Okay. I probably said it." Martin slappe
the tabletop. "I probably said that."

She slapped the table often, sometimes for emphasis, some
times for joking, sometimes for nervousness. She talked abou
how she'd always had a reputation for being gullible and trust

ng. "Is there a reason? . . . I don't know. Maybe it's the way
was raised. Maybe because I was"—she thought for a sec-
nd—"I was raised good by my parents when I was little and,
m, maybe I just had a good upbringing. . . ."

Martin then adamantly denied any abuse in her background.
lowever, she eventually noted, "I'll tell you what I was—ver-
ally abused by my parents when I was a teenager because they
old me that I was a sinner 'cause they were so religious."


Her thoughts moved to Will Busenburg, a young man she
lescribed as so mesmerizing that she couldn't resist him. "He
vasn't like this hot, macho boy. He was—what attracted me to
im was his eyes. He had beautiful eyes." And with those eyes,
he said, he looked directly into her eyes. "And he would listen
o me so intensely."

Stephanie Martin was not a girl who had been seriously lis-
ened to a lot.

"He made himself sound like a hero, like he did it for the
ountry. Ooh," she called, "that's what he used to tell me. 'I
lo it for my country.' " She laughed.

"He used to go into deep, long discussions with me about
how he felt. He started feeling bad after killing these men.
ven though they were bad men from other countries . . . he
vould go into these things about how he felt. He had a con-
cience about killing them but he did it for his country.

"And that made me look at it as almost okay. That's how I
lidn't just think that he was this hit man going out and picking
is targets and killing them. . . . But it was all very exciting
o me. Dangerous. Secretive. Like he was a spy."

There was also the sympathy factor—his physical and sexual
buse. "Now, if you want to know if this is true or not, yes,
e was sexually and physically abused. His mom and sister
old me that his dad abused all the kids. So I believe them.

"And I believe that that's the one thing true that he told me
bout because he used to have nightmares all the time." Martin

drifted off and talked about Busenburg's tale of killing his father when he was nine years old. "Now that's a serious thing to tell somebody. Especially your second night you meet 'em. And I believed him."

Sitting in the Travis County jail, she recalled, thinking about that lie day after day, night after night, caused her to want to tell her truth. "I couldn't get over how he could lie about something like that and take me in front of this man who [he] called his uncle who was really his dad," she explained.

"And then I couldn't get over the lying about the CIA missions. And, then, when my lawyer started bringing to me all this information that Chris really didn't steal this money, that Chris wasn't going to be a French assassin, that Chris had a family, that they lived in Round Rock, that's when reality started hitting me."

Contrary to what Will Busenburg had told Frank Bryan and Allison Wetzel, contrary to what Stephanie Martin had told Sergeant Gage, she now insisted that Will Busenburg was in the Yellow Rose alone the first night she met him, not with Chris Hatton. "That right there should have made me think twice—to see someone alone in a titty bar." She laughed, then turned serious. "My lawyers have said . . . he hurt his back on a job in Montana, and the money he was spending when he first met me was what was left of a settlement he got.

"I found out after I was arrested that the guy was working in the bottom as a factory worker, you know. . . . He could've just told me that to begin with, but he always wanted to tell big, dramatic stories."

"He was actually twenty-one when I met him, and had been to my high school. . . . I was shocked about everything they told me, but when they told me he went to my high school, I just couldn't believe it, because if I had opened up . . . that yearbook and looked at him and seen that he was twenty-one, that would have led me to finding [out] about all of his lies, and this may have never happened.

"You know, I think about stuff like that all the time."

Inside, the prison was cold and steel. Outside, inmates were hot, sweaty, and tired. Just barely in their view, wine cup wildflowers bloomed over gently rolling terrain.

Back in Austin, the sweet scent of the spring air drove men and boys to the shores of Lake Travis and the firepit barbeque where Chris Hatton had been found. At the Hobby Unit, a hot, sweating inmate stood outside and barbecued dinner for the prisoners. She wiped her brow of sweat.

Martin huddled her body for warmth. She sat in baggy white prison scrubs that hid her figure. She pointed again to her broken front tooth, which, she said, made her look like white trailer-park trash.

It also made Stephanie Martin look more like a growing six-year-old than a woman who pleaded guilty to first degree murder. Without a smile, she began talking about the sleeping pill plan. It had been her father's and her experiences with sleeping pills that helped her and Busenburg decide what brand to buy, she said. Unisom had knocked her father right out. Sleepinal hadn't done much for her.

"So when we considered what the Sleepinal would do to [Chris], I suggested Sleepinal because they were more natural. [Will] really had a disregard for life. He believed that Chris was after him and to the point that he didn't care. My response to that . . . well, I didn't actually agree but I didn't actually disagree.

Martin stared at the prison wall.

"The only time [Will] had mentioned killing [Chris] was . . . when he found the check missing. And that's when he said he wanted to kill him, when we were on our way home from his apartment back to my apartment."

They were driving, she said. "And he was in this rage, which is not much for Will because he doesn't ever show his feelings when he's angry. He never raised his voice at me, but he would get very red-faced. And you could tell he was just holding it all in. He said, 'That was it. That was the last straw.' "

Martin looked weak and clutched her stomach; she was suffering from a stomach virus.

"The truck conversation was very short, and it was really not even real. He said, 'I should kill him for what he did. He stole my check. I think he's after me for my money. I think he's jealous of me. He's crazy already. He wants to kill people.' . . . And he says, 'I should kill him.'

"I said, 'Okay, Will, how are you going to do that?' And that's really all I remember of that conversation. Then he said, 'I don't know,' but he could taste [Chris's] blood. Whenever he talked about killing he said he could taste their blood."

Just as Busenburg had told the prosecutors that the check had been for a payment on his truck, he told Martin, she said, that the payment was for his Lamborghini truck. "That Lamborghini made these special trucks that were millions . . ." She trailed off. "There's probably no such thing. And I asked him, 'Was there such a thing? I never heard of such a car.' He said, 'They're very, very rare.' " She uncomfortably chuckled at the memory. "Everybody laughs at that part, at those types of things."

She returned to the check. "He said that, 'Chris has to be the only one that coulda took it because he's the only one that knew where the key was to the box.' " He meant a lockbox in their shared apartment.

"He also said there was a bomb on the box that Chris knew how to detonate. Will told me he had a bomb in the back of his pickup in case of an emergency." He told her he kept it in the huge tool compartment that rode the width of his truck bed. "He never showed me his bomb, of course. I don't think he even ever opened that tool compartment."

She urged herself forward in the story. "Now me and my lawyer always had trouble with this. I honestly couldn't remember. [Will] thought up the idea of getting [Chris] drunk. I remember mentioning, 'Well, Chris drinks a lot, and you don't. So aren't you going to pass out before he does?' He said, 'Well, maybe I should try something else.' I said, 'Well, maybe sleeping pills.' I'm not for sure, but I believe I'm the one that suggested the sleeping pills.

"He said, 'Well, how am I gonna do that?' . . . Will said he could put it in [Chris's] Jim Beam . . . and he probably wouldn't taste it and that would knock him out." She took a breath.

"He wanted to take him camping and go fishing because Chris had said he'd been wanting to go fishing." That idea came about, Martin explained, as she and Busenburg walked at Twin Falls, a popular Austin swimming hole.

"It was a nice night. It was warm. We were wearing shorts. I had my dog with me, so I wanted to take her for a walk. . . ." She was actually referring to Brunner's dog. "It was wintertime, but it was warm. You know how it is in Austin. And that's where the conversation about the sleeping pills came up and the idea that he'd take him camping and that he would look for the money.

"But I said, 'No. I want to help you look for the money.' I saw this as like some secretive-type thing, and I told him that I wanted to go in with him and help him look for the money. And I didn't want him to go camping because I was also scared of Chris [being] after him. I didn't want him to be out there in the open with Chris, with these people supposedly that had been after him. Because he'd been telling me that Chris and what he said were [Chris's] Navy SEAL friends had been following him.

"We would actually be driving and he'd point out a car and say he thinks that's one of Chris's friends following him. So he had me paranoid of that. Plus, he had me paranoid of the CIA wanting to get rid of him because he had all of this information and he had left the CIA."

"After the discussion at Twin Falls . . . Friday night, we go back, go to eat, do something, didn't talk about it anymore." Busenburg had decided to stick to his decision to take Hatton camping, she said. "So he gets . . . some firewood for the camping trip."

In rhythm to the words, Martin began to slap her palm

against the tabletop. "We get the sleeping pills, the stuff for the camping trip, he goes to his apartment to say he's gonna look for the fishing poles, the tent equipment. He comes back and says—he went to his mom's to get this stuff, right—he says half of it's not there where he remembers it. 'It's too much of a hassle.' So he's just gonna ask Chris if they can hang out at the apartment. I don't think he ever intended to go on the camping trip." She slapped the tabletop again. "That's my opinion. He just came back and, and it was like, 'Oh, no. I'm not gonna worry about all of that. It's too much of a hassle.' No telling what he was doing that time while he was gone, like all those other times."

"So [Will] got some beer." She explained that the beer wasn't purchased at the same time as the sleeping pills and firewood, as well as some lighter fluid. "All this stuff was used later. So this came in as very incriminating evidence. That's why I don't think Will ever intended to go camping. I think he knew that he was going to shoot him and that he wanted to burn the body because that's what they did in the CIA."

Her voice rose. "He always told me that that's what they did in the CIA. . . . He told me his job was to shoot 'em and that that was where he stopped and another guy would come in and burn the bodies. That's the way they got rid of the evidence completely." She paused and began to laugh somewhat facetiously. "Which now contradicts itself . . . Why would he have to burn the bodies if this is ordered by the government when they want to see the person dead to confirm it?

"I'm not sure if he said that all of the bodies were burned, that that's what they did with all of them, but he mentioned that. The night that it happened, he . . . wanted to burn the body. There was no other route. No throwing it over the bridge. No burying it. 'We have to burn the body.' "

She stopped herself, realizing she was getting ahead of her story.

"This was the plan. We're gonna go over there, but I'm gonna be in my car. And as we're talking [in my apartment],

ve're pouring out the Sleepinal into a little packet . . . mini
Ziplock packets." It was the same size packet that dealers use
o package cocaine by the gram, she clarified.

"It only came to me later, what was he doing with that packet
because, well"—her voice deepened—"my lawyer thinks he
might have sold drugs on the side and that's where he was all
those times he told me he was in the CIA." She laughed slightly.
"Because he claimed to me he didn't do drugs."


"And here was the plan—for him to go over there. For me
to be in my car, behind him, and to go to the apartments. Will
would go in. He didn't want me to go with him to do all of
this because he said Chris was suspicious of everything already
because he's paranoid. Will says Chris knows that he knows
that he's after him." She again chuckled facetiously, almost under her breath. "Which is ridiculous, because he knows there's
no such thing.

"And plus, they had been falling out and having problems,
so he said he was going to have to go there and try to talk to
him and act like it's about trying to get along again since they
supposedly had been friends for a long, long time. But really
Will hated Chris." Busenburg was going to pretend he was
trying to reconcile with Hatton, she said. "And that was going
to be while he was putting the sleeping pills in his drink. So
he was gonna fake and act like his friend."

She stopped to think. "He went over there about eleven-
thirty. He said he would come out by two A.M. and get me. He
said that's when we would go inside and look for the money.
Now this is Saturday night. I had my dog with me that night.
And I had a bottle of pepper spray"—she laughed—"for my
own protection, in case something went wrong, which I never
told Will that. I just did it on my own, 'cause I was a little
scared.

"I told Will to bring a knife. Because I was—he was all
calm like it was nothing because he said he could always take

anyone out no matter how many people there are. He's that good. But I was scared, so I told him to at least bring a knife. . . . He got the knife out of his truck. . . . The seat where the crack is, he kept a knife right there all the time, along with his sawed-off shotgun underneath the seat.

"So he took the knife. He said, 'Okay, I'll take it for you, in case something happens and I have to use it.' He told me it was the knife he used for some of his killings, but now I think it was just a deer knife."

She rambled about the knife and her attorney, trying to recall what Ira Davis had told her about the knife, before moving on.

"There're three nights we go over there. The first night he comes out at two o'clock. He's laughing and joking and says he's drunk. He says he put the pills in Chris's drink and nothing happened. He said [Chris] yawned a few times but he didn't seem like he was gonna be passing out.

"Now, do I know if he really gave Chris the sleeping pills that night? No, I don't know. But if he didn't, then he got rid of the packet. But he says he put the sleeping pills in his drink. He said it was no problem. [Chris] didn't see them. He didn't suspect anything. So, he says we'll try it the next night.

"The next day was when we decided to go look for the money in his bedroom during the day while he's at work. . . . I believe Will picked his lock because Chris's bedroom door was locked, which is very strange—because the fact that he was keeping his bedroom locked and I believe that Will had said that's because he must be keeping the money in there."

Busenburg had made no mention to the prosecutors of picking any lock.

"He picked the lock, and we went into his room and looked everywhere." *They,* she said, looked under Hatton's bed. Busenburg had told the prosecutors that *she* had looked.

"When we were in the closet, [Will] came across his file box." She meant Will's file, a tiny box only about the size of a recipe box. "But the file box now was in Chris's closet, and Chris had put all his things in it. Credit cards. Receipts of things. Bills. Personal letters. Okay. So whose file box is it? To this day, I have no idea."

Prison doors slamming could be heard as Martin spoke.

"There's a fly in here." She looked at it momentarily distracted. "This one has an odd color.

"First he's mad that he finds his file box in there. 'Oh, that asshole, he's got my file box. He's got the nerve to steal my check and then he just wants to use my things.'" Busenburg said Hatton had taken Will's personal items out of the file box and put in Chris's papers, Martin recalled. "And I'm sure this was all set up by Will." She snorted an irritated snort.

"He says, 'Well, let's spend his credit cards. I'll get some of my money back like this.'" The girl who was brought up in the Baptist church confessed that she honestly, absolutely had no qualms about stealing Chris Hatton's credit cards and using them. "I was no saint during this whole thing. Trust me. I don't claim to be." She did claim, at the moment, to be ashamed of everything that had happened.

"Like when [Will] mentioned killing [Chris], I didn't freak out and say, 'You don't do that to people that just steal your money or are after you.' . . . My mom thinks I was brainwashed. A lot of people think I was brainwashed. I think I was partially brainwashed. He kind of dehumanized Chris to me to the point where I didn't even—I started to see him as like—like when Will talked about his orders to do a hit"—her voice briefly cracked, ever so slightly–"he made me start to see him as the enemy. That he just did these lousy things. Stealing his money. Fixin' to go out to be a French assassin and he doesn't care . . . And [Chris] had gotten that notion that he would just go off and be a French assassin and see when his fate was. If he died, he died. That's what [Will] told me."

She returned to the credit cards. "I personally myself haven't stolen other people's credit cards except my mom's. I snuck my mom's credit card when I was young, like everybody does, and got some clothes." She snickered at herself. "That's the only time I ever took anybody's credit cards. Then she caught me, so I didn't do it anymore." She laughed nervously. "And that was kind of bad, really. Disrespectful to my parents."

Martin thought for a moment and spoke of Busenburg. "I said, 'I agree. We should take his credit cards and go get what we can.' Plus, I was mad, kinda. Will had told me he had all of this money. Then he slowly tells me he doesn't." She rambled for a moment. "Since he's saying, well, you know, let's spend these credit cards, maybe I was kinda more for it because it's kinda like Will spending something on me. . . ."

# Twenty-nine

Prison personnel believed Stephanie Martin was easy and well behaved when not in love, but a manipulated and manipulating troublemaker when in love. The description backed both the prosecutors' and Martin's versions of the murder of Chris Hatton.

"We went to the Levitz store and got furniture," Stephanie Martin continued, ". . . on Sunday night." Their purchases, she said, were a bit Southwestern-looking, in off-white with splashes of pastels. "It's sorta kinda like something my mom would have. It wasn't all that much my type, really. I think we were just in a hurry to spend something."

As they drove away, recalled Martin, she listened to a football game on the radio. Stephanie Martin loves football.

"Oh, this is the night we also went over to Lynn Carroll's . . . the night we went to Albertsons and got a different brand of sleeping pills because he said he'd given him the Sleepinal sleeping pills and they didn't do anything.

"We thought we would try a different brand, which we got Unisom. Really there's not very many brands of sleeping pills. There's maybe two or three. So, we got that. I think that's the only thing we got," she said, rapping the tabletop.

She kept rapping. "Okay, I had talked to Lynn already. . . . She had wanted me to come see where she lived. . . . And I brought my dog with me because she had wanted to see my dog. . . . Okay, so we went over there." After they'd bought the sleeping pills. "We stayed for about an hour." Martin patted the tabletop. "So I told her we could only stay a little while.

"We mention Chris. And we didn't tell her about the sleeping pills, but I had already told Lynn that Chris had stolen some money from Will—like a week before. Right after it had happened, I told her. I was like, 'He's no good.' "

"And Lynn had met [Chris], too, I think once and he was kinda rude. Wasn't very sociable," said Martin. So that night, when we were about to go back to do the rest of the plan, I told Lynn, 'We're trying to get the money back.' "

"Now this is the part that's—it's not funny, but it's strange. [Lynn] said, 'Y'all aren't gonna kill him, are you?' And she said it as a joke. Me and Will just looked at each other . . . and when we got in the car, he said, 'Did you say that I had mentioned that about him last week?' " Martin almost whispered. Then her voice rose to its usual level. "He got kind of paranoid because he had made the comment about killing him. I said, 'No. She was making a joke.'

"That comment really didn't have anything to do with anything. She just totally said it as a joke. Like the night that she said to him, 'You're going to kill me now that I know that you're a sniper.' She was joking. And he said, 'No.' "

Again, Martin emphasized that Carroll had been joking. "She had a little smile on her face . . . and she kind of said that to Will because Will did the CIA hits."

The comment concerned Busenburg enough that he brought it up as he and Martin drove back toward Austin. "He asked me had I mentioned anything he had said about Chris the week before. And I said, 'No. She must have been saying it on her own.'

"I'll never forget that comment she made, and then it actually happened. I'm sure the whole thing freaked her out when she heard it on the news."

Martin spaced out for a few seconds. Then she recalled watching Busenburg, with a bottle of Jim Beam in his hand, walking up to Hatton's apartment later that Sunday night.

"When we drove in—I was in my car, he was in his car . . . still had my dog. . . . I felt safer with her. Because this whole thing is scary to me . . . it was all the excitement and the scariness. . . . I think that these guys are after Will but he's going to handle himself if something happens. But yet I was still scared because I brought my pepper spray"—she laughed at herself—"and my dog, and I felt a little better with her there in case somebody crept up on the car. When I was sitting out there in my car for that two hours waiting for him to come out, I was nervous—for Will, for me."

She just sat in the car, waiting, quietly listening, she said. "Because I was always afraid somebody would drive up to the apartments and it'd be one of those Navy SEAL friends or somebody like that."

There was knocking outside the prison interview room, and a door buzzed open.

"I just had my radio on, barely. Very low. And I would turn it down, turn it up, turn it down, turn it up.

"Now, on Sunday night, Chris wasn't there. [Will] went in and Chris was not there. He waited for about an hour, in the apartments, while I was sitting out in a parking space. He comes back out and says it's been an hour, he's not gonna wait.

"Will had brought something to eat, to take over there. His excuse to go see him [Chris] the second night was to share something with him." She laughed nervously.

"Tacos, I believe, and burritos and chips . . . And that was his reason to go see him again a second night because he didn't want Chris to think that he was coming over there looking for his money.

"I didn't mention this [earlier, but] the first night, his excuse to go over there was to talk to him, you know, as a friend but also because me and Will were having problems. He was saying that I was at work these nights, that I was working and we were kind of arguing and he needed a friend.

"The second night he goes over there and says he's by him-

self while I'm at work again and he wants to share his foo
with him and have a couple of drinks.

"So he left after about an hour that night and said, 'We'
try it again tomorrow night.' Nothing else happened that nigh
We went to my apartment and watched TV or ate or something
I don't remember.

"Now, the next day, which was Monday, Todd came by from
his snow skiing trip and got the dog. . . . It was in the morning
like ten A.M. . . . He mentioned to me later that he remember
looking at Will and Will looked at him crazy." She chuckle
again. "Which he probably did. . . .

"This is the day that Will went to work, at three. And befor
he went to work, we went and spent the jewelry card, at Kay'
Jewelers."

"We were in a hurry that day, too. We had actually forgo
about the jewelry card and came across it maybe like two hour
before Will—like we didn't have anything to do or something
and he said, 'Remember the jewelry card, you know?' And w
went to, ah, to get the jewelry, and, yes, I picked it out and
liked it. But I think we were only there for maybe thirty minute
total."

She sniffed as if suffering from spring allergies, then wen
silent.

"I was just thinking about how his mood was that nigh
when he went. The first night he was more upbeat, you know
we're going to get my money back, you know, came out laughing saying he was drunk, then got the bike.

"The second night he was more quiet, calm about it. I
seemed . . . kinda like . . . he started to be confused. . . ." She
seemed confused herself. "I'm not sure. But I think, the firs
night, oh, it had been exciting, going and getting the pills, we'l
look for the money. Then the second night it was kinda like
oh, here I go again.

"Then the third night . . . which was the night he actually
shot him, he seemed more determined. . . . When I look back

at it now, I think he—now we don't know if he went in knowing that he was going to shoot him.

"But if he did know, I think he was . . . like . . . it was a job." She huffed a small laugh. "He was in a very serious mood that night. And it's either because I think he knew what he was going to do, or he was confused about what he was going to do. And he just didn't talk to me much. But he was kind of distant." She repeated herself. "He was kind of distant that night. And this is just my opinions, you know."

She clarified that at that time, she didn't have those thoughts. They came only after she had been jailed, she said, and she tried, and still tries, to figure out what happened.

*Her* mood, though, the first two nights had generally been excited, she said. By the third night, "I'm not going to say it was boring, but it was kinda a hassle, maybe." She added, "Now things change when I get to the apartments. I got scared. Everything changed then. When we drove over that night, and I was in my car behind him, Chris's truck pulled in right after us.

"This was an old beat-up truck, which made sense to me about him going to the French assassins, because I figured he wasn't going to buy anything fancy, since he's about to leave the country. And I think Will had said Chris had said the truck was maybe fifteen hundred dollars. So we knew that there was forty-five hundred, five thousand dollars left. And some new cowboy hats." She slapped the table.

"So, when we drove in, Chris's truck drove right [up] after us. I started to panic. I thought that Chris had been following us, you know. Will had already mentioned to me Sunday as we were driving somewhere, whether to the gas station, to my apartment, to the Levitz store, whatever, that he pointed a car out and said that he thought that looked like one of Chris's friends in the car that he had been in the Navy with. So he would throw in these . . . things to get me scared, to make me believe that Chris and these people are after him.

"When I pulled into the Apartments, and Chris pulled in after me, I thought, he's been following us, and I got scared."

She got even more afraid, she noted, as they drove to the back of the Aubry Hills, where Hatton's apartment was. "I remember seeing a car with some guys sitting in it, and it looked like they were just sitting, you know, waiting for something. I thought, you know, that these people are after Will. And I waved for Will, I kept driving, I didn't stop, and I waved for Will to keep going, from my car. Right? And he didn't. He stayed.

"And him and Chris, their trucks pulled in side by side."

She explained, "I was behind Will's truck. Will kept driving by the Apartments, went around—there was no parking places . . . and came on the other side. I drove past Will, because I'm not supposed to even be there. . . . I was waving for him to come follow me. When I was going to see him, I was going to say, 'Forget it. I'm scared. Let's forget this. We'll try to just get the money another way, you know.' Or maybe I was gonna say, 'Let's take off, you know, leave somewhere, go—' Because I was thinking these people was really after Will when I saw that he pulled in after us and then when I saw that group of guys sitting there, and I didn't want him to stay and go in that apartment.

"And he stopped, so I went on. But I was waiting at the front gate, looking back to see if he was coming. He wasn't coming. . . . Him and Chris stopped, and whatever discussion there was, they ended up going into the apartment."

Her accent was slow and Oklahoma thick.

"So I went to my apartment thinking that maybe he was just gonna go in and come back out. Because I figured that he would be suspecting something and nervous, too.

"I went to my apartment, waited there for about twenty, thirty minutes. . . . When I came back this time, I saw Chris's truck. But I didn't see Will's truck. . . . I'm trying to think . . . if I saw Will's truck. There was some confusion about where the trucks were parked, because at first I didn't see both of their trucks, then I saw one of their trucks. And because I didn't see both, that's when—this was like an hour, two hours later—that's when I had thought, 'Oh, my God. That's it. These guys have killed my boyfriend and—' "

She again tried to remember which truck she saw, Chris's or Will's. She wanted to refer to her attorney's notes. "Because its been a few years for me." She continued debating with herself about the truck. Then she rapidly rapped the tabletop. "Okay, now I know exactly. I never saw Chris's truck until the next day when Will pointed it out to me, and that's why I had panicked. . . . And I thought if he and Will had gone into the Apartments together, why wouldn't his truck be right there in front? But actually, he'd parked it somewhere else because there's no parking places.

"But I did see Will's truck, and he wasn't in it. Now I never got out of my car, because I was scared. And I wouldn't go up to the Apartments, because I was too scared. But I would keep driving around, and I would keep driving around. When I went to my apartment the first time, and I came back, I left the car running and I sat far enough away from the window where I could see. They had that sliding glass door."

As the car engine ran, she said, she tried to see if there was a light on. "I couldn't see a light. It looked like the TV might be on. . . .

"The nights before this, I had been . . . a little nervous, but it was nothing . . . I was just, you know, supposed to be off waiting until he came out and got me. Well, this night, everything changed." She rhythmically pounded the table. "I was in a panic. I wanted out. I wanted us away from this whole thing.

"I'd gone to my apartment. About thirty minutes later, I had gone back and sat there with my car running, and I decided to wait till two, like he said, to see if maybe he would come out because he said that he would come out by two."

That was about 1 A.M., said Martin. And it had been around 12:00 or 12:30, she said, when she had first spotted Hatton at the Aubry Hills.

"When I first went back over there and I saw his truck,"

Martin continued, "but not Chris's truck, I had started to
have . . . a . . . panic [attack] a little bit. . . . So I sat there and
I waited, until two o'clock, thinking maybe he was in there and
he would come out. Then comes two-thirty. So I did sit there
at least an hour, an hour and a half. . . . I would drive around
the Apartments because I got nervous sitting there, because I
had these thoughts that maybe [Chris] had gotten to Will and
he was going to be coming after me.

"Now I remember three o'clock coming, and by that time,
I was crying. And I was sure that he had killed—"

Martin then stated that she feared he had been killed. "And
I was [in] full-blown panic attack. Couldn't hardly breathe. But
I drove back to my apartments to keep looking, I went in, real
fast. I came out. I went back to the Apartments.

"Now, at this time that I went back, I got out of my car. I
was too scared to go up to the Apartments. . . . I went kinda
under the . . . sliding glass window, to try to see if I could hear
anything, see if I could hear the TV, wondering if anybody was
there. I didn't hear nothing. It was just—nothing.

"I ran back to my car, because I was scared, got in it, drove
around wondering what I was going to do, crying. I remember
I said, 'I'm gonna go back to my Apartments one more time,
and if he's not there, I'm gonna call the police' "—her voice
was deep and serious—" 'or call my parents, or call Todd.' "
Her voice lifted and lilted as she mentioned Brunner's name.
"You know, I didn't care. I was scared to death. I thought they
had killed him and they were gonna be after me. I wasn't even
thinking what crazy story it was gonna be, that I was gonna
tell 'em.

"I probably would have just told them the truth . . . that he
had gone over there looking for the money. I was gonna tell
them that he had said that he was in the CIA. I was just gonna
tell them everything."

Martin didn't mention the sleeping pills, which she had taken
months to confess to Frank Bryan.

"But I think the person I was really gonna call first was my

arents"—she paused—"before I called the police. But [it] had
>een in my mind that I would check my Apartments one more
ime, and then I would check his Apartments one more time,
and then if he wasn't there, I was gonna call somebody.

"I remember as I was driving back to my Apartments, I was
crying so much, and I was so upset, I almost had a wreck. . . .
t was the worst I've ever felt in my life. And when I went to
he Apartments . . . I had to use the bathroom." She huffed a
oreathy laugh.

"Funny the things you remember. I was so nervous, my
stomach was so nervous, I had to use the bathroom, kinda like
he stomach virus I've had today." She giggled nervously. "
'Cause I was in this kinda major panic attack, and I was crying.
I . . . didn't know if I wanted to go back and look one more
time. I decided, okay. Because I always had in my head that
night, I never completely one hundred percent thought he's
dead, but I was ninety percent afraid that he was."

Doors slammed and slammed again in the prison. They
slammed so often that they became white noise.

"I kept driving around, I kept looking, thinking I would see
him, and by four, four-thirty, I was thinking he's gotta be dead.
Because Will was very punctual. If he ever said he was gonna
do something, he was gonna do it. He was always on time." Her
speech was rapid-fire. "He was always the type of person that
said he was gonna be, like at work, he would go early. If he ever
said he was coming to the apartments sometime, he was very
punctual. So I knew it was not like him to not come out of that
apartment at two o'clock like he'd said." She stopped to breathe.

"When I went back to the Apartments to look one more
time, and there"—she paused—"I was five minutes"—she
slapped the table—"from calling, my parents or the police.
And, uh, there he was in his truck . . . in the front of the [Aubry
Hills] Apartments, the very, very front. And I believe that's
where he had called me from," referring to the call on her caller
ID that Drew McAngus had identified, "because the phone,
you know, the phone in the Apartments was out of commission.

"He was getting out of [his truck] to stop me. I pulled in stopped my car, and rolled down my window, and I started screaming at him. 'Where the fuck have you been? I thought you were dead! And you said you would come out by two o'clock and I've been driving around crazy. I thought you were dead!'

"And the whole time he's just staring at me. He's calm as can be, saying"—and she whispered—" 'Be quiet, Stephanie Be quiet. Calm down. Calm down.'

"I said, 'How can I calm down? Where have you been?' I was gonna be mad. I was mad. I was upset. I was relieved that he was alive." Her voice cracked as if tears were about to flow, as if reliving the moment and the relief. "I couldn't believe"— she then started to laugh—"I couldn't believe he was alive. So I was relieved [and] at the same time angry because of the fact that he didn't show any emotion.

". . . And he walked out of that truck like it was just nothing. And I'm screaming and everything, crying, telling him I've been driving around all night thinking he's dead, thinking they're after me. I said, 'I was just about to call the police or my parents—or Todd.'

"And he says, 'Be quiet.' He needs to tell me something.

"And I'm still, you know, whatever, hollering and everything, 'What! What! What!' you know.

"And he says"—she paused—"he shot him." She thumped the table. She swallowed loudly and dryly. "Exactly those words." She thumped the table again. "He said, 'I shot him.'

"Actually, I asked him, 'Where's Chris?' I asked him, you know, as I was, you know, when he was saying, 'Be quiet. Be quiet. I have something to tell you.' I'm like, 'What happened? Wher-wher-, where's Chris?'

"He says he shot him.

"I said, 'You shot him?' I didn't believe him. 'Cause he said it so calm. Plus, there was no mention of shooting him. There had been no talk of shooting Chris." She stopped for a moment.

"Of course," she said with a bitter laugh, "the detective—" Her voice was froggy and needed clearing. She started over.

"The detectives and the prosecutors don't believe—half of them believe I was there and that we had planned to shoot him, he had planned to shoot him. There was no talk of shooting Chris. There was talk of sleeping pills."

Will Busenburg had told Bryan and Wetzel that he and Martin had spiked the burrito with rat poison.

"That's something Will made up," Martin said emphatically. She laughed. "That's something that Will came up with clear after two years after we had been in the county [jail]. And I had been set to testify against him. And, when he took that forty-year plea, two weeks before his trial, then they asked him, 'If we took her to trial, are you gonna testify?' He said yes, that [Stephanie] was the one that shot him. My lawyers came to me sometime between then and before I took my plea, and told me he's saying bad things about me. He's making it worse.

"He's making me look like this horrible person. Grotesque person. That really, really wanted to kill someone and wanted to do horrible things to the body. He even told them I said I wanted to have sex with the dead body."

On the burrito note detectives found in Hatton's apartment, there was a second notation by Busenburg about eating the burrito.

"Yeah, he said horrible, gruesome things about me. And I guess to him . . . the way he thinks, now that I try to figure him out, he thinks that society did this to him. . . ." She mumbled for words. "It was always poor Will, poor Will, and he ended up blaming me, putting all the blame on me and saying I was the mastermind, and he just went along with it."

To the contrary, prosecutor Frank Bryan believed Busenburg's last version of the homicide implicated Busenburg more than any of the other variations of the story.

"After I was gonna testify against him—I think he really felt like I'd betrayed him, and he must've been trying to really get me back, or take me down with him."

Martin was warned by a guard about time constraints.

"I gotta get through this, Miss Mays," Martin pleaded.

"Girl, are you begging me?" the guard laughed, then left.

Stephanie Martin returned to standing outside the Aubry Hills with Will Busenburg on the night Hatton was murdered. "My first reaction was, 'You shot him?' I didn't believe him.

"He says, 'We need to park your car and go into the Apartments.'

"When we go up to the Apartments, and I walked up there—"

The guard interrupted again, briefly. Martin barely reacted.

"Now, at the point that I'm walking up the stairs . . . at this point I didn't go into any kind of shock." She still didn't believe that Busenburg had shot Hatton, she said. "I was in the shock already of crying all night. But I was still in that state [of] . . . 'I can't believe you're standing here, Will.' I said, 'I can't believe you're alive.'

"It's almost like I didn't even almost hear him when he told me he shot him. And so when I went to the Apartments, I didn't know what he was, you know, what we were going to do. But he had told me that . . . we had to go into the Apartments."

A prison door crashed closed.

"I was just always saying, 'I can't believe you. I can't believe you. I can't believe you're standing here and you didn't come out.' And he was very, very calm, very, like I said, joblike. You know, when I look back now, I think he was kinda in the mode that this was a hit.

"So when I went up to the Apartments, I still didn't know what to expect. Then I actually remember starting to kinda get scared, wondering if they're both playing some kind of joke on me. I never really was scared of Will, even though I knew he did that for a living, but that night—after everything I had been through—believing that he's, you know, and then being paranoid of these people—as I was walking up those stairs, I considered there was some kind of joke being played on me."

# Thirty

Stephanie Martin had been in the fields at 6:30 A.M. Just before 8 A.M., the sky turned charcoal-black. She prayed. It started to sprinkle. She prayed more. She wanted the day off. The wind banged, and a Texas gully-washer stormed through. Both inmates and guards were drenched to the bone as they raced for the indoors.

"It was fun," said Martin. "I enjoyed it. I like doing stuff like that. It reminds you of being in the real world."

Between black clouds, blue skies opened briefly. Even radio waves seemed confused as FM stations from more than two hundred miles away were picked up.

Perhaps, it was a warning. Stephanie Martin was confused and wanted answers. "I'd like to know why [Will] picked Chris of all the people in the world. Why they really fell out. Who, what he was doing those times when he was on the missions. I mean, I have no idea."

Holly Frischkorn wanted to know why adhesive had been found on her nephew's upper lip.

"No," shouted Martin. "The prosecutor one time asked me, 'Did you ever put anything over his mouth?' And I was like, 'No! We never put anything over his mouth after we took the body out. . . .' " She momentarily stuttered and mumbled.

"Now, Will—I have no idea. He never said anything like that. And I don't understand why he would or how he could."

It all frustrated the hell out of her. "Well, I can't play detective forever. I mean," she said, lightly slapping the table once, "it's almost pointless. It's not going to get me out any earlier, but, yet, I wonder these things all the time. Yeah, I'm just doing fifty years of my life behind somebody that I don't even understand why they did what they did. And it bothers me all the time."

With that frustration vented, she was ready to finish telling her side of the story.

As Martin had walked up the steps to Chris Hatton's apartment, as she had watched a very calm Will Busenburg, "like it's all a big joke or something, I start actually having doubts of him. And that's the first time I really have ever doubted Will —thinking that maybe he was setting me up for some kind of sick joke. Maybe him and Chris are in the apartment waitin' and they're gonna attack me or they've got somebody in there.

"I guess I was probably disoriented out of my mind, but in reality it kind of flashed to me as I was walking up those stairs that I'm really around someone's who's a—killer. . . . I didn't trust him [Chris] anyway, he seemed so strange and, you know, wantin' to kill people. So the whole thing just was not right, and I was walkin' into the apartment—because I didn't think Will had really shot him.

"When I went into the front living room, I didn't see anything. I said, 'Oh, okay. What kind of joke . . . are you playing on me? I wanta—let's go. And because I didn't see anything in the living room, I thought, well, it must be nothing. Because if he did shoot him, I figured this was kind of a struggle. . . . If Chris attacks, you know, I'll do what I have to do and I'll kill him, right. That's why he brought the knife."

The knife that Martin had earlier said she'd insisted Busenburg carry.

"So there's nothing in the living room, so he says, 'Let's go back to the bedroom.' I'm just following, talking the whole time." Martin laughed heartily and began pounding the tabletop as she listed her conversation topics: there's nothing here; I'm

still upset with you; you didn't come out of the apartment; I
don't understand what y'all are doing. The laughter stopped.

"And I go in there and it's dark, so I didn't see anything at
first. And he moves to the side of the bed and says, 'He's in
the bed.' I go into the bedroom and I saw a figure laying there.
At first, it looked like he was just sleeping. Then I kinda took
a few steps forward, and that's when I saw"—her voice grew
quiet—"that he had blown his head off."

Her voice rose to a normal level. "That was probably the
worst moment of my entire life, because I walked in and saw
that somebody was dead. And his head was gone from his—
half of his face was still intact. It was gone like from here up."
She pointed from the nose up.

"So when I saw that, I said, 'Oh, my God.' I looked at Will,
and I was like, 'You really shot him.' " Her voice quieted again.
"I said, 'I didn't believe you.' I said, 'I can't believe you really
shot him, you know.'

"And he says, 'We need to move the body.'

"He's like functioning . . . like he's on a job, you know.
Okay, you see, you believe, now let's move the body. That's
what I remember now, when I look back on it, you know, how
in control he was, like he was really had done something like
that before.

"I almost threw up, I remember. It kinda rose, and I kinda
felt weak and dizzy and everything, because when I saw the
blood, it was splattered all over the walls. Of course, it was
still dark. The lights weren't on, but I could see it.

"We didn't turn on the lights that night—because there was
light from the . . . streetlamps, you know. And I could see when
he . . . when I looked up I could see there was blood splattered
on the walls. That part wasn't so disgusting because I couldn't
really see it, but it was realistic. Gosh, you know, he blew his
head off and there was blood splattered all over the walls.

"The most horrible part, disgusting, grotesque part that I
remember is next—when he tells me we have to move the body
to the bathroom. So he puts . . . oh, . . . he did put plastic . . .

over part of the—it was some kind of bag, like from H-E-B [the grocery store], and he did that because of the blood. I can't remember if he pulled it out right there. . . . I think he must've already had it because he never left the room with me once I was in there."

At that point, she said, Busenburg was referring to his dead friend's body as Chris—we have to move Chris to the bathroom.

"So he puts this bag on the head, and when he moved him—when he rolled him over to put him in the blanket—there was comforters on the bed and one of them was thrown back. He was actually in a . . . sleeping bag. I guess Chris had been laying on his sleeping bag, and then there was a comforter on the side. And the comforter was white. So it was soaked with blood.

"And when he rolled the body over to put him in the sleeping bag, I remember that's when you could hear the blood gushing. . . . But that's the truth because I remember that. I'll never forget it. I could hear the blood coming out of him when he moved him over. Gurgling. I mean, you know, this—this is probably gallons of blood this person is losing . . . out of the top of their head, what was left, out of his neck, almost."

She paused.

"Now, do I think I went into shock? Yeah. I think"—she chuckled nervously—"I went into shock. I think during this whole time, for the next two days, I think I was in shock because I really couldn't think, move, do much. I kinda just became this pawn. Whatever he said I needed to do, I did."

He rolled the body over, said Martin. "And I helped him put the comforter over it, because there was so much blood. So we dragged it off the bed. I never touched the body. I never had to touch the body. He was wrapped up in blankets at this time. We had wrapped him up."

Tonya Williams had told Frank Bryan that Martin had said she'd stuck her hand inside Chris Hatton's open head.

"That was a lie," Martin laughed. "It was like a year and a

half to two years after I had been locked up. I had told them everything. There was nothing left to tell." The inmate, said Martin, left TCCC and got her charges dropped. "And I think this is why she did this—because she wanted something to give the DA. She went to the DA and told them these things. She knew that they wanted to pin me down by saying I was there.

"So, she told the DA that I said I was in the apartment and I could hear—we could hear Chris breathing, and we were in the other room deciding how should we kill him. I can't remember the rest of what she said, but I remember her saying that I said we could hear him breathing before we shot him. Then she said I had said that I did something . . . like . . . put my hands in the head. . . . But, no, I never touched the head. Never had to touch the actual body."

Her voice was deep. "What on earth, what . . . reason would I have to put my hands in the head? Now Will sort of did because he was putting the bag on the head, but he didn't actually put his hands in the head."

Martin recalled that for fact. But other things, she couldn't recall. "Certain things you can't remember. I don't know if I was so out of it when it was happening, but I remember that we did drag the body. . . . I don't even remember putting the body in the bathtub, but we did. But I remember cleaning up some blood that had gotten on the floor, like a little string of it."

Her voice changed from deep and serious to high and almost questioning as she said, "He would always have me do those things, like clean this up. Had me cut off the hands. . . . Had me go—and I don't know if this was . . . he wanted me to be more involved with it or what, but he had me, uh, go into the front room and put the gun in the gun case. When I got there, the gun was in the front room next to the gun case." She meant a cloth carrying case, not a furniture case. "Now, when I went in, I don't remember seeing the gun"—seemingly contradicting herself—"but when he—when we had put the body up he said,

'Go to the front room. There's the gun laying there. Put it into the case.' So I did.

"Now, thank God my fingerprints never came up on the gun." She laughed lightly. "I mean, I wondered—the way Will's mind thinks, I wondered did he want me to purposely have my fingerprints on the gun? But then he wiped his off, too.

"Now, when he put the body in the bathtub, we left all the— the comforters and the sleeping bag on . . . and then closed the shower curtain. Then we went into the bedroom, and he put clothes—there was blood all over the mattresses. I mean, you could tell it was just soaked in. He put jeans and clothes on that to cover it until he said we would come back. Now he didn't mention to me we were gonna come back until we were driving home."

Martin had told investigators and attorneys time and time again that she and Busenburg had been in separate vehicles.

"But he put [the clothes] on the bed in case for some reason somebody came in and went to the bedroom, you know. Of course, the body was in Will's bathroom. This is the back bedroom bathroom. Then he closed that door. I remember he turned the temperature . . . down real cold, the AC. I guess that was so the body wouldn't get hot and stink. It was winter already."

It had been a warm winter. Martin, she said, had worn shorts the night they came up with the sleeping pill plan, three nights prior.

"Now this night I remember I had jeans on—or pants, I can't remember. . . . Jeans. I had jeans on," she confirmed, "I had on a pair of black jeans and a purple . . . turtleneck." She sighed deeply. Will, she recalled, had worn jeans and a sweat-shirt.

"After we were putting the jeans on the bed, I remember that's when I first started thinking cops. And believe it or not, it didn't even hit me until then because I was just so amazed that this had happened, that we were moving this dead body, and he had actually killed this guy. I started realizing, oh, my God, he just shot this guy in these apartments at four-thirty, four-forty-five in the morning, it's four—where's the cops? Then I started saying, thinking they're going to be here any second, what are we doing?

"I started asking Will, 'The cops are gonna be coming any second.' " She stuttered and stumbled for a split second. "And then I was like, 'How did they not hear you?' I told him, 'I'm sure somebody has already called. We need to get out of here.' And he's just still as calm as can be."

He didn't even seem worried about it, said Martin. " 'Okay. Yeah. Be quiet. Don't make any noise. Don't turn on the lights,' " she quoted him.

"[He] gets whatever he needs to get. Maybe his wallet, his keys. And of course, I didn't come in with anything. I left my purse in the car. And we leave.

"I get in my car. He gets in his truck. And we drive home to my apartment."


"When we're at the apartment . . . we're being quiet, you know . . . I asked him, 'Can we talk? I wanna know why you decided to shoot him?' Because he was so . . . quiet and so reserved . . . and every time I tried to ask him anything, he just told me to be quiet and said wait . . . he'd talk to me later and just do what he says."

It was the same way Busenburg had acted back at the Aubry Hills Apartments, said Martin. " 'No, no, no. Be quiet. Just help me move the body,' " she again quoted him.

He was somewhat cold to her. "Like this was like a-a professional thing he was doing," she repeated, "and I was being loud or something by talking. . . . And now I look back and I realize he was probably acting it out, acting out what he wanted to do. He wanted to go do one of these CIA missions.

"So, he says he has to go to the bathroom." She digressed for a moment with her litany of questions to Busenburg that preceded his need to go to the bathroom. Then she laughed and said, ". . . earlier in the evening I had had diarrhea because I was so nervous. Well, he had it, so I guess it did affect him. Guess he wasn't so in control after all. He just kept it in. He actually had to go to the bathroom.

"So he comes out of the bathroom and he goes and lays down on my bed and covers up and rolls over. That's funny I remember these things. I mean, I guess you can't forget something like this. I go in there and lay down next to him. I said, 'I want to know what happened.'

"He said he didn't want to talk about it, but he'll tell me that it's something that he had to do, it's part of his job, and he just felt . . . like this was . . . his moral duty, this was something he needed to do.

"I'm like, 'Okay. We didn't talk about this. You know, you didn't tell me you were going to shoot him.' We did talk about he would, could—I knew there was a possibility a death could occur because of the fact that he went in with a knife and he'd already told me that Chris was after him and there might be some kind of confrontation. . . .

"So, I wasn't completely shocked . . . like if I'd never known someone was gonna be shot, but I was shocked that he actually shot him. I was shocked that he shot him in his bed because that didn't make any sense to me. So that's really what I wanted to know. . . . 'What happened that you would shoot him? What were y'all doing, you know, talking? Did he say something about the money?'

"[Will] doesn't really give me good answers. He says that he knows . . . [Chris] stole the money. . . . The money thing just wasn't even thought of anymore, after he shot him. That just faded away. I don't think we ever even talked about it anymore."

According to Martin, what Busenburg did say about the shooting was that "he knew for sure that Chris had stolen his money. . . . I can't remember what he said in order, to be honest. But he did sometime in this conversation tell me that he did give him sleeping pills, that Chris did get tired, and that he did go to bed, and that this was about three, three-thirty . . .

and that Will was going to come out and tell me that we were going to come up and look for the money but that he went into one of his trances at this point and thought Chris had reminded him of—something, they had talked about his dad or something and he reminded him of his dad, and plus, he'd been stealing his money and he said when he stood over him for thirty minutes before he shot him thinking about his dad and that that's what got him into the mode of wanting to kill him and that when he shot him he saw his dad's face. I remember that he said that exactly.

"I asked him, 'Well, you didn't talk to me about shooting him. You didn't say that you were gonna . . . this sounds really horrible." She laughed. "Sounds really horrible, like I'm a cold-blooded killer, but I kinda like said, 'We didn't talk about this, you know. We talked about . . . you going in there and you coming to get me and us looking for the money and that something might happen to you, you might have to kill him.' " She slapped the tabletop with every phrase. " 'You didn't tell me you were gonna shoot him. That you were just gonna get him drugged up and shoot him.'

"And I said, 'I don't understand what made you decide to do that.'

"And he says he doesn't . . . really have an answer. It's just something he had to do, and that he was thinking of his dad when he did it. He went into one of his trances.'

"And that's really the . . . best explanation I've ever gotten from him that he shot him, which is not much of an explanation at all, really. His whole life flashed before his eyes?

"It's hard for me to understand because I've never been abused. I mean, I saw Will have his flashes of his dad a lot. And I saw him crying. And I've held him . . . but it was hard for me to imagine that . . . this suddenly happened to him. It's like, in some ways, the way he talked about the trance he went into and the way he stood over the bed for thirty minutes before he shot him, thinking of his dad, it's almost like he wanted to shoot him in any way. He had decided to shoot him anyway, and thinking of his dad is what allowed him to do it, like pretending it was his dad. That's kinda how he described it to me.

"That's about as much as he gave me, then he says he wants to sleep. He wants to sleep! And I didn't sleep. I walked around the apartment for a good two hours, pacing the apartment, waiting to hear sirens any minute. I'm thinking about the cops. I'm thinking about what's happened. He's just in another world, I think. I think he was gone, out there. I think he was in a trance this whole time, really. Had to have been. I mean, he didn't show any emotion about what he'd done, actually, you know, killing someone, the fact that there was gonna be probably people that had heard it. But they didn't.

"Now after I paced around the apartment, freak—thinking about everything and afraid the cops were gonna come any minute, he comes out of the bedroom. I don't know if he slept. I doubt it. But I had closed the door and left him alone, and I think I would go in there and check on him. Look at him. See what he was doing. And his eyes were closed. But I doubt if he was sleeping because he didn't sleep that much when we were together anyway. Seems like he was always awake or he was always waking me up.

"I went in there, and he said—all of a sudden he needs me to go to the apartment . . . and get some things that he left. He wants me to get Chris's car keys, Chris's wallet . . . the bottle of Jim Beam and the glasses. Okay." She slapped the table and laughed. "This is so stupid. What is fingerprints on a bottle gonna matter when you have a dead body in the apartment? . . . I had to have been in shock because that didn't click to me. Why would you want to worry about fingerprints?

"So I said, 'Okay, wait a minute, I don't want to go over there by myself.'

"And he says, no"—she stumbled for words—"he can't go, he's sick . . . he's going to the bathroom, he's sick. Of course he already told me he had a disease. So he says his stomach's really hurtin' now. And he can't go. It'd be better if one of us just went in the car. So he had a way with ordering me around after this—this happened. I just did what he said.

"It wasn't mean," Martin said of the way he ordered her around. "It was just"—she stopped to think—"like, professional. It was always real calm. . . .

"So I said, 'Okay.' Even though this was all a real horrible experience, in a way, I felt like I was trying to be strong, you know," she stuttered, "really, not necessarily trying to impress him . . . because that didn't matter to me at this point. But, like I had to be strong for him and for me since he had done this, and I kinda got in that mode of like I was his partner or something." Again Martin laughed.

"Not really like I'm thinking this CIA-thing, because I wasn't even thinking of that really. . . . I don't know how to put it. I just had to be the efficient one because he seemed like he was . . . breaking down and sick. . . . I always had this pity thing for him. He'd throw his disease in, and he'd throw in his views or something, and that just always got me." She slammed the tabletop again. "I felt like I had to be strong for him.

"So, I go over to the apartments in my car. It's about ten o'clock. . . . Now the time we got back to my apartment from his apartment after he had shot him and after we had moved the body . . . was . . . between five-thirty and six [in the morning]. We talked a little bit. Then I think he had laid down at about seven . . . seven-thirty. So this is about ten o'clock. I'll say he was in bed for about three hours then. It was something like that. . . . I remember looking at the clock, and it was ten.

"So I went over to the apartment. . . . I was nervous as can be, looking behind me in the rearview mirror, thinking there's gonna be cops coming any minute, and I was really shocked that none had come. And by this time, I—we realized by this time that no one had heard . . . the gun go off. Or no one had called."

She stumbled before finally saying, "Weird, isn't it?" Then she asked, "Is a shotgun loud? The only time I actually shot one I was, um, I was twelve years old and shot a jackrabbit with my dad, in West Texas. And that was a little 22/22. This was a twelve-gauge. I think those are pretty loud.

"They asked me did I think he muffled it. And I didn't see anything that showed he muffled it, like a blown pillow or anything.

"When I went over to the Apartments, like I said, I was real nervous. . . . I parked in the back alley, because I didn't want to park around the front, because I wanted to watch the Apartments first to make sure I didn't see anybody going in and out . . . like [the] landlady, manager, cops, whatever.

"So for ten, twenty minutes I sat there and watched, and I didn't see anything. So I went in. Now, I may be superstitious, but I was scared to death to go into that apartment with a dead body." She laughed. "I got in there, got the stuff, and got out as quick as possible." It took her maybe five minutes, she said. "I didn't have to go back into either bedroom. I got the stuff— so actually I probably wasn't in there two minutes. . . . Well, five minutes probably because I rinsed the glasses off, put 'em up, got the Jim Beam bottle, got Chris's wallet and keys, which were on the . . . the bar, by the kitchen, by the sink. They were right there. And then I left.

"And I was wanting to get out of there as quick as possible because I"—she stuttered—"have always been kind of superstitious, you know. I've watched a lot of horror movies, so when I saw that dead body," she laughed, "from then on out, it was living in one." She meant a movie, not a body. "So when I . . . went in there, just knowing that the body was in there really freaked me out."

Her voice went soft. "And another thing, you know how they say you can smell death? It's the blood, you can smell it. It has a bittersweet smell. It's actually kind of nauseating. . . . To this day, I remember it. I've heard other people say it and talk about it, like people that've been in war. It's not a horrible, gross smell. It's just kind of bitter. Kind of sweet. It's the blood."

Her voice strengthened a mere mite, but her throat smacked with dryness, "So I left [Chris's] apartment, went back to my

partment, and by this time I think Will was up and had taken
shower. And I gave the stuff to him. And he—I don't remem-
er him putting—but I remember this is where later they found
, he put . . . the wallet in one of my drawers. . . . He was
ying to hide it.

"He actually went to work that day. And he told me the
eason . . . was because he wanted to go to work like every-
ing was normal for the benefit of the people he worked with.
's like . . . during this whole thing, he would think of some
ings teeny to cover up . . . like for instance, he suddenly
inks of these fingerprints on these glasses. But then other
ings, he would just completely miss.

"Now, me," she defended, "I missed everything." Martin
uckled. "I did. I didn't think of anything. I couldn't hardly
nction. . . . I had some . . . Vicaden that I took for my head-
ches, and I took me a couple of those for my nerves—that
ay when we got back to my apartment."

She added, "And I continued to take 'em, a couple here and
ere when I needed them, for the next couple of days—because
had real bad nerves, I was very paranoid, and I was upset and
was in shock, everything.

"[Will] calls me from work. I don't remember how long he
as there. I know he ended up getting off early, because he
aid he told them that he was sick." She yawned deeply. She
xplained that the coldness in the interview cubicle was making
er sleepy. "He called me from work, and he told me to go to
et a tarp. This is to wrap the body up in, which he doesn't
ay over the phone, but I know. . . . He says he needs me to
o that by the time he gets home.

"So, at nine P.M., I go to Academy [a sporting goods store],
hich is on Burnet Road . . . and I get a tarp. It was almost
losing because it closes at nine . . . I got in right before it
losed. The manager had to open it for me. I said, 'Oh, this is
n emergency. I'm going camping,' or something. And, uh, paid
or the tarp. I don't remember how much it was.

"At one point I went to my mother and dad's house, and I

can't remember if that was Tuesday or Wednesday." She playe
with her memory for a moment. She fluctuated between th
days. She couldn't recall. "There was some point that I wer
to my parents' house, during the day, while they were at worl
to get"—and all of sudden she began to recall—"the pain
But it had to be Wednesday or Thursday because he didn't eve
tell me that we were gonna go back and paint until that nigh
So it was Wednesday or Thursday."

She still tried to recall, as if the detail and lack of memor
bugged her.

"It had to be Thursday because we slept all day Wednesday.

Martin still wanted to figure it out for certain. Maybe sh
could think it out as she talked, she said. Then she changed he
mind. "That's not really that important, anyway. But really, it
really horrible that I went and got something from my parent
to use to cover up a murder. I mean, I could've almost got m
parents involved.

"But I wasn't even thinking about that. And"—her voic
rose as if excited. She slapped the table—"I called them an
asked them for a tarp before I called Academy to go get th
tarp." She rhythmically rapped the table.

"My dad said it had holes all in it, that it was messed up. . .
When he asked what it was for, I said me and Will were gonn
go camping. That's so horrible." She laughed at her audacious
ness. "That's just horrible—that I called my parents for
damned tarp and went over to get some paint." This time sh
seemed to be slapping the tabletop out of anger or frustratio
"I mean, I didn't even realize what kind of jeopardy I'm puttin
them in."

# Thirty-one

Just hours before purchasing the tarp in which to wrap Chris Hatton's corpse, Stephanie Martin drove to Intermedics Orthopedics to take Will Busenburg dinner, an "Egg McMuffin" she'd made for him.

As they sat in her car, with Busenburg eating the food, there wasn't much conversation, just a little talk about his upset stomach. He said he'd call her later and went back to work. It was the first time Martin had seen Busenburg at his workplace, the place he'd claimed was home base for his CIA missions.

"This is so funny. This is really weird. I remember—this is so dumb. In fact, I don't even know what it means. . . . As I was driving to get him [Busenburg] . . . I remember looking up in the sky and seeing this star." She laughed. "And I felt like the star was telling me"—she laughed more—"that we needed to go." The laughter left; her voice grew deep. "That we needed to leave. That we needed to follow. I was thinking clear back to the Bethlehem thing." The laughter returned.

"Really. . . . I mean, why God would speak to me at this time, I'm not sure. Maybe He realized what kind of distress I was in. . . . This was a cold act that had been done. . . . I'm not any saint in any part of it because, you know, I knew a lot of things. But . . . when I looked at that star, I felt like we needed to—it was telling me that we needed to leave."

She stammered, "That something bad was going to happen, and we should just leave. Not go back to the apartment. I never wanted to go back to the apartment and do any of that anyway. . . . I didn't see why we had to go back and get rid of the body. But that was immediately cut off when I suggested that. . . ."

Martin had suggested that they leave and not return to Chris Hatton's apartment, she said, earlier that day. "Why are we gonna get rid of the body? . . . The cops are gonna be coming. Let's—let's just go. Let's leave. Let's get out of town."

Martin said she had suggested it just as they had arrived back at her apartment, just as the sun had been rising.

Busenburg had replied, "No, we have to get rid of the body." According to Martin, "That was it. No more discussion about it."

Sixteen hours later, though, as the light in the clear winter night sky of Texas had shone like the North Star over Israel, Martin had still wanted to run.

"I think about that sometimes. I don't know if it was my imagination or it was my head talking to me." She chuckled. "Or if it was deliriousness." Her tone turned serious. "Or if it was really something that was telling me that we—but why would God tell me to leave with a killer and go out of town?" She laughed again at herself and slapped the table. "You know, that doesn't really make sense."

Her voice went very solemn. "My parents are absolutely sure to this day he would have killed me. I don't know if he would have or not." She laughed. "Most people generally think that if I would have stayed with him and had never left him, he probably would have killed me.

"That night, when I took him back from work . . . he told me the details, that he had a plan." The plan was that they would put the body in Chris's truck. "Not Will's truck because Will didn't want a dead body in the back of his truck. That's what he said. . . . And we would take it out to some deserted place. And he wanted *me* to come up with the deserted place because I had been living in Austin, and he didn't know where to go.

"And I thought of . . . out on three-sixty, which is not deserted at all." Three-sixty was a loop that wound through the rugged hills, high-tech offices, and millionaire homes of Austin's west side. "On three-sixty, there's that wildlife preserve."

The Wild Basin Wilderness Preserve, as it was officially named, had one winding, climbing dirt road with a postcard view of the city and gave frequent nature tours, even at night.

"We'll take the body there," she continued, "and then the next day we would go back to the apartment and cover up the blood on the walls.

"He decided that we would paint over the blood and we would scrub the blood off the floor if there was any, which there was," said Martin as her intonation lifted with cynicism, as if Busenburg's idea that there might not be any blood on the floor was ludicrous.

"Now"—she began to correct herself—"when we decided to scrub the blood from the floor, I don't think [that] was until we got there and saw it. Because the only blood on the floor was a big—there was a big blob of blood, and it was—it looked like it was—must have been the impact of when he shot him. It must—the way this blob of blood was, 'cause it was, it was— ooh, man . . . it was disgusting." Martin seemed about to smash her fist against the table from her own disgust.

"It didn't even look like blood. It was a big, round, thick blob"—her words came slowly—"of blood and it looked like kinda fluffy." Then she chuckled briefly. "That's a terrible word," she laughed. "It had foamed up. . . . And it was very odd-looking to me. . . ."

She stopped. "I'm getting ahead of myself. This was the next day when I saw this blood because it was after we had moved the bed out of the way."

"This is what I saw with my eyes [in Chris's apartment]. The first time, I didn't see anything but splatters because it was dark. . . . After we had gone and took the body out and then we slept that day." She once again began to rap the table-top. "And then on Thursday, we went back to the apartment to clean up. Uh, and that's when I saw it in the light, okay? Okay. I didn't see any, any head parts. I didn't see it.

"I guess it disintegrated into micro-micro-," she couldn't find the word, "you know, tiny, tiny, tiny droplets of blood, maybe skin, or skull. Okay, now, bones, I did see. Well, when we were scrubbing the floor and painting the walls, I saw bits of bone and that was from his skull. And it was—maybe the biggest"—she circled her fingers into half-dollar size—"this big."

Quizzically, she added, "And I didn't see very many. . . . When I think half of this person's head was blown off in this room, I didn't see all that. I guess it disintegrates into nothing, into powder, maybe? I don't know. The blood, though, I saw, you know, the blood. And I did see in the wall—you could see some pieces of tissue. It was embedded in the wall, with the blood, and the pellets from the shotgun were in the wall, and they were in the carpet.

"Now that big blob of blood . . . it's like that was just where the brunt of where everything went. . . ." She repeatedly pounded the table, then stopped. "Because, like I said, it was thick, and it was an odd color. It was brighter than normal blood. I guess that's because it had thickened up." She sighed. "It was hor—it was disgusting."

She stopped and seemed to try to rest. "Whenever I get done talking about all of this, I'm exhausted." She laughed tiredly. "It exhausts me."


"I remember it was about midnight, Tuesday night, Wednesday morning. . . . We took the body out of the bathtub. The blood had—seemed to have all drained out. It was pretty—he was pretty much dry. He was getting stiff, because his arms were kinda out, like this." Martin outstretched her arms. In the bed, though, she said, his arms had been out to his side.

But for further specific description of Hatton in the bathtub, to confirm or dispute the rumors that Hatton had been tied up by his feet, Martin was no longer free and forthcoming. She had to be quizzed, detail by detail. She answered only in short, three- or four-word phrases and "yeahs."

Hatton lay faceup, lying on his back, his legs and feet propped on the edge of the bathtub, propped against the wall. "Yeah." He laid simply like someone taking a bath.

Martin was ready to move on.

They dragged him out of the bathtub, she said. "And I remember there's a little bit of blood left in the bathtub, and we ran the water, and cleaned that out. Not cleaned," she corrected, "but washed—rinsed it out. Then we dragged the body to—we laid the tarp out as big as it would go on Will's carpets, in his bedroom. And dragged the body from the bathtub, across the tile floor to the bedroom onto the tarp.

"It was very heavy. Deadweight, right. Because it gets—they get stiff. He didn't have blood flowing from him anymore. It must have drained out the top of his head."

Up until then, the prison had been unusually silent, no slamming doors, no loud talking. But slowly, the faint sound of distant voices began making its way into the interview cubicle.

"He lifted one end. I lifted the other end. At this point, we had on dishwash—no, we had on those gloves he brought from his work. Plastic gloves. Surgeon gloves. He had those at work. They worked with them, so he brought a bunch of those."

Thick and slow like a child's voice, her tone seemed to have grown weary. She had carried, she said, Hatton's feet. Busenburg was still calm. "Calmer than ever." Martin laughed weakly. "Always calm." Her throat rasped with the syllables. "At this point, I'm calmer than I was"—she could barely get the words out—"when I first saw the body, but paranoid every second that we're in that apartment, and around that dead body, and the whole situation in general."

She had felt like evil spirits might be flying into her, she noted. Martin stopped for a moment. "I'm like that. I'm very—I believe in [the] supernatural. I didn't like being around someone that had been killed and"—she paused—"not to mention, I'm not going to say I had any friendship really with Chris, so there wasn't that kind of feeling there.

"But to be honest, [it] never really hit me that—we had just taken someone's body out and that Will had taken someone's life. That all never really hit me until I had been in the county [jail] for some weeks. I was so out of it, and so brainwashed by him, and so into him and feeling sorry for him." Her voice had become bitter.

She returned to the facts. "Then [we] folded the tarp around him, and then tied both ends tight with some string, and I don't know where that string came from—either Will's truck or there in the apartment. I think he got it out of his truck, at some point. Okay. Now, it's . . . about twelve-thirty to one o'clock. We have to take this body down the stairs and get it in the back of the pickup. I can't believe we did this." She breathily chuckled. "It was killing me. It was heavy. What I'm saying is that I can't believe that we did this in a public apartment."

With each carrying an end of Hatton's body, they lugged the corpse outside. Said Martin, "We thought that if maybe we carried it like that and someone saw us we could say it was the carpet." She laughed. "You know, rolled-up carpet."

"The mood had definitely become somber—ever since this happened, between us. There wasn't much hugging, kissing"—she chortled—"talking, in general. It was just kinda what we needed to do and—like the eating, you know, getting something to eat and . . . and me taking the pills to stay calm."

She did ask Busenburg some questions, and made a few comments about the body's appearance, she said.

"His head's half blown off, but he didn't really look like a person anymore to me. He looked like a dummy because he was so white." She even mentioned that to Busenburg, she said. Martin stopped. "But I don't remember much conversation about anything else."

She stumbled for a moment. "He leaves me alone for a minute to go get Chris's truck . . . brings the truck around and parks it in the alley, which is in the back. . . . I remember we looked at the other windows to make sure we didn't see anybody. And, waited until we thought it was a good time and then we just"—her words suddenly shot with speed—"took off. As fast as we could. Picked up the body. Went down the stairs. Went in between the apartments in the back, and then threw the body up over the back end of the pickup.

"Now I started panicking because I couldn't get it up. It was so heavy, and I started panicking, and I was like, oh, my God. Someone's gonna drive down this alley right now and we're gonna be standing here trying to put this body in this truck. Now I don't remember if I was saying that, but I was like, 'Will, Will, I can't—' And I started panicking. 'I can't get it up.'

"And finally he just said, 'Come on, one, two, three,' and we got it up. Then [he] puts the [lift gate] back up, gets in the car, tells me to get in my car.

"Okay, now I was driving my car. And I had in my car the firewood, the lighter fluid, the, uh, that's it." The hacksaw, she said, had been in Busenburg's truck, then he moved it to Hatton's pickup.

"At some point he said *he* was going to cut up the body and put it in the fire. Okay. Now"—she chuckled—"obviously you can't just cut up a body. But at the time being. . . ." Her words faded for a moment, then turned serious. "Since I had the experience of having to do such a horrible, gruesome thing as cutting off hands, I realized you're not going to be able to cut up an entire body. I mean, it's gonna take you hours, and you're not—you've gotta have a big stomach to do it." She laughed uncomfortably. "I don't know."

They drove to the Wild Basin Wilderness Preserve, said Martin, and she laughed again. "We drove out there, but when I drove by, something told me no, this is not the right place. . . . This is public, you know. People might go down here, for all I know. . . . I made the motion, come on, keep following me.

"You have to realize I've been up for two days now and it's one-thirty in the morning. So I'm thinking, thinking, thinking, thinking, thinking." Her words were as fast as automatic gunfire. Then stopped, as if the gun jammed. "So I thought of . . . this deserted, abandoned—what's the word—it doesn't exist no more. They don't go out there. Sandy Creek Park, at Lake Travis.

"This was out in the middle of nowhere, 'cause you had to go down that long"—she stretched out the word long—"winedee road to get to it. In the middle of nowhere. . . . Okay, so we drive down this winding road, for about thirty minutes." She started to laugh at herself again.

Almost all of Martin's laughs, giggles, and chuckles seemed to be laughter at her own stupidity, the ludicrousness of the situation, or laughter of nervous embarrassment and shame.

"And I cannot find it." It was the laughter of a child at her first funeral who giggles simply because she doesn't know what else to do. "I can't find this Sandy Creek Park exit. I've"—she stuttered—"had been there a million times during the day . . . but—but I couldn't find it. And we kept going back and look-ing, going and turning around. Finally it's like two-thirty, three o'clock . . . and I say, 'Oh, Lord, Will, I can't find it.'

"So I say, 'Okay, Pace Bend Park.' We drive out there. That's another good thirty minutes. All of this time he's driving with the dead body in the back of his pickup. At one point, we saw a cop. . . . We panicked to ourselves, made sure we went the right speed limit. But it was no problem. . . .

"So we get to Pace Bend. Now, it's three, four o'clock . . . and I'm exhausted. When I got out to see him, because every-body was in the pickup, I don't think he was very exhausted." She laughed. "I think he was just perky." She continued to laugh. "No, I'm not gonna say perky, but he didn't seem tired or anything. . . . So we was just in the mode of okay, now we're here, let's get the body out."

Martin then explained that she knew all the coves at Pace Bend Park because she'd been to them all. Pace Bend Park was where she had shot the Yellow Rose calendar.

"But I didn't know which cove I was gonna go to, but when I drove by Kate's Cove, I remembered that it was the . . . big-gest and farther away than the other coves, and that you could keep going on it to a part that they didn't camp on. So, that's why I picked that one.

"We go as far . . . as possible as we can go. The water goes

ack into an inlet there, kinda. Park the car, get out, drag the
ody out the back of the pickup, and lay it on the ground, and
ut the fire—now we didn't get any more firewood. We were
oing to try to get some out there. But," she said, breathing a
uff of disgust, "we didn't find any. Scraps. So we were like,
Okay, let's just use this.'

"We put what firewood we had in the fire and lit it . . . put
he body down . . . put lighter fluid all over the body. Now, he
lid that the first time. And then threw a match on. We had a
ox of matches. It lit up decently.

"It burned through his clothes. . . . Now only his top half
s on the fire. From his waist up . . . so his feet and his waist
nd below are not even hardly getting burned. We assumed"—
he began to stammer—"that—that's when I, that's, um, Will,
h, assumed that he would have to cut the body up if it didn't
tart burning, better."

Martin seemed to stop herself. "I know that he never even
lanned to cut up the body. I don't think he ever thought he
vas going to do it, even though he said he was. . . . Or maybe
e thought he was gonna do it, and then he looked and realized
e couldn't do it.

"But he didn't even make an attempt to cut up the body."
he sounded a tad angry. "He never even got the saw. . . . I
hink he wanted me to cut off the hands all along. He wanted
ne to do that. That's what I think. I think he wanted me to do
omething." Her anger seemed to grow with the memory. "To
e tied into it more with him. Me do something grotesque since
e had shot him. That's what I think."

She returned to the facts. "I helped put the lighter fluid on.
thought it was going to be a horrible . . . smell—burning
lesh. It wasn't. . . . It was a smell, but it was not gagging,
orrible, because I've smelled burning flesh. One time I
melled . . ." She began laughing somewhat uproariously.

"That's a whole 'nother story. I've smelled a cat burning
efore." She laughed more. "I didn't burn a cat. Me and my
riends walked on leftover grounds where a cult had been. And

there was leftover burnings of a cat. This was back in '91, whe
me and my friends went out to that church. This is a whol
'nother story." Then with giggles, she vowed she wasn't a Sa
tanist, to rebuke the investigator's constant questions.

However, Martin admitted, "I had a run-in with a cult. It
actually kind of funny." She continued giggling. "There's m
bad curiosity. Gotta go out here," she spoke as if telling a ghos
story at a slumber party, "and see where this church has bee
that we've heard about." Her voice matured. "And we ende
up walking up on where we think a cult had been burning
cat. We saw the hair and the bones. We smelled that, and
was an awful smell.

"But this smell, maybe it was me, maybe it was because
was in shock, whatever, but I didn't smell anything horrible. .
In fact, it was"—she stopped and sighed as she thought—"
smelled just like burning wood almost. . . . The smoke wa
black, though. Dark smoke. It wasn't real windy. So it kind
went up. Maybe that's why we didn't smell it too bad becaus
it wasn't real windy. It was very still. Very"—she stretched ou
the word—"still. Well, you have to remember it's four o'cloc
in the morning. That's a still time.

"When I got out there . . . before we even took the bod
out of the truck, I remember looking out at this place [an
thinking] how peaceful it was. And, then," she stuttered, "I-
almost, you know, felt like we weren't even doing anythin
crazy. Then it flashed on me, oh, my God, we have this dea
body . . ." She laughed lightly. ". . . and we're about to bur
it. Maybe I was delirious." She laughed again, breathily.

Martin admitted she always laughed in embarrassing or se
rious situations.

"We've been there about thirty minutes burning the body
and it's not burning. It's gonna take a barn fire to burn thi
body. I remember asking Will, 'I thought you had done this i
the CIA, right?'

"And he said, 'Someone else always did it.' That he just sho
'em and left 'em for someone else to do that. . . . He says, '

lon't know what's wrong. Maybe we don't have enough fire-
vood.' Blah, blah, blah. 'It's not gonna burn.' He says, 'But before
ve go, you do need—we do need to get rid of the fingerprints.'

"So I go and take the lighter fluid to pour on the fingerprints
ind think we're gonna light the fingerprints, and he says, 'No,
need you to cut the hands off.' "

"I say, 'Cut the hands off! Why can't we just burn the fingerprints like this?'

"He says, 'No, that's not good enough. You can still see them.'

"Which is a lie," Martin simmered. "He doesn't know. He
ust wanted me to . . . do something. So I said, 'Why can't you
lo it? I thought you were gonna cut the body up.'

"He says, no, he's not gonna do that. He can't do it. He's
eeling sick. Now"—she slowed—"this is a pretty important
phrase he made. He said he couldn't do it because he was sitting
here and it dawned on him that that was his friend." She paused,
is if for punctuation. "Now, he didn't show a whole lot of emo-
ion when he said this. He didn't cry. He didn't break down.

"He just said, 'It's kinda dawning on me that this is my
riend. I don't want to do anything else.' He said, 'I need you
o go and get that saw and cut off the hands.'

"I said, 'Will, I don't wanna do that. That's hor—I don't wanna
lo that. I can't do it.' " Her voice was almost soft and distant.

"And he said, 'No, you're gonna have to do that before we
go.'

"Now, I don't know if you take that as a threat or what,"
he laughed. "At the time, I didn't know what to take it as. I
mean, he was so calm about everything. He didn't actually
make threats, but he gave orders." She mentioned the word
menacing. "That's a good word. Everything he said was so
bitterly calm. I don't know how to describe it.

"So, I said, 'Okay. I'll try.' So I get the hacksaw." While wear-
ng surgical gloves, she said, she began to saw. "It's kind of hard
or me to describe because I kinda blocked it out. But I do remember that I had to hold on to his hands"—she paused—"with
my hand, and I just started cutting at the wrists. And there was

no blood. . . . It was dry," she said in shock, or awe. "It was dry,
I remember," she stammered, "I do remember that. When I was
cutting through his wrists, there was no blood."

Martin's voice moved from soft to firm. " 'Cause I expected
this to be a horrible thing, that blood was gonna come out, you
know. I didn't think I was gonna be able to do it. . . . Now, the
gross part, the part that made me, I mean—not almost be able
to do it was . . . when I hit the bone."

As if for tension relief, there was a knock on the prison door.
Martin muttered, "Shit," as she realized how little time she had
left to tell her side of the story.

"It wasn't as bad when I was doing skin, it was when I hit
that bone." She came down hard on the word "bone."

"And it took me a good five to ten minutes to get through
that bone. . . . It was hard." For the first time, in a long time,
she slapped the tabletop for emphasis and said "will" got her
through it. Not Will Busenburg, but *self-will*. "I tell you it was
hard. I was tired." She laughed.

"I was exhausted. But I wanted out of there." The laughter
vanished and was replaced by determined words. "I wanted
away from that dead body. I wanted out of that whole scene.
And I wanted to go. And that was probably what it was"—a
nervous chuckle arrived—"you know, that probably gave me
some more strength to—" Martin's laughter faded.

"And he watched," she said, as if stunned. "He watched me
do it." Her words seemed shock-filled. "[Will was doing] nothing but staring, but you know what comment he made while I
was doing it?" Suddenly anger dripped from Martin's voice as
she quoted, " 'You're sick.' And laughed. He said, 'You're sick,'
and laughed.

"I said, 'You're the one that wanted me to do it.' Oh, I was
mad at him . . . for this, for making me do that, because he
had never said I was going to have to cut any hands off. . . .
He was just staring, watching me. I didn't really—we didn't
really talk. I just did it."

Martin stopped talking. Then she gasped, "Oh!"

A long silence ensued as she contemplated her next words.

"I don't know if I should—maybe it's not right to say this about Will. Why not? He said horrible things about me that weren't true.

"He made some jokes during this whole thing." She stumbled over words. She stopped and thought. "He even made one joke at the apartment right after he shot [Chris], when he was wrapping him up. What was it?"

The prison was quiet.

"No head," said Martin. "He said, 'No head' a couple of times as a joke. . . . He made a joke about him having no head, and this was during the time that he was rolling the body—after he first shot him. I remember. And then he made a comment, a joke out there at Pace Bend about him having no head then."

She stopped. She was silent. She tried to recall more.

"Like he called him 'Mr. No Head.' I can't remember exactly," and with that, Martin slapped the tabletop with laughter.

She grew more serious. "I mean, it's kinda funny that he said it later on, but it's, it's really crazy that he said it right then—right after he shot the guy. But that's how he dealt with things.

"I'm over the hands and the body. The only thing that still bothers me is when I think about when I first went in and saw that blood and that dead—that's what I remember the most. That was worse to me than cutting off the hands. Much worse. No one under—can believe that when I tell them. But I guess you have to be there to experience it. To walk in and see someone's lifeless body in a bed, with blood pouring out of their head, and then to smell that smell of blood in the air . . ."—she paused—"that's the worst. That was the worst of the whole thing." She stopped again, then added, "And to know that he had done it."

# Thirty-two

For the last interview session, Stephanie Martin looked sexier than usual. Her smile beamed, her makeup appeared more tasteful, and her eyes shone. She'd removed her glasses, she said, because she wanted to be remembered in a nice way.

"Why am I helping you get rid of this body?" she asked Busenburg as she cut off Hatton's hands. "I asked him at this point, 'Why can't you call one of these guys that you're supposed to be working with [at] the CIA? Why can't they do this?' That's when he says when he got out of the CIA, he lost all them types of privilege."

With those words in her head, Martin placed Hatton's hands in the fire, under the body, she said. But realizing that the body wasn't going to burn, they decided to bury it. "So, we were thinking that we were gonna have to go somewhere and get a shovel and come back and bury the body.

"Right at this point," she said, slapping the table, "that we talk about burying the body, we hear dogs barking. And we hear a car. This is still far away. But we freaked out. Jumped in our cars and took off." She laughed briefly. "We hauled ass out of there quickly."

Martin fidgeted. "Later on, when I imagined, when it hit me what we had been—what I had been involved in and everything, what made me really realize it was"—she pounded the table—"I put my brother [Jeff] in his place." Her voice went soft. "And then I saw his little brother. I didn't even know he had a brother.

"So, I . . . I got very depressed for days. For weeks. I became suicidal, 'cause I realized that we had—I had been—what I had been involved in, and someone's life had been taken. I was pretty much equally, almost equally responsible, because I could have stopped it. But, anyway," she said, "that's a whole 'nother story. . . ."

She moved forward to Wednesday after the murder. "And we took—oh, gosh, that's when," she exclaimed, "oh, gosh. That's when . . . I saw my dad. This is Wednesday, right. And this is when we remembered we had got the couch. On Chris's credit card. . . .

"It's hard to believe. And it's funny, if you were to read this story, you would say, when they got this furniture, they knew they were gonna kill this guy." She tapped the prison table with her finger, in rhythm to anxious, nonstop knocking at the door. "But it wasn't—that didn't—I don't think that that even had anything to do with his death. I really don't.

"Now, I can be honest when I say I didn't know he was gonna be killed when we were getting the furniture. Maybe Will did. I don't know."

Martin returned to the Wednesday night with her father. They called Robert Martin because they believed they needed to get the couch, she said, because they feared Levitz might call Hatton's employer. " 'Look, you've got a couch and when are you gonna come pick it up.' You know what I'm saying? Track him down to get the couch, so we thought we've gotta get the couch so that . . . they're not tracking somebody down."

She called her father to get him to help them move the couch. Martin noted that when she phoned her dad, Busenburg stood right next to her. "He didn't trust me. Obviously, or he wouldn't have stood right there and listened. . . . He thought I might say something, because after I got off the phone, he said, 'Don't call them anymore.' He said, 'Don't use the phone unless you tell me first.' "

When her father arrived at the apartment, they moved the couch, then shared a drink and visited. "After he left, me and Will were talking to each other, thinking, 'My God. If he only knew. If only he knew that we had just moved a body, [that] you had just shot your friend."

Martin and Busenburg then ordered Chinese fast food, she said. All the while, they never thought to glance at the newspapers or TV. "We thought that the body wouldn't be found for weeks. Because this was in the middle of winter, we didn't think anyone would be fishing, or out there. . . .

"Thursday was the day that I went to my parents, by myself, during the day, and got the paint and the paintbrushes." That night, they returned to Hatton's to clean. She stopped and thought back. "Oh, that's when we found Chris's camera. . . . They were wondering why we took those pictures." Just as she had told Bryan and Wetzel, she again said she had no idea where those pictures ended up.

"I just remember that we found Chris's camera, and—" Martin began to stutter and stumble badly. Finally she got out, "And that we were seeing if it worked."

With very light laughter in her voice, she said, "I don't remember. They say there's pictures of us cleaning up. They say there's pictures of it, and they were thinking that we were sick and demented, thinking that we're cleaning up while I'm saying, 'Look what we did. We're cleaning up. Let's take pictures.' " Martin chuckled. "But that's not the case."

She added, "And the mood, we were—to be honest—kinda joking around, you know. I took a picture of him. He took a picture of me. . . . By this time the mood was a little bit lighter. We had slept. We were . . . talking more. The conversation was a little bit better. Getting the body out there, I guess, lifted something off our shoulders.

"But still, you know, we're in the apartment cleaning up blood and membranes, I guess, tissue, membranes, and bones.

But I didn't see bones—Will found the bones. They were laying all over, different places, and he put 'em in a bag. I remember he showed 'em to me, 'cause he said, 'Look, here's part of the skull.' "

She continued, "Now the blood, the only thing we were cleaning up, really, was some spots and then that big clod. That big, big clod of blood. And first," Martin said as in wonder, "he had to just take his gloves and kind of pick it up. It was thick. I mean, who knows what was in there? It could have been part of his brain.

"Then we took the mattresses—oh, it started storming. Thundering. Lightning. And storming. Pouring down." It was evening, she recalled.

As Martin sat in the interview cubicle, she began to say her neck hurt. Seconds later she was back to the business at hand— covering up the murder of Christopher Michael Hatton.

"It starts pouring down [rain] because when we took the mattresses and put [them] in the back of the pickup, it was pouring. We used some type of paint to spray all over the mattresses to cover the blood. There was actually a few things we did that were halfway smart, but most of it was really stupid. We left a lot of things, as you know. You can't cover up a murder. Well, I guess some people can, but we can't.

"But there's just things you forget." She enumerated the receipts and the sleeping bag. "And then the teeth. The teeth," she repeated. "I didn't think about the teeth. Neither did he. When we left that place, we thought that body was unidentifiable.

"But now I know dental records because I've read all them true crime books and I've read cases. Back then, you didn't know much about dental records and how they identified bodies. I didn't. And when this was happening, I couldn't think of anything." Martin inhaled and coughed.

"Of course, he, the expert, was supposed to know all this. But he wasn't the expert. He was a liar. So that's why he didn't know."

She stopped to recall where she was in her story. She explained that they tried to drop the mattresses at a dump she'd been to before with her father. "But once again, I can't find it." Martin sounded frustrated with herself. "So here's what we did." They tossed the mattresses in an apartment Dumpster, just to get them out of the back of the pickup, she stated.

"Now, here comes the drama." Martin snickered. "Here comes"—her laughter grew—"Will's next acting spree. We started arguing. We hardly ever argued. We were driving home in the rain after we had got the mattresses out of the pickup, and I'm sittin' there. And all of a sudden, things started dawning on me. . . . I start thinking . . . why am I helping him and not some CIA guy. And I asked him that again.

" 'Okay, you say you don't have contact in the CIA no more because you're not in it, but you still have friends that you say owe you favors. Why couldn't you call one of them?'

"He starts saying, 'Why are you asking me questions? Do you doubt me?'

". . . I never doubted him. But if I ever did, the slightest bit, he got very offended. And he said you don't ever call him a liar. Because [once] I called him a liar. And it wasn't about the CIA or nothing. It was about something simple.

"And he said, 'Don't ever call me a liar.' He said, 'I don't ever lie.' He got very offensive [sic] and ignored me for a couple of hours."

Martin tried to remember why she'd called him a liar. She had it on the tip of her tongue, then started laughing. "No, that was when he caught me lying. Sorry."

She explained her "lie": Brunner was at her apartment when Busenburg phoned, and she didn't tell Busenburg that Brunner was there. "And he came home . . . and said, 'I know that Todd was here.'

"And that's why—most people laugh at me, but I feel like Will was somewhat psychic." She laughed. "You know these crazy people have these psychic powers. . . . I think he read my mind. Because I don't know how he could have known Todd was there."

She still tried to remember why she had called Busenburg a liar. She thought it had something to do with family. "And he said don't ever call me a liar. That's the worst thing. He'll leave me if I ever call him a liar, and he ignored me for a couple of hours. . . . He got so offended. Yeah, that's because he was a pathological liar," said Martin, bitterly. Then she laughed. "Liars are defensive."

She returned to their night in the rain. She said she asked Busenburg about Hatton's friends who had been after Busenburg. " 'Where were they, and . . . why haven't they noticed that Chris is missing? Aren't they gonna come looking for him?' " She said she started thinking rationally for the first time in days.

"He says, 'I don't know, Stephanie. I don't know. I don't know. Maybe they . . . took off.' "

Martin admitted, "Uh, I don't remember what he said. He didn't have an answer. . . . For once in his life, he had no answer." Martin chuckled again. "He usually had an answer for everything. And he got flustered. He started saying, 'Do you doubt me? Are you accusing me? Do you think I'm a liar?' "

She seemed to be saying almost the exact same words she'd told the detectives the night of her arrest. "If you're accusing me of something. . . ."

To Busenburg's question, "Do you think I'm a liar?" Martin said she answered, " 'Yes. I think this is weird. . . . Nothing makes sense. I don't understand why you shot him. I don't understand why I'm helping you get rid of the body. I don't understand why you say you have no more money.' "

She snickered. "I just got this major attitude. I don't know where it came from. Maybe I was just irritated with the whole mess. . . . But I started going off on him.

"So he says, 'Be quiet. I don't want to hear any more. Don't say anything else.' He said, 'When we get home, I'm leaving.'

"I couldn't believe that." She uttered the words as though

still shocked. "I couldn't believe he said that. I was like, 'You're leaving? Oh, you're leaving. You just murdered your best friend . . . we just got rid of his body, and—and, you're really gonna leave me?'

"And he said, 'Yeah, I told you to never call me a liar.'

"I said, 'I didn't call you a liar.' Well, actually, I did. . . . And then I just got quiet. And we didn't talk—all the way home. I got out of the car, and I went into my apartment. I thought he was gonna get out behind me, but he didn't." She spoke as if in wonder. "So, I was like, 'Oh, my God. This . . . guy's really gonna take off and leave me like"—she started snickering—"in the middle of this mess, you know. I actually thought he was. I didn't know what he was gonna do. 'Cause so much had happened, I could believe anything, right.

"I was like where's he gonna go, what's he gonna do, come on, please. . . . And I went in my apartment. I'm like he's not gonna leave, he can't. And thirty minutes goes by, he doesn't come in.

"I go out. I open my door. He was sitting on the top of his truck in Indian-style." She giggled hysterically. "He's on the top of his truck, on the top, the hood part . . . in the rain . . . it's still raining . . . with his legs crossed like this." Martin crossed her legs to demonstrate. "Looking straight ahead. And now I realize that's yoga. 'Cause I do it. He was into Buddhism. . . . so I guess he was meditating. Thinking of what he was gonna tell me, because here's what he told me when he came in.

"I said, 'Are you gonna come in, Will? What are you doing? Why are you sitting on that car in the rain?' " Martin started chuckling again. "And I didn't laugh or nothing because at the time, it's funny now, but at the time I was just like, 'Come on. Come inside.'

"So he waits another fifteen, twenty minutes, and he comes inside. He walks in, and I said, 'You need to take your wet clothes off.'

"And he goes, 'Don't touch me.' " Martin giggled as she

continued quoting Busenburg. " 'I don't deserve to be touched.'

". . . He starts crying. Sits down on the floor." She sounded irritated. "Not on the couch. On the floor. . . . Like five or ten feet away from me. And he puts his head between his hands and starts crying.

"And I said, 'What's wrong?' " She said she tried to hug him. And again he replied, " 'Don't, don't hug me. Don't touch me. I don't deserve it.' He said, 'I've been lying to you.'

"And I go, 'About what?' " Concern and sympathy tinged her voice, but then Martin began giggling. "And I thought he was gonna spill out with this story . . . about life or something." Instead, he spilled out with a story about how he lost his money, she said. "That when he was in the CIA, back in January of '94, they . . . put him in prison." Martin tried to recall, but couldn't, why he had been placed in prison.

"They were just gonna leave him there to rot, he said. And he was in there for, like, thirty days, and he had to get lawyers and bargain his way out of there. And they took everything he had. His accounts, his cars, his assets, everything but one car in Montana. That's all he had left was the Lamborghini." Martin laughed heartily.

"So I'm like, 'That's it?' " She giggled. "I mean, that wasn't a big deal after everything that had happened, you know. I'm like, 'Okay, Will. I don't care about the money.' I said, 'Okay, I forgive you for lying to me about how you lost your money.' So then I said, 'Wait a minute. So what've you been doing all this time?'

"And he says, he's still been doing work for the CIA. It's just been undercover, under another boss, and . . . it's not approved by the President. It's just a boss paying him to do these killings, in these countries and stuff. So it's like—mercenary killings?

". . . And he said that's why he was really gonna leave. It wasn't because I accused him of lying; it was because he had been a liar. And yet he was lying more." Martin chuckled. Then her chuckle rolled into laughter. "That's the ironic thing. He sat out there and made up a big, big lie to cover up the other ones, and then was upset that I—he had lied. God," she moaned, "he's unbelievable."

Martin talked about getting Hatton's truck out of impound. Breathlessly she said she had nearly told Todd Brunner about the murder, while getting the cash from him for Bernie's towing services. "I was so close. . . . I wanted to tell somebody." She laughed. "Half the time I was with Will and this was happening, I wanted away from him, and away from the whole situation, I wanted to tell my parents. But then the other half, I loved him. . . . I could see no wrong in him. I wanted to stick it out with him all the way. . . .

"And so, every—anytime I'd entertain the thought, I would just put it out. . . . I was more dedicated to Will than telling. So, when . . . with Todd"—she stuttered—"I came close. And you know why I didn't?" Martin swallowed. "Because I thought if I told him"—she began to giggle—". . . he would say something to Will, and then Will would kill him. And then kill me.

". . . I didn't think I could trust Todd to be quiet. I figured Todd would go out there and say, 'You bastard, da-da-da-da," you know. . . . I didn't know if I wanted to tell him anyway. So, I didn't."

That night, said Martin, they drove to the movies and checked to see if there were any Cinemark theaters in Colorado. She laughed and stated that they had planned to hide out in the mountains. "And, of course, we thought we were also going to be changing our names, disguising ourselves, all that."

They stayed at the theater and watched the movie *Demon Knight*. She chuckled at the name of the movie. "We thought we could get into it and relax and take our mind off things. Sad, huh? *Demon Knight,* right.

"Then we went back home. Got something to eat. We were always getting something to eat because I wasn't in the mood to cook," she explained, with a light and facetious laugh, "to say the least."

Nor, she said, was she in the mood to make love. "But at one point, [Will] wanted to. It was like on a Thursday. It was like Thursday or Friday, a few days after the murder. I remember that he kinda tried to [make love], but—" She laughed. "I was always willing in the past, okay. We had wonderful—we had a good sex life, right. But I didn't want to. I didn't.

"And there was, uh." Martin stuttered and stumbled again. "I didn't"—She paused. "It's not that I was"—she groaned— "I don't know how to explain it." She thought. "From—from the murder on out, like I said, things were weird for us. There was a dark mood. We were . . . not close. We weren't huggy. We weren't kissy."

The cops who watched the EZ Pawn video disagreed.

"It was a horrible thing that had happened, and we were feeling the effects of it. . . . That's what I felt. I don't know about him. . . . I think he was too—feeling the effects of it. But I think he was also more in another world, too."

The late-afternoon noises of prison life began. Doors slammed. People yelled.

Former friends had said Martin had wanted to kill someone, that she had been excited by the thought.

"Being around a dead body," laughed Martin, when told of the idea. "Up until—it was. All the adrenaline was pumping those few days before it happened. All of that was exciting. All of that was real exciting. But after he shot him, cleaning up the dead body, and being around all that blood, no, that was not fun. That was not fun. Wasn't fun at all."

It was time for Stephanie Martin to be led back to her cell.

# Epilogue

Just after Independence Day, 1999, Lieutenant Rick White-head of the Travis County Sheriffs Office walked into his office and tossed onto his desk a completed FBI case profile. Un-nown to Stephanie Martin, Whitehead had been at the FBI Academy in Quantico, Virginia, profiling her and Will Busen-urg.

"Neither one of them, Martin or Busenburg, is telling the truth," he said, leaning back in his swivel chair. "Chris Hatton was probably bound and tortured." Whitehead backed up and stated that "tortured" was, perhaps, too strong a word.

"They messed with him for a couple of days trying to get the money out of him. . . . They bound him and coerced him . . . before they finally got frustrated and killed him."

That belief, he stated, was based on the adhesive tape residue on Chris Hatton's mouth and the ligature marks on his wrists.

Whitehead admitted, however, that liberties had been taken in coming to such conclusions—limited information had been utilized, officers' reports, the autopsy, and photographs.

Still, there was one certainty, believed Whitehead. Martin and Busenburg consistently lied and continue to lie.

As proof, Whitehead pointed to his FBI study on statement analysis. "It works best if you're the suspect but claiming to be the victim," he noted. Stephanie Martin had first claimed to be the victim of attempted rape.

The way an alleged victim writes his or her statement, the

words he or she uses, the order of the words he or she uses, raise flags, Whitehead explained. If Stephanie Martin had said "I," then stuttered and stumbled and changed it to "he" or "we," he subconscious had been voicing the truth the first time.

The same, said Whitehead, applied to where Martin gaze while speaking. According to the officer's studies, if Marti had stared at the wall rather than the interrogator while talking that indicated deception.

"I thought it was right in line with what we suspected," sai Detective Manuel Mancias of Whitehead's report. He recalle Martin's statements to others that she had wanted to know wha it was like to blow someone's head off. "And lo and behole poor Chris Hatton gets his head blown off."

To Detective Mancias, there was little difference betwee saying one wanted to blow someone's head off and clarifyin that one *simply wanted to know,* or was curious about, what felt like to kill someone.

But many would disagree: Sandra and Robert Martin; privat investigator Drew McAngus; and, of course, Stephanie Martir

# Author's Notes

"If you're a woman and if you meet someone who says they
~~h~~ave everything, do not take it at face value without some solid
~~v~~erification from somebody else," said Robert Martin, as he
~~s~~at in his Round Rock living room. He paused and thought. "I
~~g~~uess that's what went wrong. But that doesn't justify what
~~h~~appened. That just tells you how she got to know him and
~~m~~et him and he moved into her apartment. That doesn't justify
~~h~~er not running like hell after what happened, as soon as it
~~h~~appened."

As I researched and wrote WAGES OF SIN, I was wracked
~~w~~ith worry over what we could learn from this crime . . . be-
~~c~~ause for me, there is no reason to write true crime unless we
~~c~~an learn something from it.

Continually, I asked the friends, the family, the investigators,
~~th~~e lawyers, "Is there a moral or a message to this story?" Each
~~ti~~me, they shook their heads and looked at me blankly.

Then, as I sat with Stephanie Martin for the very first time
~~a~~nd heard her version of the events, focusing that day on Will
~~B~~usenburg's stories, I too shook my head and stared blankly.
~~"~~Lord, how could this girl believe this stuff?" I muttered in my
~~m~~ind.

Stephanie shivered from too-cold air conditioning. The guard,
~~b~~ored, and also freezing, joked a bit. And I, crazed by the fact
~~th~~at Stephanie could believe such "stuff," suddenly realized I
~~k~~new a woman who'd dated a guy who'd hinted that he'd been
~~i~~n the CIA. Like Stephanie, my friend had bought it.

Months later, I was on a radio show promoting my previous
~~b~~ook, WASTED, and talking about abuse and denial and how

they combine to destroy lives, when, WHAM, came the phrase "Con Men of Love." I suddenly knew what WAGES OF SI was about—women (and men) who look successful and confident on the surface, but who, underneath, are so lonely, frustrated, and scared that they will believe anything to be loved and accepted.

Often, they subconsciously are seeking self-confidence by being with someone they perceive as being more successful and exciting than they. So, they are attracted to con men of love.

I remembered another woman I know who'd been swept away by her lover's outrageous stories and I realized that this is a very common occurrence. Try to point out the inconsistencies in the boyfriend's stories and the reply is often, "Why would he lie to me? What can he gain from me? I have no money to give him."

They follow those lines by talking about how perfect, wonderful, successful, and changed the boyfriend is—just like Stephanie's love had changed Will.

I thought about what my friends and Stephanie have in common. Stephanie's father admits that he slapped her and yelled at her. My friends have fathers who physically or verbally abused them. And I'm back to abuse and denial combine to destroy lives.

Since then, I've talked to others who have worked in strip clubs and I've learned that the CIA line is frequently used and often believed. I've read about men who are sucked into financial schemes and defrauded of their life savings. Frequently the con artist says to them, "I've got CIA clearance."

1) If someone says they work for the CIA, run! If they work for the CIA, unless they're a receptionist, secretary, or the like, they can't be telling people what they do!

2) If your father hurt you physically or emotionally, find a qualified therapist and go.

3) If you find yourself asking, "What does he (or she) have to gain from me? I have no money," reply, "Self-esteem. He (or she) can take self-esteem from me." That's what Will Buser

urg got from Stephanie—it made him feel "big" that he could
get a stripper because Chris Hatton had told him that strippers
were really hard to get.

4) If someone shows up at your door who seems to be in
costume, remember that costume shops are open year-round.
If they have degrees or certificates on their walls that back up
their claims (or stuffed in their closets to purposely look non-
chalant), remember desktop publishing is easy and there are
copy shops on every corner.

5) If friends you have loved and trusted for years try to talk
to you about a new love in your life, breathe deeply, and listen . . . without trying to defend. Love can be blind. And in
that state, we often believe only what we want to believe. In
times like that, friends can be perfect eyes.

6) Find yourself a Ben Masselink.


Everyone needs a Ben Masselink in their lives. Ben was my
professor at the University of Southern California Masters of
Professional Writing program. He became my friend, then my
mentor, and finally my hero and father figure. I didn't realize
that, though, until he died in January of 2000.

I always called Ben my "Zen Marine" because he was an
old, drunken Marine who got himself sober and swam every
day off the Pacific with a hook and line tied to his toe.
That's the way he caught his supper. And that's the way he
lived. Enjoying nature while moving forward and working.

He wasn't perfect and never claimed to be. He typed his
manuscripts on a collection of old Underwoods so that keys
missed their marks and sometimes didn't print at all and typos
were left uncorrected. But his words were always filled with
humor, love, passion, and encouragement.

Every letter Ben wrote to me for the past ten years always
said, "You can do it! You're almost there! Go. Go. Go. Go. Go.
Love, love, love, love, Ben."

He loved me unconditionally.

Everybody needs a Ben Masselink in their lives. Chris Hatton. Will Busenburg. Stephanie Martin.

Just months before Ben died, he told me he'd written the Lesley Ann Warren TV movie, "Portrait of a Stripper." We laughed because with that we knew we were bound for life.

To Ben Masselink, thank you for helping me with this life.

To my mother, my sister Siba, my aunt Jeane, and my best buddy Beth, thank you for being there for me every day. I couldn't survive without any of you.

To Karen Haas, this book wouldn't exist if it weren't for you. Thank you. Paul Dinas, you keep me smiling.

Most of all, thanks to Jane Dystel. God intervened when Paul sent me to you. And I am most sincerely blessed.

Heartfelt thanks to Holly Frischkorn, Lisa Pace, Glenn Conway, Elizabeth Conway, Cathy Blackson, and Marni Broyles for sharing their love, sorrow, and loss with me. I know it wasn't easy.

Holly, thank you for your kindnesses to me and your concern for my family. You're in my prayers.

As Will Busenburg declined my invitations for an interview, thank you to Holly, Glenn, Marni, and Lisa for giving me insight. Thank you to Mike Wright of the Texas Baptist Children's Home for giving me a tour and a glimpse of life there. It is a loving organization worthy of your donations—P.O. Box 7, Round Rock, Texas 78780-0007.

A very special thanks to Allison Wetzel and Frank Bryan who painstakingly read me their interviews with Will Busenburg, providing me with his side of the story, and Stephanie Martin.

Thanks also to Chris Gunter who talked to me about Will, and Ira Davis and Drew McAngus, who talked to me about Stephanie.

Stephanie, herself, spent hours and hours with me over three days, as well as writing me countless pages of letters, and permitting me unrestricted access to her attorney and her letters to Will, other inmates, and her parents.

Thanks to Robert and Sandra Martin, who shared their love

hurt, as well as Roxy Ricks. I wish you the best, Roxy.
've overcome a lot and have a lot going for you.

Thanks to park ranger Michael Brewster, court reporter Jim
g, Rosalinda Fiero from the Travis County District Attorney's
ice, and TCSO officer Dolly Day. Dolly provided me with
otographs and hundreds of pages of reports and letters. She
up with me for more hours than anyone should have to.

Mark Daughn provided the photos of Stephanie Martin as
ll as insight into the life of strip clubs. Thank you. Thanks
o to Don King, manager of the Yellow Rose, for not throwing
out of the club and a special thanks to David Marion
lkinson and Frank Campbell for accompanying me to the
se. I know that was tough research, fellas.

Detectives Manny Mancias, Tim Gage, and Lieutenant Rick
itehead were more than generous in their help. Sgt. Man-
s, thank you for your patience.

Jim Bob McMillan, executive director of the Austin Writers'
ague, thank you always for your constant support.

And a very special thanks goes to my favorite novelist Louise
dd. The words you write inspire me, make me laugh, make
cry, make me work harder, and make me applaud you both
an author and a friend.

# MORE MUST-READ TRUE CRIME
# FROM PINNACLE